EP Sports Series

- ○ All about Judo
- ○ Backpacking

D0861034

Swimming
for Sport

cs

- ○ Football
- ○ Golf
- ○ Hockey for Men and Women
- Improve your Riding
- Learning to Swim
- ○ Men's Gymnastics
- ○ Modern Rhythmic Gymnastics
- Modern Riding
- ○ Netball
- ○ Orienteering
- Rock Climbing
- ○ Rugby Union
- Sailing
- ○ Snooker
- ○ Sports Acrobatics
- ○ Squash Rackets
- Start Motor Cruising
- ○ Table Tennis
- Target Rifle Shooting
- ○ Tennis up to Tournament
  Standard
- ○ Track Athletics
- ○ Trials Bike Riding
- Underwater Swimming
- ○ Volleyball
- Water Polo
- ○ Weight Lifting
- Wildwater Canoeing
- Windsurfing
- ○ Women's Gymnastics

- ○ Denotes titles currently
  available in paperback as well
  as hardback

ADAM AND CHARLES BLACK
LONDON

ep sport

All about Judo

Geof Gleeson
7th dan

Cover photograph by Tony Duffy

ISBN 0 7136 2572 4

Published by A & C Black (Publishers) Ltd,
35 Bedford Row, London WC1R 4JH

First edition 1975, reprinted 1984

Text set in 9/10 pt. Photon Univers, printed and bound in
Great Britain by Netherwood Dalton & Co Ltd,
Huddersfield.

Contents

Acknowledgements

First, I would like to thank Keith Cannaby and Les Hudspith for again helping me in producing the photographs. Not only are they very good fighters (both have been in British teams), but they are both knowledgeable and experienced in judo skills and how to perform them. I have appreciated too the support they have given in many ways other than just taking bangs while I take pictures! My thanks too go to David Gauntlett, not only for taking all the pictures, but for his enthusiastic support and help in many ways over the past few years. Much of the information contained in this book has been accumulated while I have been Chief National Coach to the British Judo Association. By and large it was a very enjoyable period, and much work was done in changing the face of judo – both in Britain and in other parts of the world. For that, I would like to thank the many coaches, both men and women, who have taken the time and made the effort to learn many of the things I have advocated over the years. They have done sterling work and British judo has much to thank them for; not only have they been instrumental in increasing the number of people participating in judo, but they have also helped to enlarge the fund of judo knowledge.

My visits abroad too have been very exciting, and my deep appreciation and regard go to people like Gene Doerrsam in Canada, Jim Bregman and Phil Porter in the U.S.A., and Øivinn Tveter in Norway. They have done much for judo in their respective countries and when it is realised by the establishment that progress has been made, it will have been largely because of the efforts of these men. Finally my greatest thanks go to my Senior Coaches, Messrs. Hicks, Barnett, Silver and Welsh – and particularly to Mrs. Margaret Johnson – for the assistance and support they have given me over the years. They have shown great faith in the principles and ideas I have tried to promulgate and have put them into practice with great effect. For that I shall always be grateful. I think between us all we have contributed something very special and worthwhile to judo over the past decade or more. Finally, my wife, she is, therefore I am.

G. R. Gleeson,
Enfield, 1975

About the Author

Geof Gleeson first took up judo in 1947. First became member of British Team in 1949. Finalist in 3rd Dan and Open Championships of Europe in 1951, then won a scholarship to Japan from 1952-55 and won several awards there. Was first foreign student of the Kodokan (National Institute of Judo in Japan). Captained British Team from 1955 to 1957, when the British Team won the European Team Championships. Retired from competition in 1958. Was first National Coach of the British Judo Association and kept the post for over 14 years. Writes, teaches, advises, and makes films on judo. At present studying for a masters degree in sport sociology at the Polytechnic of North London.

Foreword

All About Judo summarises the research of an era – the era of Geof Gleeson. It extends from his appointment as Britain's first full-time National Coach in 1960 to his highly controversial departure in 1974. Anyone unfamiliar with the very rigid traditions that enshrined judo teaching before 1960 will find it hard to appreciate the impact of the so-called Gleeson "method" which reverberated as far as Japan! Ironically it has been Geof's emphasis of the particular individual ability and potential of both player and coach rather than a rigid "method" which has transformed judo from a mysterious and elitist activity into Britain's fastest growth indoor sport. With breath-taking irreverence he swept aside ritualistic method and replaced it with the application of logic and creativity – concepts which are far closer to judo's founder, Professor Kano, than reactionaries have realised. British schools' judo has thrived on this transformation, and other conservative sports have followed rejoicing; but the tornado-like energy with which Geof has pursued his inspiring iconoclasm has regretfully, but perhaps inevitably, panicked many sacred cows into stampede! Prophetic leadership is a dangerous occupation. When Daphne Dickins of the Sports Council asked me for a copy of Geof's first block-busting book (*Judo for the West*), I thought it was for a judo coach, but in fact she was recommending it to a teacher of movement as the best book on teaching physical skills. For although Geof has been called "the foremost judo thinker in the world today", his research has transcended judo. His intellectual curiosity has led him to the study of philosophy, educational psychology, art, and much else besides – his house appears to be built of books! Concepts which have withstood his analytical scrutiny have been integrated into a formidable mental armoury, which infuriates his opponents, but which inspired a very eclectic coaching scheme. Conference lecturers used by Geof Gleeson included not only other National Coaches, but authorities in such diverse subjects as military tactics and dance notation.

A network of area coaches set up by Geof Gleeson thrived on this broad educational diet; and it was the rapport between this team supported by a new breed of provincial players that crystallised many of the ideas in this book.

I was personally involved with this team from its inception, and as an artist teacher and active environmentalist I am sometimes asked why I have devoted so much of my life to "Japanese Wrestling", and continued to do so long after whatever skill I had, has markedly deteriorated. The answer must be that, like Geof's other coaches, I have derived far more from judo than just the ability to throw someone on his back. As Gerald Gardner once said, "There is a certain high breathlessness about beauty . . ." and this includes the beauty of physical movement, or even abstract concepts. I think we all recognised the unmistakably authentic flavour of something right and beautiful; it would be nice to think that we have passed on to the players the excitement of this recognition. It seems significant that many of the coaches changed their careers into ones which I believe they have found more rewarding. Perhaps this corporate and idealistic enthusiasm which Geof did so much to generate was one of those all too rare examples of sport becoming what Norman Collins calls re-creation.

I am delighted that the results of those re-creative years are here for the first time analysed and recorded in full by the man who initiated the whole adventure; and I am deeply honoured by his request for a foreword to what I feel may be his final comment on our sport. There is so much in these pages to stimulate further developments in an emerging Olympic sport that I am sure *All About Judo* will provide a lifeline for players and coaches in the fallow years which will follow Geof Gleeson's untimely departure. It concludes the transformation of judo for the West.

Gerry Hicks, Bristol
Feb., 1975

Gerry A. W. Hicks,
Royal West of England Academician
Senior Coach of the British Judo Association
Senior Examiner of the British Judo
*   Association*
Head of the Art Department at Cotham
*   Grammar School*
Member of the South West Sports Council

Introduction

This book, as the title suggests is an attempt to look out over the whole field of judo performance. It is for the intermediate and ambitious advanced performer who wants to know something more about skill than just where to put his hands or feet. It is also for the curious coach who wants some stimulation to think anew in areas of his trade that perhaps he had thought previously were well known and hence somewhat stale.

The object is two-fold.

1. To broaden the horizons.
2. To relate to the past.

Let me elaborate.

Judo has, or should have, come of age. It should no longer be adequate to see it as some occult art, some facile performance that needs only the precise explanation of how the wrist is flicked to rocket the passive blob of opposition into outer space. Judo is far more than that. Judo is a grappling or wrestling skill, devised and developed by several succeeding generations of performers to bring about certain predetermined objectives, taking into account multifarious factors coming together at one point in time. In order to teach/coach physical skills well, they must be understood as comprehensively as possible. Anything and everything that goes to make up that skill must be known, if it is to be understood. If it is known it must be teachable. I have tried to show as many of those variable factors as I know.

Judo is now in the Olympic Games, and it therefore deserves to be treated with professional consideration. When judo was seen as some kind of peculiar activity fit only for the social and physical throw-outs, it may have been sufficient to talk only about where to put the hands or feet. But now, because of its increased status and recognition (due to the Olympics, World Championships etc. etc.) it should be realised how important it is to know, for example, the personality that puts the hand or the foot where it should be put. The second object is to show how erratic is development. There are short periods of concentrated creativity, when much progress is made; the pace then slackens and there is a comparatively long period of apparent stagnation (during which, it is hoped, consolidation takes place!), then comes another burst of activity and so on. Each burst of activity is directly related to the time, place and environment of that moment. Yet erratic as the progress appears, there is an over-riding sense of rhythm about it all:[1] a rhythm of participation (there are "waves" of people taking part in the sport), rhythms of dedication (some generations seem more able to apply themselves than others), rhythms of styles and performance (see later). I have tried to show, particularly with reference to the early days of judo, how the environment did affect its growth.

A secondary objective has been to try and show a closer connection between the three traditional forms of judo training than I feel has existed in the recent past; for randori, shiai and kata are all essential to each other, and together make up the sport of judo. Over the years I have frequently heard phrases like "I'm just a contest man, I don't like kata"; "I do kata because it's the perfect form of judo"; "I like having a pull-round with me mates, can't get interested in punch-ups or that poncing about called kata". Those and many like them have always given me some concern; they would be quite acceptable of course if the meaning of the phrases were just what they said, but too often I felt the meaning went far deeper than that. The speakers really meant they did not understand or appreciate the real role of the other two types of training. Artificial fences have been built between them, preventing people moving easily from one to the other. I want to try and knock those fences down, or at least put a lot more gaps in them! By so doing I hope all judo players will, by participating in all types of training – with understanding and enjoyment – get to like all the branches. If after that, they still prefer their "contest", their "perfection", or their "pull round", that's grand, for now they are – or should be – fully aware of what they are doing, and what they are missing.

Of course books can never replace "doing", any more than "doing" can replace books. A piece of Zen advice was to "burn the books", which has always been a great slogan for the illiterate, but a convenient blind-eye was turned to the unspoken qualification buried in the advice, which was "read them first!" The ambitious man, wanting to be a judo champion, cannot afford to ignore any possible source of information that may help him along the way to his goal. I hope this book as well as my others will at least do that.

As for the coach, I hope he will not burn it after

he has read it! I hope there is enough new material in the book to justify keeping it on his bookshelf. If from time to time, it can help him get over a "sticky patch" when he is trying to develop new skills, or "trigger off" a new train of thought, then I shall be well pleased. Because of my different view of judo as a developing skill (different from that of the recent past) I have had to devise virtually a new vocabulary for the sport. I could use Japanese terminology and where the appropriate words do not exist (which would be often) I could make my own new words (Japanese ideographs are very convenient for doing that) but I thought as I am speaking largely to an English speaking population I would use English. However, when Japanese words do already exist I have used them, for the sake of those who feel disorientated if there is not a certain amount of Japanese splattered throughout the text. I hope all the neologisms are explained in the texts, but undoubtedly a few will get through the net and remain unexplained; for those I apologise.

For example, it may not be clearly stated that "attacking action" and "throwing action" are not necessarily the same; in such cases I hope it is apparent that an "attacking action" need not be successful, whereas a "throwing action" is. When I speak about a standard grip it refers to the situation when the left hand is holding the (opponent's) right sleeve, and the right hand is holding the (opponent's) left collar.

Some readers may find my custom of including quotes in the texts disturbing. If so, for that too I am sorry. I do it for three reasons:

1. I like doing it!
2. It says what I want to say better than I can (because the authors are better informed on the subject than I!)
3. It shows that what I am saying has a point of contact with another different area of knowledge, and perhaps – if the reader is interested – he could, at a later date, explore that area for the same kind of enjoyment and inspiration that I got when I explored it.

Finally may I ask the ladies for their forgiveness? I am in many ways a lazy man. I cannot keep writing "man and/or woman", so I always write only of "men". It is not because I am anti-woman, only lazy! Please accept that the two words are interchangeable, although I must admit that there are many places where I personally would not dare replace the word "man" with "woman". I leave that to you ladies!

PART THE FIRST

RANDORI

"Art and literature can perform the miracle of overcoming man's characteristic weakness of learning only by his own experience, so that the experience of others passes him by. Art extends each man's short time on earth by carrying from man to man the whole complexity of other men's life-long experience, with all its burdens, colours and flavour."

Solzhenitsyn[1]

A Definition

Randori is free play. In Japanese RAN means confusion and TORI or DORI is a suffix emphasising, or reinforcing the meaning of the idea it is attached to. In a word like RAMBO, for example, (the same first character) the second character means violent, disorderly — the overall meaning is extreme violence, rudeness, roughness, wildness.

In judo randori is that part of training where complete freedom of choice is given to each player, in terms of his own movement. He can aimlessly play, just doing what he thinks the passing moment demands (which can be a lot of fun or deadly dull), or he can have it well planned with an emphasis on specific aspects of skill development.

The training for the acquisition of skilled behaviour needs three things:

1. OBJECTIVES SET: to achieve any objectives planned, teaching and coaching will need to be organised.

2. INFORMATION AVAILABLE: derived from the task itself, which means experience of, and participation in, the skill-learning environment.
3. RESULTS CHECKED: how successful is the effort, assessed by feedback from the training put in.

Randori can be a time of experimentation, a discovery of the existing limits of the individual's skills, with regard not only to the strengths, but also the weaknesses — so these can be strengthened if necessary. It is a time to test spontaneity, to see how quickly or otherwise the individual responds to the fleeting moment. It is a time to learn how to recognise those critical situations that are always arising in combat sports, when a specific action must be produced immediately in order to seize an advantage.

Even from such a brief description it can be seen how important randori is in judo training. Kano wrote,[2] "Randori can also be studied with physical education as its main object", and "In randori each contestant cannot tell what his opponent is going to do, so each must always be prepared to meet any sudden attack by the other. Habituated to this kind of mental attitude he develops a high degree of mental composure — or 'poise' ".

But that of course is something of an ideal. Randori is not always that; the opposite, the less respected of human frailties can manifest themselves in "free play": i.e. lack of purpose can develop indolence. The confusion of mul-

titudinous choice (as the very name implies) can produce confusion of thought and bewilderment of action. Lack of discipline, encouraged by aimless practice of nothing in particular, can develop an undisciplined mover (and can be stultifying to skill growth, see Kata.) An undisciplined movement style can percolate into the thinking style and bullying (of all kinds) and bad behaviour can result. Unless the bad as well as the good is recognised as a possible product of randori, there is great difficulty in avoiding the bad, as well as falling short of the full potential good.

GENERAL DISCUSSION

Most judo clubs in Britain, indeed in the world, spend much, if not all, of their time doing randori as their only skill programme. Randori can be great fun. The results in terms of winning and losing need not matter, so there is no need to "do well". Pleasure and satisfaction can be derived from the whole business of experimentation and finding solutions to the many problems which appear spontaneously or are self-created. If general well-being and enjoyment is the main objective of training then all is fine, all is great.

If, however, satisfaction from achieving a high rate of skill improvement is wanted, then the "confused" part of randori is a luxury that few can afford. Just as swimmers striving for Olympic standards do not just splash about in the local Baths, just as the ambitious athlete does not aimlessly jog-run round the track for lap after lap, so the judo player — if he wants high-level performance — does not just do judo, he MUST *PLAN* his randori.

The Essential Factors in Randori

Most players and coaches will of course have their opinions about this. But they have to be established, for only from that standpoint can randori be planned to ensure that these factors are given every opportunity to emerge.

Let me briefly state the ones I think are important. There are only four, although each one covers a lot of ground and in a sense may be multiple.

1. **TECHNIQUE** (the basic constant in skill development)

Technique refers simply to the fundamental use of arms, legs and body weight in physiomechanical terms, with the minimum variation in application.

The equivalent in Japanese is waza;* in both languages (English and Japanese) the meaning of technique can be extended (erroneously I feel) so that it overlaps into the etymological area covered by "skill". Skill in English, kōmyō in Japanese, means more than just technique; it concerns itself with such ingredients as consistency, internal and external feedbacks, motivation etc.[3]

2. **SPACE, PACE AND DIRECTION** (the basic variables in skill development)

Space refers to both the space contained, "sandwiched", between the two opposing bodies, and to that space immediately surrounding them. The control of these spaces,

by the appropriate crouching, standing straight, turning, twisting, is very important in the growth of all the skills. Pace refers to the speed at which the contestants are moving when the attack is launched (NOT the speed at which the attack is made, which is always as fast as circumstances allow). Direction refers to where they are moving when the attack is launched (e.g. backwards, sideways etc.)

3. **LINKING OF TECHNIQUES**

It is necessary to link techniques, in terms of space, pace and direction, both offensively (renraku-waza) and defensively (kaeshi-waza). The object of such linking is in general to restrict the variables, to a greater or lesser degree; in particular they can bring about a terminal score.

Or to put it another way, if a second attack is launched before the opponent completes his response to the first attack, it will be ineffective. The opponent must finish the first response before he can initiate the second response (to the second attack). In psychology that is called the refractory period, and can restrict the variables in any attacking situation.

4. **DEVELOPMENT OF STRENGTH AND STAMINA**

In many ways this is the easiest of the sections in which to achieve success. Much of the "slog" of this aspect of skill acquisition can be done outside of judo training proper (i.e. weight training, running of different kinds etc.). But it should not be divorced from randori sessions entirely. It is sometimes heard, in judo circles,

that strength is somehow extraneous, or even unnecessary, in skill acquisition. On the contrary, both strength and stamina[4] are essential to the growth of skill (presumably the comment refers, if anything, to superfluous strength or disproportionate stamina.) It is of course essential that technique and strength must be developed as a unit; if one is stressed at the expense of the other, then overall skill will undoubtedly suffer.

Expansion of Factors

1. TECHNIQUE

A sound knowledge of technique is essential to skill development. But how to learn it? Is it best to learn all the separate techniques first, in all their differing details, or is it best to reduce the many varieties to a couple of basic forms, learning those and letting the details develop.

Such a difference in approach could be seen as the perennial battle about which is best — the whole-part-whole, or the part-whole. But it is not as simple as that. In practice there is often no clear dividing line between them. A possible fault with the "Gestalt" approach to learning is that it imposes the concept of "wholeness" in a "part-whole" form, and can therefore bring about the very style of thinking that it is trying to avoid. Thinking, conception,

* In some contexts "jitsu" is also used as meaning "technique", but it has a slightly "bigger" feel about it than waza.

can stop at the particular "whole" being considered, which now becomes just a "part", but because it is spoken of as being a "whole", the greater whole is lost sight of. In the acquisition of skills, there are "wholes" within "wholes", and imperceptibly these "wholes" merge into the "wholes" in life. It is just like those Russian dolls, each doll is perfectly self-contained (as a doll), but she fits inside another bigger doll. By looking at, and admiring the smaller doll, we can forget that it fits into a bigger doll, but we must remember to look at that too. The "whole" skill of throwing is the smallest doll, which fits into a bigger "skill doll" of linking skills, which in turn fits into the bigger "skill doll" of winning matches. And although that may be the biggest "judo doll", it will still fit into a bigger doll — which could be the "whole" of ethics, integrity, behaviour in society.

Ehrenzweig writes at length on this and other possible weaknesses of the Gestalt approach.[5] He says, "The conscious gestalt compunction makes us bisect the visual field into significant 'figure' and insignificant 'ground'." What part of that visual field we will make the significant figure will depend upon our educational or trained bias (what Gombrich[6] calls "traditional schemata"). We are taught, in the early days of our training — be it art, mathematics or judo — what are the accepted things/standards/whatever, they then become our "traditional schemata" and are applied to all subsequent material (before it is accepted or rejected). Some people try and keep their

traditional schemata up to date by modifying it as they acquire new knowledge and experience (although it can never be entirely eradicated or superseded). Others of course make absolutely no attempt to modify their original schemata and go through life applying the same criteria they learned in the early days of their training or education.

Judo traditional teaching tends to lean towards the part-whole approach, stressing details first, heading for the general later* (the inductive approach). I tend to lean the other way, and work from the general to the specific (the deductive approach).

Here I want to use something of a compromise: for the purpose of reference, I want to list all the individual techniques of the gokyo and give the details (normally I would just talk about them generally and let the performer sort the details out). To do this fully, however, would take up more space than I have, so I am going to use a "shorthand" so that all the fundamental factors can be covered.

Analysis of Throwing Skills

All throws can be divided into three main types:

(1) can be called "lifters" (and can be divided into two sub types).
(2) can be called "rotators" (again these can be sub-divided).
(3) can be called "tricks", where surprise is the essential ingredient.

1. **LIFTERS.** These are generally used when the opponent is standing still or moving very slowly.
Lifter I. The opponent is very "heavy" and strongly defensive. A lot of power is needed to shift him. The attacker moves into position by bending both legs and getting under the hips of the opponent. BOTH legs are straightened to get the man off the ground, the (attacker's) body is turned to throw the opponent down.
Lifter II. Here the opponent is not so "heavy", not so defensively strong, so the lifting strength of one leg is adequate, whilst the other leg does something else (usually knocking the legs out from under the opponent, helping to turn him over onto his back).

2. **ROTATORS.** These are generally used when the opponent is moving, fast or slow. (It can be seen that when the movement is slow Lifter II and Rotator I can overlap; so indeed can Rotator I and II — when the pace is medium — but Lifters I and II cannot overlap with Rotator II, for the pace is too extreme.)
Rotator I. Usually when the opponent is moving slowly, something, i.e. leg, hip, arm, body, is put in front (or behind) him, the head

---

* An excellent example of this difference in viewpoint is contained in the quandary of how to teach throwing. Which should be taught first? Falling or throwing? Traditionally (in Japan) falling is taught first, presumably because it is seen as the dominating part of the whole (throw) in terms of producing the requisite confidence in the person thrown (an unexpected view when the samurai tradition of no shield in case it develops inhibiting "protective fears", is considered). I tend to teach throwing first because it gives satisfaction (and motivation) to the thrower and justifies fully to the partner the importance of learning to fall.[7]

Fig. 1. Not a spectacular throw, but left leg thrusting well sideways. It will score!

is pulled down (by the collar), and he is rolled over the obstacle; the hand on the sleeve helps to twist him onto his back. These I usually call Rollers.[8]

Rotator II. Usually when the opponent is moving fast; the upper and lower parts of the (opponent's) body are made to move at different speeds, so that either the upper trunk is driven over the slower-moving legs, or the legs are moved faster from under the slower-moving upper body. These I usually call "Drivers."[8]

3. TRICKS. These are throwing actions, which are seldom based upon sound physio-mechanical pirnciples, but depend almost entirely on the element of surprise and the unexpected. To say that in no way denigrates their value in the repertoire of winning throws. However, their life-span is usually short, due to the invariably intrinsic weakness. As soon as the element of surprise has been lost, they can be stopped or avoided comparatively easily. One way of postponing this termination is of course to use them at very infrequent intervals, so that the opposition does not get a chance to recognise what they are. In general, the pattern of these "trick throws" is to snatch up one or both legs of the opponent, and crash him down! Speed plus surprise is of the essence!

FORCE AND THE WAY IT IS APPLIED

Depending upon the degree of defensive resistance on the part of the opponent, will depend the amount of force applied by the attacker. In general basic terms, force is produced by the dynamic body weight, and that force is transmitted to the opponent via the hands.

Seeing throwing actions, and indeed grappling actions too, from the viewpoint of just a two-factor contribution – body-weight force and a transmitting system (of arms, hands and legs) – is useful for the purpose of analysing. Some techniques will use the body weight force as the primary factor (with the limbs as secondary), others will use the limbs as the primary factor (because they have the sensitivity to discover the essential subtle manipulations that are needed to produce success), and the body weight force as the secondary factor. For example, sutemi-waza and osaekomi-waza are primarily body weight skills, whereas shime-waza and tai-otoshi are primarily limb skills. It should be realised that as always, in practice, it is not always easy to draw a line clearly between them all.

USE OF HANDS

In the Lifter, both I and II, the hands of the attacker pull in tight (equally), trying to ensure the opponent does not slip off the lifting action of the hips and leg(s).

In Rotator I (Rollers) the collar hand is the most important or dominant hand, for it has to pull the opponent's head down (to facilitate the rotation), and the sleeve hand comes in late to twist the opponent onto his back.

In Rotator II (Drivers) it is the sleeve hand which is most important or dominant; the driving leg and body weight tend to pitch the opponent sideways, and so it is the sleeve hand which, working early and strongly, twists the opponent so that he lands on his back.

THE DRIVING LEG

With the few exceptions where just timing is the most critical factor (with its usual implicit big difference in skill standard between the competing two) it is the body weight being thrown against the opponent that moves him in any desirable direction. The direction of that moving body weight is controlled by the driving leg and in particular where that driving leg is put.

In the Lifters I and II it is, very simply, the driving leg (the one that thrusts against the opponent's "heavy" weight) which is placed directly underneath the opponent. When it straightens it lifts the opponent. When considering the Rotators, the driving leg (or foot) is placed on the outside of the attacker's body weight, on the opposite side to where the opponent is to be thrown. It thrusts mainly sideways and then forwards or backwards.[8] See figure 1.

POSITIONING OF THE HIPS

With both Lifters I and II, and the Rollers, the hips (of the attacker) are usually deeply inserted. With the Drivers, they are shallow. Sometimes of course they do not touch the opponent at all; this will apply in some of the body throws, and the fast Drivers (e.g. see gokyo nos. 1, 13, 34, 39).

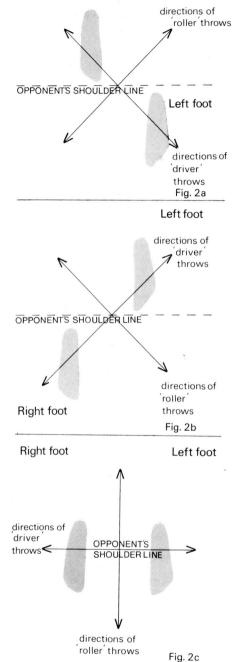

Fig. 2. Direction of throw, as affected by the position of the opponent's feet. Note: the opponent is looking down the page.

Right foot

directions of 'roller' throws

OPPONENT'S SHOULDER LINE

Left foot

directions of 'driver' throws

Fig. 2a

Left foot

directions of 'driver' throws

OPPONENT'S SHOULDER LINE

directions of 'roller' throws

Right foot

Fig. 2b

Right foot

Left foot

directions of 'driver' throws

OPPONENT'S SHOULDER LINE

directions of 'roller' throws

Fig. 2c

OPPORTUNITY – THE POSITION OF THE OPPONENT'S FEET

The positioning of the opponent's feet in relation to each other can facilitate or hinder the attacking action of a throw. In general there are three (see figure 2).
Some throws prefer just one of the opportunities while others can use any.

GENERAL COMMENTS

The above classification into Lifters and Rollers and Drivers is not always easy or so clearly diagnosable. Some are easy of course, e.g. sasai-tsurikomi-ashi can only be done as a "Roller", although the opportunity can vary. Sometimes the dividing line can get very vague between throwing actions in each group (e.g. where do osotogari and haraigoshi stop and start?) and even a traditional (judo) text book[9] says that soto-makikomi could be classed as sutemi-waza (normally it would be a Lifter II). So in the following I am only going to try and indicate the usually accepted form the techniques take. This does not mean in any way that the description I have given is definitive. There will be many more ways these techniques are done than those shown below.

The Gokyo

Both the *Illustrated Kodokan Judo*[10] (published 1955 in English) and the magnum opus of Maruyama, *Dai Nippon Judo Shi* (The History of Japanese Judo, published 1939[11]) claim the Gokyo is the gateway to the understanding of judo technique (tora no maki is the phrase used in both and it means "key", the "authority", or "bible"), yet neither of these authoritative text books, nor even *Judo Koza*[12] (the 5 volume "judo bible" published by the All Japan Judo Association in 1955), nor Mifune's last work, *Do to Jitsu*[13] (Method and Technique published 1953 in Japanese) make any attempt to explain why. Mifune in his book, and *Judo Koza* give no introduction to the Gokyo at all; both dive straight in, explaining each technique in detail. Geesink (ex-World and Olympic Judo Champion) in his book, *The Gokyo*[14] speculates that it is some kind of historical account of throws' development from the start of judo. This hypothesis would appear to be discounted however by Maruyama's brief notes on the development of the Gokyo. He tells how it was first devised in 1895, mainly by Messrs. Yamashita, Yokoyama and Nagaoka and "others". By 1920 the concensus of opinion was that the original Gokyo was now out-of-date, and should be revised. Yamashita and Nagaoka, both 10th Dans (Yokoyama had died in the meantime) plus Mifune 9th Dan and "some other 8th Dans" got down to the job of sorting out what should be left in and

Fig. 3. A schematic "bird's-eye" view of the positioning of the attacker's driving foot in relation to the direction of the throw. Note: the "driving" foot goes in the opposite quadrant to the direction of the intended throw, preferably on an extended line, but that is not strictly necessary as long as it is in the general quadrant.

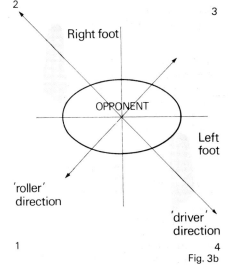

Fig. 3a

Fig. 3b

The imposition of "driver" and "roller" directions should clarify the situation.

what should be cut out, and what should be added.

Out went obi-otoshi, osoto-otoshi, hikkomi-gaeshi, seoi-otoshi, yama-arashi, daki-wakare, tawara-gaeshi, and in came techniques like kosoto-gake, harai-tsurikomi-ashi, o-guruma, hane-makikomi, sukui-nage, tani-otoshi. No explanation is put forward as to why the one lot was thrown out and why the other lot was brought in. No attempt is made to explain why they are put in this traditional grouping of 5 sets of 8 techniques (go = 5; kyo = a "teach" or set — hence gokyo). The implication behind the whole approach to the "key of judo" — the gokyo — is that it is some form of teaching order. You start by learning deashi-harai, then proceed to hizaguruma and then go right through to yoko-gake. It could be said that the difficulty of performance does increase in some rather nebulous way from start to finish, but on inspection is it true?

There appears to be very little rationality as to why any one technique follows any other; for example, what kind of overlap or transference could there be from No. 23 tomoe-nage to No. 24 kata-guruma? Indeed Kudo, the author of this particular part in *Judo Koza*, hints very strongly that in his opinion at least, the present Gokyo should not be considered to cover all or even the best of the throwing techniques. To make his point, he adds to the "official" list of 40, 23 of his own, and included in those are such beautifully-named throws as

kuchiki-daoshi (rotten-tree-fall) and no-waki (field separation).

THE KEY TO GOKYO

To save space, and the reader's patience, I have made a key that is simple and can be read if required.

The code is:

NAME (Japanese)	seoi-nage	
TYPE (Japanese)	te-waza	
TYPE (Gleeson)	L I (Lifter I)	R (Roller)
POSITION OF DRIVING LEG	Underneath	the third quadrant
DOMINANT HAND	Both equal	collar hand
OPPORTUNITY	foot level	foot back
PACE	fast medium	slow

This key tells the reader that seoi-nage can be done either as a Lifter I (both feet on the ground), or as a Roller. The feet are underneath if a Lifter, and as a Roller the driving LEFT foot is in the third quadrant (see figure 3). In the Lifter both hands work together; in a Roller, the collar hand is the more important. As for the opportunity; done as a Lifter the opponent's feet should be level, but as a Roller the foot is back (see figure 2a). As for pace, this is just a very rough guide as to the speed both are moving at when the attack is launched (see Page 38).

It is very tempting and indeed difficult not to write many kinds of qualifications and variations on the many techniques listed, so

extending the list considerably. An obvious one for example is No. 28 sukui-nage. This one is usually done as a counter (as indeed are Nos. 4, 18, 26, 29, 37, 38), in which case it changes its superficial appearance and would need a lot of description to cover all variations. But there you are, how do you make a finite list of the infinite ways of performing combat skills?

IKKYO 1st kyo

deashi-harai
ashi-waza
driver
3 quad
sleeve hand
foot forward
fast

hiza-guruma
ashi-waza
roller
3 quad
collar hand
foot back
medium

sasai-tsurikomi-ashi
ashi-waza
roller
3 quad
collar hand
foot back
fast

uki-goshi
koshi-waza
roller
3 quad
belt hand
foot back
fast

1.

2.

3.

4.

osoto-gari
ashi-waza
driver
4 quad
sleeve hand
foot back
medium/fast

o-goshi
koshi-waza
lifter 1
underneath
both hands
feet level
medium

ouchi-gari
ashi-waza
driver
4 quad
sleeve hand
foot back
medium/fast

seoi-nage
te-waza
lifter 1   roller
underneath   3 quad
both hands   collar hand
feet level   foot back
slow/medium

5.

6.

7.

8.

NIKYO 2nd kyo

kosoto-gari
ashi-waza
driver
1 or 4 quad
sleeve hand
foot forward
fast

kouchi-gari
ashi-waza
driver
1 or 4 quad
sleeve
foot forward
fast

koshi-guruma
koshi-waza
roller
3 quad
collar hand
medium/slow

tsurikomi-goshi
koshi-waza
roller
3 quad
collar hand
slow

okuri-ashi-harai
ashi-waza
driver
4 quad
sleeve
fast

tai-otoshi
te-waza
lifter 1   roller   driver
to suit
to suit
slow/fast

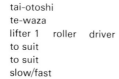

harai-goshi
koshi-waza
driver
3 quad
sleeve hand
medium

uchi-mata
koshi-waza
lifter 11   roller   driver
to suit
to suit
slow/fast

SANKYO 3rd kyo

kosoto-gake
ashi-waza
roller
1 or 4 quad
collar hand
foot back
slow/medium

tsuri-goshi
koshi-waza
lifter 1
underneath
hand at back (of opponent)
feet level
medium

yoko-otoshi
yoko-sutemi-waza
driver
4th quad
sleeve hand
foot forward
slow

ashi-guruma
ashi-waza
roller
3rd quad
collar hand
foot back
medium/fast

17

18

19

20

hane-goshi
koshi-waza
lifter 11   driver
underneath   4th quad
feet level   foot back
medium/fast

harai-tsurikomi-ashi
ashi-waza
driver
3rd quad
foot forward
fast

tomoe-nage
ma-sutemi-waza
roller
2nd quad
collar hand
foot forward
medium/fast

kata-guruma
te-waza
driver
3rd quad
sleeve hand
foot forward
medium/fast

21

22

23

24

sumi-gaeshi
ma-sutemi-waza
roller
2nd quad
collar hand
foot forward
slow

tani-otoshi
yoko-sutemi-waza
driver
4th quad
sleeve hand
foot forward
slow

hane-makikomi
makikomi-waza
lifter 11
underneath
both hands
feet level
slow

sukui-nage
te-waza
trick
to suit
to suit
medium/fast

 25

 26

 27

 28

utsuri-goshi
koshi-waza
lifter 1
underneath
both hands
feet level
slow/medium

o-guruma
ashi-waza
roller
3rd quad
collar hand
feet back
medium

soto-makikomi
makikomi-waza
lifter 11
underneath
both hands
feet level
stop/medium

uki-otoshi
te-waza
driver
3rd quad
sleeve hand
foot forward
fast

 29

 30

 31

 32

osoto-guruma
ashi-waza
roller
1st quad
collar hand
foot forward
medium/fast

uki-waza
yoko-sutemi-waza
driver
sleeve hand
foot forward
slow

yoko-wakare
yoko-sutemi-waza
roller
3rd quad
collar hand
foot forward
medium/fast

yoko-guruma
yoko-sutemi-waza
roller
3rd quad
hard round body
foot forward
medium

ushiro-goshi
ura-waza
lifter 1

ura-nage
ma-sutemi-waza
driver
3rd quad
sleeve hand
foot forward
slow

sumi-otoshi
te-waza
driver
4th quad
sleeve hand
foot back
fast

yoko-gake
yoko-sutemi-waza
driver
3rd quad
sleeve hand
foot forward
medium

The Onset of Speculation

Having looked somewhat superficially at the Gokyo, and realising the importance that the Japanese establishment gives to such an arbitrary list of throwing techniques, it is intriguing to speculate why a gokyo-no-katame-waza was never formulated. One rather desperate, and forlorn, explanation I have heard was that the Kodokan (the abstract "it", not the personal "them") did not consider ne-waza important enough to have a gokyo of its own! Plaintive as the explanation is, it is relevant to note that Kano did not have a hand in the formulating of the existing gokyo (which I feel is very significant, for I like to think that Kano thought about it as I do). But to suggest that the Kodokan was so parochial as not to realise the importance of grappling skills (katame-waza) within the framework of the total competitive skill, is too far-fetched to accept.

What I hope happened was that the powers-that-be realised the many daunting problems within the project of setting-up such a gokyo, and this stopped progress. To give but three examples:–

1. By the very fact of making a list, it would mean that some techniques were left out, and who is to decide which are omitted? It has already been seen with the gokyo-no-nage-waza that present authorities complain about omissions. There will always be people who think those missed out are better than those included!

2. What is the purpose of such a list anyway? To lay down which are "correct" or "fundamental"? Again what – or who – is to decide?

3. If such a task of compilation IS to be tackled, what are to be the criteria for classification? Four techniques will cover all the locks and strangles (i.e. straight and bent arm-lock; pressure on windpipe or blood-vessels for strangles), anything else is only a different way of doing one of those four techniques. Much of the same applies to osae-waza (pins), which is simply how to put force/body weight on the opponent's head, shoulders, arms, hips; anything else is just a variation of doing that. There must be dozens and dozens of ways of applying those eight techniques. At best it is just a personal opinion (the more experienced the selector is, the better the opinion is presumed to be); at worst it is an arbitrary selection which only breeds restrictive and repressive attitudes.

At one stage I did contemplate trying to devise a Gokyo-no-katame-waza, in an attempt to fill the gap that some traditional instructors felt was created by the very presence of the throwing Gokyo. But I gave it up, for I just could not find forty – or anything like that number – ne-waza techniques (although there does not *have* to be 40)! This paucity of fundamental techniques is also very evident when considering the katame-no-kata. There are of course plenty of variations, on a basic few techniques, but once, and if, variations are to be considered as being worthwhile extracting from the whole welter of ne-waza tactics, then some form of kata is more to the point, for kata is the place for isolating situations (see Part Three), and certainly in ne-waza, situations are more important than just techniques.

However, I do want to show some kind of "basic" range of ground-play technique, so I will lay out the more common ones – in groups, but the groups will be different from the traditional ones, leastways in osaekomi-waza. There is little to disagree with in locks and strangles – arms are either bent, or straight, necks are squeezed from front or back, but osae (pins) can offer differences and variations in approach. Traditional grouping has been based upon the direction of attack (NOT the purpose), e.g. kami-shiho-gatame = (attacking from and) pinning the (opponent's) upper body; yoko-shiho-gatame = (attacking from and) pinning the (opponent's) side-body. Tradition has also decided what is regarded as a "standard" pin form and indicates this by the prefix "hon", while anything that looks similar, but differs in details is called a "variation" and then "kuzure" replaces the "hon" prefix.

When I teach pinning techniques I like to stress the object of them, so that when I group them, I base these groupings on the objective. There are four main parts of the opponent to fix – his head, arm, shoulders, waist. Of course not only are these parts controlled; when the head is pinned an arm is often held also, but these parts are the dominating ones and I have listed them in order of priority. See Fig. 5

The reader will no doubt conclude from what has gone before, relating to both the gokyo and the Analysis of Throwing Skills, that I am very much against any approach which attempts to make a definitive statement about what is "right" or what is "acceptable". I think general principles can be formulated, based upon extensive empirical experience, but how these principles are put into practice is the responsibility of the performer – possibly with the help of a sound coach or teacher.

Fig. 5

b   kuzure-yoko-shiho-gatame

e   kuzure-kami-shiho-gatame

c   hon-yoko-shiho-gatame

f   kata-gatame

a   kuzure-yoko-shiho-gatame

d   hon-kesa-gatame

g   kuzure-tate-shiho-gatame

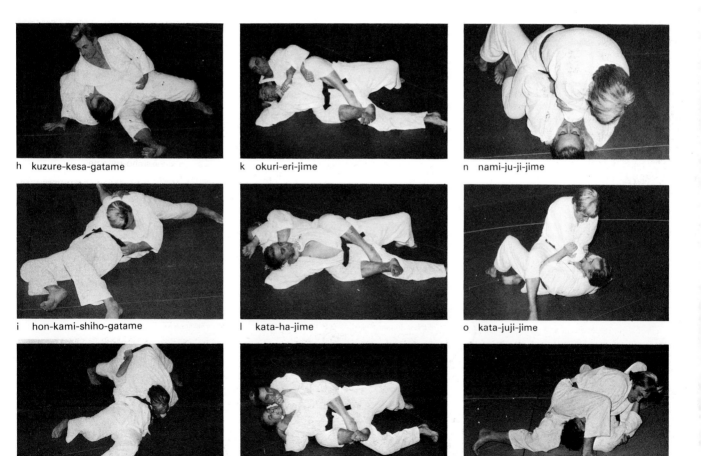

h   kuzure-kesa-gatame

k   okuri-eri-jime

n   nami-ju-ji-jime

i   hon-kami-shiho-gatame

l   kata-ha-jime

o   kata-juji-jime

j   obi-gatame

m   hadaka-jime

p   kata-te-kata-ashi-jime

q tsukikomi-jime

t ashi-gatame

w ude-garami (up)

r ju-ji-gatame

u hon-ude-gatame

x ude-garami (down)

s hiza-gatame

v sangaku-gatame

CONCLUDING REMARKS

The way of learning is also individual. Whether the alphabet is learnt first, and then the letters made up into words; or whether the words are learnt first and which letters make them up learnt later; or even whether the learning of complete sentences (tactical situations) are tackled first, is dependent upon the mental make-up of the player and/or the coach, and the total situation.

Observation and Empathy

Information from cybernetics can be used to get a differing view on the subject of skill acquisition and learning. Skill improvement can be seen as the result of information received from feedbacks, of both an internal and external kind. External feedback is based mainly upon the perceptual ability; internal feedback is from what is called the "kinaesthetic loop" or the "feel" of it.

By and large, the skilled player will work mostly on the kinaesthetic feel of the movement, whereas the novice will work on the perceptual feedback. (It is interesting to note that research seems to point to the development that as the skilled performer goes past his peak, he reverts back to the perceptual feedback.) It means, to put it a different way, that cues (which "trigger" off the skills), change as improvement takes place. It should go without saying (but perhaps sometimes it should be said) that what the skilled player needs to know about what starts an attack off, is not always the same as for the novice!

For the inexperienced player the watching, critical watching, is an essential part of his training (even the Japanese acknowledge this, for they have a phrase for just that – midori keiko – the watching of, and learning from, practice). He must know what to look for, what are the technical factors he should note (if necessary the coach should help him directly with the task). What are the "displays"? What does the attacker do BEFORE he launches an attack (i.e. bending his head forward, stamping with his right foot etc. etc.). These factors and display need not be copied (see Imitation), but they can be realised as being a part of the total skill of throwing. Colour cues are very useful in the watching/learning process. If the coach is illustrating his teaching by demonstration (of throws etc.), dramatically highlighting the important parts of the "display" or visually isolating cues can be of great help; and the mark of a good coach is how simple and understandable he can make these cues. For such a purpose I may wear red trousers (to show clearly what happens to the legs and feet) and black gloves (to show precisely where the hands go). Having an all-white demonstration (white suits, white skin etc.) can present a very bewildering splurge to the novice.

The kinaesthetic loop is concerned with how the body "feels" the action; does it feel "right"? To create this kind of training situation, differing types of kata can be devised (see KATA). Mechanical aids can be used to check that the body (and its parts) are in the right position. Apparatus can be designed to isolate the required points. Even such obtuse aids as "mental rehearsal" can be included here, and have real value. That means the player goes through the whole throwing action in his head; he thinks about every part – when he does that, he will then do this, and then that, and so on. He "rehearses" what he is going to do.[16] All is grist to the mill of getting the "feel" across to the learner!*

SPACE, PACE AND DIRECTION

These are the first of the many additions to technique that convert it into a skill. I have given some definition of technique – the physio-mechanical systems of the body driven by the force of the dynamic body-weight – so now what about "skill"? I have a definition in my book *Judo for the West:*[15] "Skill is a set of movements made to achieve a predetermined objective with the least amount of effort and with the greatest degree of certainty and regularity." Although it was written before 1967 it does not appear to need any basic alteration. What I would like to do here is to bring to the notice of the reader that part of the definition which refers to the consistency of result.

Habitual movement is very similar to skill; indeed there is a large overlap of characteristics but it is the relation to success that differentiates the two.[16] Once the habituated

---

* I once designed and built a piece of apparatus which allowed the trainees to do the throwing skills in a controllable situation (the coach could control it). The throwing action could be stopped at ANY point during the movement, so that verbal and physical correction could be given immediately at the standard necessary. Because, incidentally, the partner could also be prevented from being "pile-driven" into the ground, the thrower could concentrate fully on the corrections that were needed, without concerning himself about the partner. Improvement was fast.

sequence is triggered by its stimulus, then it goes to the end, irrespective of the situation. Skill, however, should be able to "absorb" the changes in situation or environment, by changing slightly in order to achieve the preconceived end – with the greatest possible regularity. The changing feedback from the performance must be continually monitored by "tracking tasks". Is what happens the result of so-and-so? If it is not, then some part of the movement will need to be changed (the kinaesthetic loop). For this to happen effectively, the performer must know what should be happening – in as much detail as possible, suitable for the individual.

What Sort of Players are there?

How, or indeed if at all, these factors are to be introduced into the training – randori – situation, is a problem for the conscientious coach. The trainees will no doubt cover the whole range of intelligence – from the very dull to the very bright (just as there will be a full range among the coaches!) Without trying to make any value judgments whether it is better to be brighter or duller to be a champion, the coach has to decide whether the group, as a collection of individuals, is capable of intellectually appreciating what the skill factors are, and therefore how they are to be practised. If they are dull, it may be best to stick to just physical rote-learning (see Ritual/drill). Intellectual explanations will only confuse them. If they are intelligent then perhaps unexplained per-

formance will bore them and drive them away from training. The coach must do some self-inspection and decide which he is best at – for example is he good at physical demonstration, or intellectual explanation; whichever is his forté (and no doubt he will never be completely incompetent in the other area of coaching), he will naturally utilise that the most, but he must remember to develop the other style, so that he can use it when required. In practice of course what often happens is that the coach gathers about him, unintentionally or otherwise, a group that reflects the general characteristics of his personality, which makes adoption of other teaching styles unnecessary; for similar personalities will get from him what they need.

What Sort of Coaches are there?

The coach may be a "part-thinker" or a "whole thinker"; that is he may normally think in terms of details and parts (an approximately equivalent idea in some psychology schools is called "field independent".[17]) Now these people will no doubt be best at teaching/coaching in "parts". Whereas the person who thinks in "wholes" (what can be called "field dependent") will be best at coaching in total concepts. Of course a really capable coach will be able to change his approach (and WILL change) to almost any to suit the individual or group he is facing at any one time. But without a doubt, he will have a preference for just one sort of approach. That is he will be best at the

method which is "him"! It is the person, not the method that is important.

Space and the Two-part Concept

What happens sometimes, when throws are being taught, is the instructor forgets a very obvious fact – which is it takes two to make a throw! Instead of considering the two as parts of a whole, the coach inadvertently talks to only one person in the combination – the thrower. This I feel is a mistake. It is the whole which is important, the interplay of the two. I suggest there are two general ways in which the idea of throwing can be approached:

(1) from the two part concept (this is the traditional way of doing it), or
(2) from a one-part concept – which refers to the SPACE contained between the bodies, and around the bodies.

Let me fairly quickly go over the two-part concept first, but possibly giving a different slant to it than has usually been given in the past.

The Two-Part Concept

Certainly one of Kano's biggest contributions to the development of judo theory, was his attempt to break down or to analyse a throwing action, and give names or titles to those parts. It would appear that jujitsu did not attempt any such analysis – either through ignorance or choice; for example I have a book in my possession on the Yabe School of Jujitsu (published in 1904). The author claims that it is identical to the instruction of the Ten Shin Ryu jujitsu (one of the schools attended by Kano). In it there is no mention of "preparation for throwing".

Kano differentiated and named three phases of an attacking action, tsukuri, kuzushi and kake. Tsukuri (from the verb tsuku (reru); the suffix "ri" emphasises the "body" of the action) means to make, manufacture, prepare. It would appear as though it refers to the action of the attacker done to the opponent, preparing him, or "setting him up", for the throw. Kuzushi (from the verb kuzu (reru); it is the suffix "shi" here which emphasises the "body" of the action), means to crumble, to fall apart or down. This appears to refer to what happens to the opponent. It is the control of his physical stance which breaks down – as a result of the tsukuri of the attacker. Kake (from the verb ka (karu), the suffix "ke" turns the verb into a noun) is a very complex word (the dictionary lists 20 different, subtle meanings!). It is to do with "hanging on to", "hanging together" and so can be seen as the joining together, or "hanging together" of tsukuri and kuzushi, in terms of an effective result.

COMMENTS

The recognition of these three phases of throwing, in terms of importance in throwing theory (for it is curious that no-one appears to have applied them to newaza skills) seems to be somewhat irregular. In Kano's own small book (*Judo Kyohon* published in 1936, "Judo Reader"), he only discusses kuzushi; in 1922 Yamashita (later 10th Dan) published *Kogakko Judo Kyujin no Jissai* ("The right way of teaching judo in Primary Schools"), and he only writes of tsukuri and kake; the very famous newaza specialist who finished as a 9th Dan, Oda, in his two volumed *Judo Taikan* ("Judo Vista" published in 1930) only writes of kuzushi. This inconsistency can be seen reflected in the many different interpretations that exist of these three "basic" terms throughout the judo world. It has also produced a lot of confusion in the teaching approach. Because of the different emphasis given to each part by different authorities, lesser mortals have often come to the stage where the parts are more important than the whole. For example, tsukuri is too often taught as being something done separately from the throw; tsukuri is done first, then the throw. Tsukuri can only be an intrinsic part of the throw. It is something like practising the run-up, isolated from the long jump, which would be nonsense. Tsukuri must be a part of the total throwing action. It is because these terms have caused such confusion that I will not use them; not because they are wrong (Kano has my greatest respect for tackling the problem of analysis in the first place – at the time he did), but because they do not go far enough, they are not flexible enough, to cater for all possible situations that arise in randori. If these terms (tsukuri, kuzushi and kake) are to be used, I feel they should be approached with much freedom of thought. Kano, when he was illustrating his hypothesis of the inter-relationship between tsukuri, kuzushi and kake, frequently used the analogy of tilting men onto the corners of their base (heels, toes etc.) thus showing in one small, but dramatic manner how control could be taken away from an individual in terms of "loss of balance". Unfortunately, like so many other great teachers, before and after him, his dramatic analogies (because of their very drama) have become dogma instead of illustrations. Balance breaking is at best only one way of manifesting tsukuri, kuzushi and kake (and in practice, a very inefficient one). There are many others – much better than the dogma of tilting!

Let me give but six examples of the kind of "disturbing of equilibrium" that I would use when teaching the fundamentals of judo skills. Which one I would use as the dominating one would depend upon the group I was teaching:

1. Take a leaf from the pages of Behavioural Psychologists, a simple refined stimulus/response pattern; a push or pull (or both) by the attacker, and the opponent could over-react, so putting himself into an unstable position.

2. A gross stimulus, in the sense of physical aggression, in the form of combination attacks; again the purpose to be achieved is an over-response, yet again putting the opponent in an unstable position.

3. Reduce the opponent, by fatigue, to an un-

stable state; this can be done by a continuous linking of attacks, not to achieve a score – only fatigue.

4. Shock: by doing something totally unexpected and startling, the opponent will "freeze" into a position that he cannot defensively respond from (see "choke" in Shiai).

5. By laying "traps" (in the form of bogus opportunities) so that the opponent is tempted to launch an attack; that very launching is the "breaking of his stance".

6. Utilisation of the Rules (of competition). This can be done in many ways, e.g. force a man to the edge of the fighting area, and as he reacts, so as not to step off the area (a penalisable action) he can be attacked.

NOTE. If such actions as these are seen as tsukuri, kuzushi and kake, they can be applied with equal facility in katame-waza as well as nage-waza.

SPACE

The above range of conditions showing how to prepare an opponent for an attack is not just for the player who already has some knowledge of judo performance, but can be just as beneficially used as a starting point for initial learning. When Kano said that tsukuri, kuzushi and kake should be taught at the first stage of learning (judo) I agree with him entirely – provided they are not restricted to his analogy of "balance breaking"! It is not just a matter of eight different directions of pushing and pulling the opponent (happyo-kuzushi). Any of the above listed six can be used, and I indeed do use any and all of them in an early

learning situation, depending upon the particular group I am dealing with. For example, if it is a young group, orientated towards contest, I would start with No. 6, making point-scoring and point-avoiding the core of the lessons; if it were an older group, less active, I might start with No. 1 or 3; if another young group, but not so competitively minded (girls for example) then 2 or 4 might be better. In addition, I would not hesitate to devise other starting approaches, even more "tailor-made" for the group. As always it is people, not method, which is important.

The following is a way that I have devised for a general situation, which stresses a "unity" of approach, instead of a "duality" (i.e. two separate bodies). The "unity" refers to the seeing of the bodies as one single unit. Or, put another way, to consider the space around the two bodies, and how it is affected by the bodies moving within it. It is a way that will not suit everybody, but used with consideration it has many advantages over the "two-body" approach. One of the reasons I like it, is that it does cover every situation, both in standing play (tachi-waza) and ground-play (ne-waza), with all the sub-sections of combinations and counters etc. For one of the most important elements in a learning situation is the one of transfer.

The degree of transference of training from the learning environment to the performing environment is critical. If the transference helps the final skill it is called positive transfer, if not, then negative transfer. The closer the similarity between the learning and the perfor-

ming environment, the better the chances of a positive transfer; the less similar they are, the better chances of a negative transfer (which means the final skill could be worse!) I have found that approaching the business of skill acquisition from the point of view of the "space concept" the transference is very positive.

Unit Space Concept

Internal Space

A throw, or any form of attack, can be divided into two simple types of space: Attacking space, the distance existing between the two combatants, and through which the attacker has to move in order to achieve . . . Throwing Space, which is the space or gap between the two bodies when the opponent is taken off his feet. In very general terms, the attacking space needs to be big – to allow the attacker to move in and build up momentum (he may, for instance, need to turn anywhere between a half and a full turn during an attacking movement); whereas the throwing space needs to be as small as possible, so that the transfer of force (developed by the technique) can be as direct and efficient as possible (and at the same time provide the minimum space for the opponent to construct a defensive action).

Of course the above is an over-simplification. For example, if the throwing attack is to the opponent's rear (Nos. 5, 7, 9, 10 etc. in the

Fig. 6a. Opposing stances, closed space on one side, open on the other

Gokyo) the attacking space could be small, for there is no need to turn. But the pattern, as a pattern, is good enough. Now, change the attention to the opponent, who will be trying to do the opposite to the attacker; he will be trying to keep the space between the two bodies small, so giving no room for the attacker to move in; if by chance (or plan!) the attacker does get into a throwing position, the opponent will be trying to make that space as big as possible, thus giving himself room to escape in and make inefficient the transfer of power.

In practice of course neither man is the attacker or defender, both are attacker and defender simultaneously; the role changes from moment to moment, depending upon who controls the situation at any instant. Control depends upon planning. Planning is for control of the space!

With developing sophistication of space sensitivity[18],* the attacking space can be further sub-divided into two — lateral and longitudinal. The bending or crouching of the fighters are the ways of affecting longitudinal space; the turning or twisting the body, by changing the positions of the feet, or moving the shoulders, is how the lateral spaces are controlled.

* People have an extremely varied capacity for movement as a part of skill acquisition. Some require movement as a part of their learning environment, others prefer static conditions in which to learn. Some have a greater intrinsic spatial awareness than others, and hence will need less help to develop in this direction. They are usually the ones who are said to have "natural talent". However, that does not mean they are automatically champions; they will still need a lot of discipline to turn that latent ability into an effective skill.

Fig. 6b. Parallel stances, space more or less the same on each side

Fig. 6c. Crouching opposing stances, closing space at shoulders, opening at hips

A CROUCHING STANCE

Frequently, restrictively called a "defensive" crouch, (figure 6c), possibly because of the Japanese term jigotai, which is always illustrated by a man standing with his legs bent, and translated as "defensive" stance. It could have been more advantageous in the early days of judo development in Britain to have used the more relevant meaning of the central ideograph, which is "protection", for protection has a more latent meaning of attacking — in order to achieve that protection — than defending, which is more negative and almost totally lacking in aggression. Certainly in free-play situations a crouching stance should not be assumed to be defensive. It can be of course, but just as equally it can be an attacking stance. The trainee must learn, as early as possible, what are the physical differences between the two crouches, so that he can recognise them, and plan his attack accordingly. In spatial terms it is a very useful shape; it closes up the upper spaces, thus making it difficult for the opponent to move his shoulders and so restricts his capability to make lateral attacking spaces; but by keeping space lower down open, at the hip level, he can move/swing his hips through that space and so develop enough power to make a dangerous attack of his own.

Such a stance therefore is very effective when it is concerned with DEFENDING against Driver attacks from the opponent. (Drivers are flank attacks, i.e. throwing from one side to the other.) It is also very effective for ATTACKING with "Roller" throwing actions. The opposite is also true. It is not so good when Rollers have to be stopped (especially back Rollers, i.e. No. 17 and all the other "gakes"), or the Lifter (both I and II); or when it has to facilitate the user attacking with Drivers.

AN UPRIGHT STANCE

The Japanese is shizentai, the upright or "natural" stance, (figure 6b). Here too it must be realised that this can be just as much a defensive stance, as an attacking stance, as it is effective for the opposite set of conditions to the crouched stance. In general, it is to limit the space at the lower hip level, so defending against, or protecting against, Roller attacks, whilst facilitating Driver attacks. The upright stance provides a good base for twisting the trunk, getting maximum effect on the sleeve side of the opponent's body.

Again to use the stance against the opposite set of conditions would be dangerous, i.e. to stop Drivers, and facilitate attacking Rollers!

RIGHT AND LEFT FIGHTERS

The terms, left and right handers are frequently heard in judo parlance. Superficially it seems straight forward enough, but in learning skills it can be slightly confusing. It depends on what Left and Right is referring to. If it is referring to which way the opponent is being thrown, to his right or left side, then there is no problem. If, however, it refers in any way to the thrower, it is not so simple; it should now refer to which leg he uses as the "driver" (it seldom does however!), e.g. a left throw would mean that it is the left leg which is being used and he can therefore throw the opponent — to his right, with turning throws, like harai-goshi, or to his (the opponent's) left with "no turning throws" like sasai-tsurikomi-ashi (the same driving leg is used in each case). Very few judo players can use both legs as the "driver" with equal facility (unless a lot of training is undertaken); most are "natural" left or right leggers (see Kata).

IN THIS BOOK, A RIGHT HAND THROW MEANS THE OPPONENT IS THROWN TO HIS RIGHT — *NOTHING ELSE! A left hand throw is the opposite!*

Side Space

In terms of utilisation of side spaces, it is important to realise how the driving leg affects the problem. By and large, a fighter will keep his driving leg back, furthest from the opponent (see figure 6a); which means he can, by pivoting on the forward foot, swing the driving foot into the correct position (for the technique being performed, see figure 7); the pivot foot then moves on to do the job it has to do — "blocking" or "sweeping". The shoulders tend to line up with the fore and aft positioning of the feet, so giving an oblique line of body to the opponent. If the same "leg drivers" fight together the obliques are parallel and the side spaces are roughly the same. If, however, opposite "leg drivers" fight, the side spaces are

opposed (see figure 6c) — that is close on one side (the shoulders very close) and very open on the other (shoulders far apart). Because most of the time left leg-drivers fight left-leg-drivers, they become accustomed to fight through constant side-spaces. Right-leg drivers meet far more left-leg drivers (both in training and competition) than other right-leg-drivers, therefore they become accustomed to having open spaces on the throwing side. When two "right-leg drivers" meet in contest, they invariably have many difficulties (and the match is a very dull one) because the unaccustomed spaces hinder their skills considerably. Two important training exercises arise from this simple observation.

1. Fighters must train in situations where the side spaces (on the throwing side) are both closed and open. Simulated conditions must be set up in which the opponent provides different space situations on the throwing side.

2. The balance-breaking analogy crops up again, creating problems. Because of the misreading of this analogy (see page 27) it has become assumed that the space on the throwing side must always be closed, or to put it another way, the attacker must always initially pull the opponent's shoulder forward on the side he is going to throw on. THIS IS NOT ALWAYS NECESSARY! Indeed it can be seen that sometimes it is advantageous if the attacker pushes the opponent's shoulder BACK, so making more space on the side he wants to throw. (When the feet leave the ground

Fig. 7

(kake), he can then pull the shoulder forward to close up the throwing space as the man falls, to make him land on his back.)

Drivers are very frequently used in the open-side situation (although Rollers are by no means excluded) which has an implication that all good competitors should recognise. Throwing attacks, which normally have the throwing direction one way, e.g. tai-otoshi forward, can be used to throw in the opposite direction – tai-otoshi backwards!

This change of throwing direction can often happen when the opportunity is considered in detail. Another good example is kouchi-gari to the front.

RANDORI EXERCISES

Look at ways of opening attacking spaces when the opponent is keeping them closed. Examples: hold under opponent's arms, by snatching up arms/elbows, lift the opponent's arms up – make the space; use each arm separately, so getting rid of one arm (of the opponent) at a time – make the space; push one or both arms off– make space; the attacker pulls his sleeve (hold) arm or his collar (hold) side back, breaking the grip of the opponent – space is made!

The difficulty is to keep the attacker's body flexible and loose, able to move into the throwing position fast, when the arms and shoulders are very hard and strong, busy making space.

Do lots of alternative pushing and pulling with the hands (readily reinforced with a large, gross, shoulder movement) in order to make side spaces. Fit throwing types into the spaces. Make determined attacks on open side spaces, with no intention of closing them until after the throwing action has been made. Techniques to try first are Nos. 5, 7, 14, 16, 20, 21, 30; these are the "easiest", then try Nos. 8, 12 – but as Drivers NOT Rollers! After that, well! who knows what can be done!

Now try for the longitudinal spaces. Here another leaf can be taken from the traditional book – use tsurikomi. Tsurikomi refers to a very complex hand action, which is pulling forward and upward; it also has a scooping feeling about it. It is good for getting the opponent up, if he is crouching. Push down first, then "tsurikomi", in other words, in the same way that the opponent's shoulders can be pushed and pulled (simultaneously) to get the side spaces, so he can be "bounced" to get the length spaces. Techniques to try first are Nos. 8, 11, 12, 14, 16.

When the trainees have "felt" and "played" with these spaces in standing play, they should experience them all in ground play too. When using any of the arm-locks plenty of space will be needed before the locking attack is launched. If an escape is needed from a pin, then space (between the bodies) must be made first – just the same as the opponent has to expand the throwing space if he wants to avoid a terminal score. Length spaces will be necessary to apply strangles (shime-waza) if done from the (opponent's) front, i.e. kata jujijime and tsukikomi-jime, side spaces will be needed for strangles like kata te-kata ashi-jime.

Starting Training

External Space

Till now, it has been the space "trapped" between the two bodies which has been closely looked at, in order to see what happens to it during the many phases of attack and defence – the internal space. Now let us talk about the space immediately surrounding the two – the external space. This has seldom been discussed before in judo textbooks although many "space-aware" fighters have known all about it empirically.

It is, by definition, something of an area of desperation, although spectacular action is common there. In other words, it is by and large, an area in which point-scoring falls are avoided. To obtain a terminal score, a competitor must be landed on his back with impetus (see Rules of Competition). If he can make sure that he does not do that, then he reduces the score according to the degree of withdrawal he achieves.

NOTE: If a 10 score attack is made, the match finishes at that moment.
Pins have to be sustained for 30 seconds to get 10. For more detailed information see International Judo Federation Rule Book.

SCORING			
Points value	Throws	Pins Secs.	Locks and Strangles
10*	Fully on back (with impetus)	30	only submission, which gives terminal score
7	On side/back	25–30	
5	Hips and side	20–25	
3	Hips only	10–20	

AVOIDING SCORES

The immediate object of competitive throwing is to get the "other man" to land on his back, and if possible to make him stay there. The job of the "other man" is to avoid that. It can be done several ways; stepping or jumping round the attack, countering or stopping the attack, or if late and the throw has succeeded, by twisting or turning out of the fall. There are several ways of introducing twist and turn outs into the training plan, but whichever way is chosen it should be incorporated into the first-ever judo lesson – if the learner is competitively orientated (motivated) (see page 28).

First step is to inculcate into the trainee that the back (of his body) is something which he does not allow to touch the floor – at any time. For him to voluntarily allow his back to touch, there must be a specific instruction from his coach, for a specific purpose (probably to practise a specific aspect of skill – as done by the other man (i.e. terminal score throwing); or it can be an idea of his own, but again only in order to practise a specific aspect of skill. By and large however, the trainee should not allow the back to touch, or to stay on his back for a moment longer than he need. If the back does touch, he must jerk, twist off it, as fast as possible.

Fig. 8a. Cartwheel—off the elbows, not the hands

Fig. 8b. Land on the front, feet hitting first

1. VERY SIMPLE INTRODUCTION

In pairs, they roll about on the mat, helping each other to roll, i.e. hands are being continually moved to different places e.g. belt, trousers, sleeves, in order to help the partner roll over. It is continuous movement, with no breaks. They then begin to "keep the backs off the mat". As the back touches they quickly twist off.*

2. NEXT STEP: OR NOT SO SIMPLE AN INTRODUCTION

Lots of "cartwheels". A simple gymnastic exercise. "Cartwheels" are a much better general head-over-heels exercise than forward rolls (of any kind). Forward rolls always land the performer ON HIS BACK – it can be negative teaching. "Cartwheels" have a lot more possible variations too, e.g. land on feet, land on front, cartwheel on the elbows (see figure 8a and b). There can be a much more positive transfer.

3. A DIFFERENT STARTING STEP

Head stands, roll over; head stands, roll over, twist to land on front. This can be taken on a stage, so that it is done over a partner.

---

* When a teacher takes on his group or class for the first time, one of the very earliest tasks he must tackle is the assessing of the ability of each individual making up the group. All aspects of the total ability must be considered, and only then can he devise a training plan that will help each individual – taking into account the particular abilities. One of the occasions to begin to assess the physical ability is in the "warm up" sessions.

Fig. 9a. Twisting out—on the collar-side (grip)

Fig. 9b. Twisting out—on the sleeve-side (grip)

GENERAL NOTE. Apart from the specific aspect of "teaching" body twists in "external space", such gymnastic exercises help enormously towards improving general body awareness and spatial awareness. Indeed gymnastics, of any kind, is a very useful adjunct to judo training.

4. A DIFFERENT STARTING STEP.

There are simple twists, which are not so complex as the twist outs (but that does not necessarily mean they should be the STARTING step). They can be learnt very simply in a back throw situation (see figures 9a and b). Sometimes it is better to start with a more difficult approach, for it can be easier to "come down" to a simpler task than to "go up" to a harder one.

Fig. 10. Turning *out* of the throw

Fig. 11. Turn-out *with* the throw—he will land on his front

Combining the Approaches

Cartwheel "turn offs" can be started easily with very low modified shoulder throws (No. 8 gokyo); chest-stand "turn off" can be done to a very low tsurikomi-goshi (No. 12 gokyo). In the early stages of training or practice, "turn offs" are usually found to be easier turning OUT of the throw (see figure 10), therefore these may be done first, and the turn outs going with the throw (see figure 11), may be done afterwards.

Needless to say, both ways will need to be done sooner or later. In a competitive situation, the "avoider" will have very little choice! To reiterate, but in differing terms, the "turn out" away from the throwing direction is done early in the fall, whereas the "turn out" into the throw is done late (and is therefore not always possible). In randori many situations of varying difficulty will need be devised to allow the players to practise these turn-outs. Practising twist-outs is much easier. Start with any and all of the back throws, and facility can be acquired from them. Moving on, "front-throws" can then be tried. If for example tai-otoshi is used, the opponent steps round as he is falling, sits down and twists onto his front.

Using External Space to Win

Early in the training, it is just the avoiding of scores that is made the most important part of the exercise. However, once facility has been achieved, this somewhat negative approach should be avoided, and the more positive approach used – that is, the "turn-offs" and "twist outs" should be used to BEAT the opponent. The "avoider of the fall" has a great psychological advantage – for a moment – over his opponent. The opponent is confident that he has won (or at least gained a good score) because he HAS THROWN his opponent, but instead of that he is now suddenly faced with an opponent who is trying to get a score from him!

It can take several forms.

1. If the avoidance simply moves the (thrown) man onto a different position (but he has not fallen at all), then a counter-attacking throw can be used.
2. The avoidance fall can be used to throw the attacker with.

3. The avoiding fall can be used to initiate ground play, into pins, locks, or strangles (see figures 12 a, b, c, d and e).

COMMENTARY

Randori is a place where these situations can be explored. If they do not arise often enough in "natural" conditions, then they must be made to happen, and this is where randori overlaps into Kata.

Fig. 12b

Fig. 12a

A throw has been made, a fast cartwheel into . . .   . . . a "solid" pin attack.

Fig. 12c

Fig. 12d

Fig. 12e

A poor attack, which gives the opportunity for . . .

. . . a fast, unexpected, arm-lock in space, falling into . . .

. . . "normal" ju-ji—gatame!

Dynamic Factors

Pace

This factor, the pace or the speed at which the players are moving when the attack takes place, has been mentioned briefly in the earlier texts. As I said at the beginning of the Gokyo section, this is a factor in skill which "trad judo" has never really discussed. For example, because both deashi-harai and uki-waza were shown and taught when both players were standing still, no-one recognised the most obvious of facts, that all would be different when they start moving — especially if it were fast or slow. An indirect hint has sometimes been "built-in" when they, the performers, were put into "jigotai" (as in uki-waza) at the start of the movement. This could tell them, if they were experienced, that they should be moving slowly and strongly. But when it comes to differentiating — in speed terms — between say harai-goshi and deashi harai (see "An Exercise in Comparison") nothing is mentioned about speed, pace or tempo.[8]

Randori is the place to experience pace! From the beginning of the training (the first night) some kind of awareness of at least three levels of pace should be introduced; fast, medium and slow. Such a crude classification may vary with each person (i.e. one person's "slow" may be another's "medium"), but that does not matter, providing he knows, "feels", what differing paces are like.

FAST

If the pace is very fast, then of course there is not enough time even to turn (in order to do throws like harai-goshi, uchi-mata) so the most suitable attacks are those in which there is the least gross bodily movements i.e. ankle trips. Yet even at this level there is a differentiation built into the various types of trips, e.g. harai-tsurikomi-ashi is for a faster pace than sasai-tsurikomi-ashi.

It is easier to snatch an arm-lock when moving fast in ground-play, than to try and slow it all down in order to organise the "power" for a pin.

MEDIUM

In the early days of training, it is here that most of the throws will be done. The experienced player of a couple of months will not be able to handle the skills at either end of the pace range very well (fast or slow), but here in the medium range there is enough time to get a movement going, and also to build up the necessary power to make it work. Later on, when a year or two's work has been done on the skills, pace appreciation — in this middle range — will be critical. Yet even at an advanced level it is still the most ENCOMPASSING pace range, covering all the long standing, proven, effective throwing actions, e.g. uchi-mata, tai-otoshi, seoi-nage, ouchi-gake, osoto-gari etc. Therefore experienced players will need to know the extent of the pace range of the medium pace section well, so that they are able to fit quite subtle pace differences with the appropriate throwing action. For example, harai-goshi and uchi-mata (of the Driver type NOT the Roller) are very similar, (in terms of pace-range), but usually the harai-goshi is done at a slightly faster pace than the fastest of the uchi-matas; ashi-guruma and hane-goshi are much of the same pace, but again, ashi-guruma will be that shade the faster.

SLOW

At a slow pace range, there is of course the implicit inclusion of power. Sometimes players do move slowly with no increase of power from that they would use at a fast pace, however, usually moving slowly does mean there is plenty of power available (see "go" in Kata). Caution too is very evident, therefore few mistakes are made, either in opportunities given (for an attack) or in performance of attack (technical errors). Body control, in terms of stability, in terms of discipline, must be of a very high order. To attack with something like No. 25 sumi-gaeshi, or even No. 8 seoi-nage at a slow pace needs courage as well as very correct (organised) technical application. The body shape, the positioning of the feet (particularly the driving foot) has got to be accurately done, and such accuracy can only be learnt in movement at the right pace.

COMMENTS

Many ways can be utilised to bring home to the trainee how important pace is, and how he is to feel pace. Areas on the training mat can be given over to different pace ranges, as the players move on to these areas they must move according to that pace specified.[8, 19] Music can be played, at different tempos; they can learn much about pace from that medium. A pace key can be called out by someone, all must change accordingly. Providing the message is getting across – recognition of pace through the body sensors – any way will do! Some throwing attacks depend almost entirely on a pace-change. One of the 1972 Japanese Olympic champions won his medal on just that. The technique was not that good, but because he could make the change of pace momentarily confuse his opponent, in that moment the technique was good enough!

In ground-play many attacks are made at the moment of pace-change. A slow move is made for a pin, the opponent moves quickly to avoid, automatically moving up into the arm-lock pace range, so that is what he is beaten with.

Speed of movement can compensate for poor technique, but slowness needs accuracy.

In the early days of training, three levels of speed or pace, may be all that the novice is capable of recognising, but later on in his training he must be able to recognise, and preferably work at, something like 7 or 8 (or even more) levels. Only in this way will he be able to extend his attacking repertoire, and to organise a better defence against the many opponents he will meet during his competitive life.

Direction of Movement

Again this refers to the general direction that both competitors are moving in at any one moment in time. Another simple truism to keep in mind (like the "it takes two to make a throw") is "you can move faster going forward, than you can moving backwards!"

MOVING FORWARDS AND BACKWARDS

If the opponent is moving backwards, he is tending to OPEN the attacking space (good), yet by extension he also tends to open the throwing space (bad). By and large the novice prefers the situation which facilitates the throwing action (because he thinks that is the toughest space to control) whereas the experienced player will tend to go for the situation that facilitates the attacking space, because he knows that is the toughest space to create.

Again many exceptions will be found to this general pattern outlined above. But it does indicate the kind of thing that needs to be looked into.

MOVING SIDEWAYS

In general, if the opponent moves to his left (when the attack being used is RIGHT handed) then it will be similar to him moving forward; that is it will tend to close the attacking space (bad) and tend to close the throwing space (good). When moving to his right (in a similar attacking situation) it will be like him moving backwards, for it will tend to open the attacking space (good), but also open the throwing space (bad). Variations on these four main directions will modify the spaces according to the actual direction considered.

COMMENTS

In specific conditions, relating to specific individuals, whether the attacking spaces will always need to be big and the throwing spaces always small, will depend upon the techniques chosen for performance and the personality of the fighter. An ostentatious person frequently chooses an ostentatious attack and therefore needs all the room/space that he can get. He will choose a movement direction that will give him the maximum benefit for making large attacking movements. The quiet type may prefer the situation that requires the least movement from him, so he selects the "closing space" movement patterns. Space – big or small – as affected by the direction of movement, will affect considerably the way a technique needs to be done. Again randori.

Linking Techniques

Before trying to ascertain how techniques are to be linked, let us establish first what is the objective of linking them? There can be said to be three main objectives:

1. To achieve a terminal score; this is the conventional (recognised) objective; by linking two or more attacks — either in standing or ground play — the opponent is brought to a vulnerable position whereby the last attack finishes him.
2. To tire the opponent; every time an attack is made the opponent needs to make emotional and physical tense responses and adjustments. This can be very exhausting and after many such attacks the effect can be highly debilitating.
3. To change the location of the opponent within the contest area; if for example, a competitor tries to stay near the edge of the contest area in order to restrict the attacks (of his opponent) then he may need to be moved away from there to the centre area of the mat.*

Offensive Links (Renraku-Waza)

It can be seen, therefore, depending on the objective of the series of attacks, that the type of attack can vary considerably. The player should recognise that all attacks are not necessarily made to achieve terminal scores. An uchi-mata done as the FIRST of a terminal scoring link, is not the same as the LAST uchi-mata of the same type of link, and in turn is not the same as an uchi-mata done to exhaust the opponent, and will probably be different again from an uchi-mata attack intended to shift the opponent from A to B.

Too often, in the past, have combination attacks (renraku-waza) been seen as a failed terminal attack (either because of poor execution or opponent's defensive action), with a second attack thrown in, in an attempt to retrieve what is in fact a lost situation. No doubt sometimes this desperate volte-face (in terms of intent and body movement) happens and even proves successful, but it is not good enough to incorporate into a training plan. For consistency is most important in the smallest of the "wholes" (e.g. throwing) and certainly in the bigger of the "wholes" (e.g. tactics and strategy). A direct terminal attack, by definition, should mean complete mental and physical commitment; any reservations will only weaken it and lessen the chances of success; but because of that very essential commitment, a change of anything (direction of movement, body action, speed of movement etc.) is extremely difficult. Most terminal attacks, consist — or should consist — of ballistic movements[21] (full commitment); once such movements are launched they have to complete their intended journey.

Attacks launched to achieve objects other than terminal score, will necessitate something less than total commitment of body weight, the degree of reserve being dependent on the objective. For example, in the first objective (terminal scoring) each linked technique would have to give the impression that it is the last attack, therefore commitment would have to be high (say 80–90% of terminal attack) in order to "fool" the opponent, which means that the link would have to be practised as a link, for consistency of effect — kata! In the "tiring objective", commitment would be much less, but with a lot more strength included (say 50% terminal); change of location may need a very "exploding" type of attack (as distinct from the compactness of a terminal one), encouraging the opponent to move away from the "flailing" arms and legs of the attacks.

To say that a movement is not destined for terminal attacks, does in no way denigrate the quality of that movement. It will need to be just as disciplined, just as carefully trained and nurtured as any terminal attacking movement. Hence why these qualities must be cultivated in the freedom of randori. Here are some suggestions for a training scheme, but of course specific plans can only be designed for specific people.

* It is interesting to note that in Kawamura's book "Judo Combination Techniques"[20] he makes no attempt to classify — in any way — objectives of renraku-waza, or to introduce factors such as pace or direction of movement. Presumably he considers combinations are only for terminal scoring.

It will no doubt be appreciated that what links the objectives is change of pace and direction. Indeed it could be said that the linked attack to achieve a terminal score is to get the opponent moving at the pace most suitable for the attacker's strongest attack. Similarly in "fatigue-making linkage" it is the continual changing of pace and direction which is exhausting. "Changing location" is of course mainly concerned about direction of movement. Therefore the information acquired by the players during space, pace and direction training can easily be extended into this area of specialisation.

EXAMPLE 1

Let the trainees make up a series of attacks, say alternating Rollers and Drivers (what sort is left to them but at least four for a start). With anything less than four it is difficult to cultivate a sense of rhythm of movement, so essential to combination attacks. Indeed it may be necessary at the start, for them to (mentally) count themselves from one attack to another — like a metronome. Certainly the four attacks should be done whilst both are moving freely, but cooperatively, around the mat. There must be several steps between the attacks, so that there is a sense of MOVE-MENT. As the rhythm improves and confidence accumulates, the partner must try and respond in as normal a way as possible; that is he should show some resisting power, so that the attacker can feel it and organise his own

body to cope with that power (see how near the training situation is getting to kata (see Part 3). The same kind of arranged linking attack should be done in ground-play too; different attacks to change the movement pace of the partner. An arm-lock attack will tend to slow the man down, now suitable for a pin attack, to avoid the pin the pace will go up again, good enough for a strangle attempt(?), slowed again so another pin and arm-lock can be attempted. Again rhythm plays an important part in the linking.

EXAMPLE 2

When "tiring links" are being used, strength and control is more important than appreciation of pace and direction. Practice time should be given to "manhandling" the opponent with the least risk to the attacker, in terms of stability. Type of attack (i.e. Roller or Driver) is immaterial.
I suggest, for instance, that in any kind of "tiring attack" both feet (of the attacker) are on the ground. Allowing one foot/leg to wave about in the air— for whatever reason — would offer some form of "weakness" for the opponent to counter-attack.
In ground-play the principle is the same. Undulatory pressures — of all kinds — must be brought to bear on the rib-cage of the opponent, restricting and hindering his breathing, so that tiredness is brought on by shallow and intermittent breathing (see Restricted Oxygenation).

EXAMPLE 3

When trying to move an opponent from one area to another in a total fighting space (contest area), then big attacking movements are necessary (usually of the Driver type). In point scoring attacks, for example, the attacker's hands are pulled in close to his own body, giving the opponent the least opportunity to break away and create space. In the situation above, the opponent is expected to break-away, so the attacker will push (in the direction he wants the man to go) not pull. If the attacker's legs are to be used in sweeping actions, then the sweeps will be very big and much "looser" than if they were done for scoring points. In ground-play specific sides (of the opponent's body) would be blocked, so allowing no escape route that way, and then routes would be deliberately, but very surreptitiously, opened on those sides where the attacker wants the opponent to move.

EXAMPLE 4

This example, the last form of linkage to be suggested, is that of joining standing and ground attacks. It is very important that trainees can move very simply and quickly into ground-play situations.
It is not enough to say this should happen; physical guide lines must be offered. For example, after a couple of standing attacks, a back attack could be used (i.e. ouchi-gake); as the partner falls he twists to land on his front (so saving a terminal score), the attacker

cartwheels along the length of his body and on landing immediately attacks with –well, anything will do, lock, pin, or strangle. That could terminate the sequence, or several more could be practised in the ground-play situation.

Some kind of transference would then be practiced from a forward throwing attack. All forms of somersaults, cartwheels, twists and turns should be experimented with, in order to get a smooth change from standing into ground play. The originating attack is very strong, but the opponent manages to twist out and only loses say three or five points. The attacker has got to react spontaneously and move quickly down into the best ground-play situation he can contrive. On the other hand this failure could have been a deliberate plan to start ground play. For some reason a 10 terminal throw score is impossible (the opponent's defence is too strong, he is too skilful, etc., etc.), but if he can be got down to the ground there may be a better chance to win. (Perhaps the attacker's standard of ground-play is higher than his standing play.) However, the rules of competition prohibit a direct "pull-down" into ground-play, so the attacker must camouflage it with good/skilful throwing attacks – preferably on the end of several such attacks. These he will have to practice! Randori is the place!

Defensive Links (Kaeshi-Waza)

Just as in the offensive links, there is more than one objective in doing defensive links.

1. To win points;
This is the commonly recognised objective. An opponent's attacks can be beaten by countering the technique or by countering the attacking movement; in both cases the counter can be early or late. A general statement could be that early counters are "go"; later ones "ju" (see page 108). The early ones are preferable if possible, because of the lesser risk necessary, whereas late counters can go wrong – if so a loss of score is certain.

2. To shatter the confidence of the opponent: these counters are not designed primarily to score, but are used very early in the opponent's attacking movement (before it really has got under way), the object being to destroy the attacker's confidence! It shows that the one fighter can apparently foresee the attacking movement of the other and can stop it before it is even begun. The result can be psychologically shattering!

3. "Stonewalling."
For some reason a fighter wants to waste time, so his whole approach is to close up all the attacking spaces, minimising (eliminating if possible) any opportunities for his opponent to utilise.

SOME EXAMPLES

Countering the technique early: a good example of this is No. 28 sukui-nage; the opponent starts to launch No. 5 osoto-gari, at that instant the defender "walks" forward, using the inclination forward of the attacker (for he has hardly started to actually move forward yet) combined with his own surge forward (to close up tight the throwing spaces). He does sukui-nage before the opponent knows what's happened. (See go-no-kata). Countering the technique late: the attacker gets through his attacking space, and starts to close up for the throwing action of osoto-gari, but now the defender opens up that space (which is giving him an attacking space!) and turns – moving his driving foot into a more advantageous position – throws with what is in fact virtually the same throw – osoto-gaeshi.

Countering the movement early: a fighter likes to use (right) uchi-mata when he has manoeuvred his opponent to move towards his attacking side (his own right side). The opponent recognising this, instead of vacuously moving in that dictated direction, moves determinedly into that position and throws with his own attack before the first man even gets the chance to launch his uchi-mata. Such a counter requires a lot of movement sensitivity, and an empathy with the whole physio-mental build-up of the opponent's attack.

Countering the movement late:
Here the attack has been launched (it could still be uchi-mata – but not necessarily). It is stopped or blocked by the opponent; retreat is the order of the day! The original attacker quickly goes back to where he started (where he feels safe); as he does so the opponent follows him back, and before he can settle down, throws with a direct attack. One of the

commonest forms of this type of counter is ippon-seoi. One fighter attacks with ippon-seoi, the opponent blocks it, the man retreats quickly to his original position, the opponent immediately attacks him with ippon-seoi and scores.

Confidence Shattering

In any kind of confrontation, from politics, through war (and Klausewitz claimed that war was only an extension of politics!) to any combat sport, one of the most important areas of skill manipulation (it can be called a part of 'tactics') is the mental domination of one opponent by the other. Innumerable examples of sabre-rattling can be given from the frightening to the assinine (e.g. stamping out of a man-made holocaust by the bare feet of Shaka Zulu's impis, done to frighten the Christian missionaries; to the painting of innumerable cannon images on the walls of Peking to frighten away Ghengis Khan); so in the lesser world-shattering context of judo! The domination of the opponent "mentally" is just as important as the physical domination (see Shiai).

In this concept of countering, the idea is that the opponent must not be allowed to even start his attack! As soon as he makes the faintest flicker — even of an eyelid! — which looks like the start of an attack, the opponent crashes straight through it breaking him down — whether for points or not is quite immaterial (although of course getting points is a

Fig. 13a. The defender (left) crashing through the attacker—posed!

Fig. 13b. The defender (right) crashing through the attacker—real!

useful "bonus"). If possible, it is not enough that a defender stops the attack by opening the throwing space, for the attacker has won a moral victory in as much as he has created the attacking space and got through it; the attack

must be killed even before the attacking space has been made (see go-no-sen). In this way the attacker feels totally incompetent, not only is he unable to throw his man, he cannot even start an attack! (See figures 13a and 13b).

"Stonewalling"

This area of skill development is not countering as such, but deals only with the ability to stop the other man from attacking at all. There are many reasons for doing this, ranging from good to bad. Let me give a few examples. A type of fighter wants a fast pace and lots of space to facilitate his throwing attacks. He is very good at obtaining these conditions. His opponent knows he must keep the match in low key, pace must be kept slow, space tight. Another situation is when a man wants a "rest". There has been a flurry of attacks and blocks, the man wants to get his breath – and composure – back, he slows the match down, temporarily. Another obvious example; a man has just scored, he does not want his opponent to catch up, so again low-key fighting is needed. In all these cases, the man must tighten up and control the attacking spaces. It can be helped by suddenly freeing the spaces, and allowing the pace to go up, but then quickly clamping down again – but slower than it was before.

"Acting" in these situations is important. It is against the rules to be "passive" (a fighter can be penalised for passivity), so he must learn how to "fight" without fighting. He must learn how to keep active, but without giving his weight away (becoming unstable). It sounds as if I am adovcating "unsportsmanlike behaviour" and certainly in some situations "stonewalling" is just that (and that I would not like to be associated with). However, in the situation where one man wants space and fast pace, the other man has got to slow the match down; it is an essential part of his match-winning skill. In my opinion a referee shows unintentional prejudiced severity by telling a competitor to "speed up" when he is fighting a "fast pace, big space" man; he is condemning the man to lose! Because of such "blind-spots" in the rules, the fighters have to learn how to "act"; they have to learn how to comply with the requirements of the rules, but also to do what they have to do.

COMMENTARY

Remember, the easiest time to throw a man is when he is just standing still (the shape of him is not really important), that is when all factors are constant (i.e. no movement – for any reason – shape constant, strength constant, attitude constant). The more these factors vary, the harder it is to throw (one of the purposes of combination attacks is to limit the number of variables, see page 40). The inexperienced player will tend to keep rigid and move about like a frozen puppet, under the impression that his strength and stability will save him. Quite wrong of course. The "fortifications" can be mapped out and a simple plan made to breach the walls. (Very few medieval castles, however formidable-looking, were ever really impregnable; most were stormed sooner or later.) It is the flexible, variable opponent, who is difficult to beat; the whereabouts of his centre of control is always doubtful and hence difficult to get at. (Hannibal, in his Roman campaign, never really had a centre that could be attacked.)

When the opponent settles down (to reorganise further attacks) that is the time to "hit" him. With practice, it is possible to learn to recognise the signs which tell when a man wants to wait, wants to hustle, wants to "coast"; if he needs to be "put off his stride", then at those times the opposite conditions are imposed on him. Sometimes these "opposites" will manifest themselves in (what is in fact) bogus attacks – for the benefit of the referee(!), but the unsettling effect will be there.

It takes practice. Mistakes can be made, the trainee will speed up just when his opponent is going to use a fast pace attack, which is just what that man wants – he then scores a beautiful full score throw! But it is in randori, so it doesn't really matter! Better there than in the shiai, where any mistakes can be the last!

Development of Strength and Stamina

A convenient shorthand to cover these two factors would be "fitness". Fitness has a somewhat amorphous meaning and like so many other words among the jargon of physical skills, it can be both general and specific. It covers the aspects of physical development (in terms of simple muscular bulk), cardio-vascular (respiratory) efficiency, and mental attitudes towards the tasks that need to be done. Attempting to define fitness as succinctly as possible does give an indication of what it is, even if the definition does not cover every possible presentation of all the items involved.

Fitness is the ability to meet all of the possible demands of the challenge to come: having adequate and relevent reserves to maintain that capability for as long as necessary, so that effectiveness (physical) and satisfaction (mental) is not marred, and recovery from the effort is quick and efficient.

As usual, it is beneficial – to the building of a training scheme – to realize why fitness is needed in judo. It was after all a skill factor which took a long time for the judo establishment to accept. Because of such things as the misunderstanding of "ju" (see Part Three) and the limited deliniation of "skill", fitness (with its intrinsic qualities of strength and stamina) was seen as something antipathetic to skill – or to use the word of that time, technique-development. Indeed strength was frequently denigrated and was even said to be unnecessary or detrimental to the acquisition of "pure" technique.* What of course was being referred to was the use of unrelated or irrelevant strength to the object of the skill (which is of course the "curse" of all early skill training). No-one bothered to differentiate these two kinds of strength (necessary and unnecessary), so when "unnecessary" strength was thrown out from the accepted training development, the other baby went out with the denigrated bath water.

Now of course, strength – fitness – is fully accepted, both at national and international levels of competition. I would even say it is taking a too large a part in some training programmes. As frequently happens when a pendulum swings too far one way, (in this instance against the need for strength and stamina), when it gets reversed, it invariably swings too far the other way. It is after all comparatively easy to improve fitness, therefore too often it gets the training scheme's main emphasis (for the quick "improvement" can be used as a simple motivator) rather than skill improvement – which should be the main objective of any such scheme.

In brief, strength and stamina should be seen as a part of the whole skill, not as something separate from it. Skill is an "umbrella-word" covering technique, fitness, awareness of space, pace, direction, etc., etc. All these factors or items are interrelated and interact on one another: for example, if strength is increased (by the use of weight-training etc.) then the form of technique must be modified to cope with that increase in strength. Too often, a competitor could develop – say – an uchi-mata, which is quite effective at the standard he is fighting at – say 1st Dan; he then decides he is too weak in the shoulders, so he goes on an intensive strength building programme. At the end of six months his shoulder girdle is very much stronger. Now, if he tries to use the same TECHNIQUE of uchi-mata as he did BEFORE he started weight training, it could be much worse – in terms of effectiveness – because the greater power being used to "drive" it, the greater power available, will throw everything out of balance (somewhat analagous to taking the engine out of a mini-Morris and putting in its place a Jaguar motor). The technique would need to be modified to cope with the greater power available.

Fitness Outside Judo Training

As was mentioned earlier, much of the fitness work, especially of the general type can be done outside of the actual judo sessions. Because it is general fitness, I do not intend to go into any great detail here. Specialists in the field can be consulted, or recognised books can be read. Much of the following medical information has been gleaned from the material accumulated by Dr K. Kingsbury, who has worked much with national judo teams and has compiled a large body of information on and for judo players.[22]

NOTE: A word of caution: beware of deep knee bends under load or stress; that is, either full squats with weights, or long journeys round mats or playing fields doing "bunny hops". Such exercises as these can be, potentially, very dangerous for the knee-joints. Knees can easily be strained by such extreme forms of punishment, and therefore become susceptible to subsequent injury in the stress of competition. Anyhow strength at such an extreme range of the knee-joint is not necessary in Judo! Squats, with weights, or any other forms of stress, should not be deeper than having the knee-joint at a right angle.

GROSS MUSCLE TRAINING

Judo is truly a total-body usage activity. Too often this truism is overlooked when physical training is being organised; therefore when dealing with shuttle-runs for example, it is better to put small weights (say 3–5 lbs.) in each hand. This simulates, much better, the kind of stress (on heart and lungs) that happens in competition. So forms of gross-muscle training could be:

1. Shuttle runs with hand-weights (about 3 lbs.)
2. Maximum rate skipping.
3. Sprint swimming (if the person is good enough!).
4. Rope-climbing at maximum speed.
5. Stressful running: if running is to be done, it should be of the variable pace type (hard sprints, uphill running, running up long flights of stairs, interposed with jogging, etc.). Running for judo men is not the same as for "runners", because of the difference in bulk and body-type (i.e. somatotype).

CIRCUIT TRAINING

Care should be taken to ensure the severity of the circuits are related directly to the individual, and that cardio-vascular development is adequate. Circuits take two main forms:–

1. Each exercise in the circuit is done as quickly as possible, in order to get the maximum repetitions in – for example – a minute. A rest period is then taken (ranging from 3 minutes for the unfit to a few seconds for the fit!), then all is repeated. Another rest period, another whole repeat. The number of total repreats again depending on the standard of fitness being aimed at.

2. The circuit of exercises can be taken in the individual's own time, the idea being that the unfit can do 'X' repetitions on each exercise (a number that he can manage comfortably) and the fit as many as he can stand. In both cases as the total sequence is repeated – with the same kind of rest period in between – the number of repetitions are increased.

INTERVAL TRAINING

Here the objective is to put the individual under a lot of pressure, to improve the oxygen uptake (oxygen uptake is that part of the oxygen intake (inspiration) which is converted into energy; the greater that part is of the whole intake the better, and the percentage can be improved by training). The trainee is expected to put in 80– 90% maximum effort, then rest for a couple of minutes or so (depending on standard): the work is repeated at something less than 80%; another rest, then a repeat of 80–90% – and so on!

WEIGHT-LIFTING

Use of HEAVY weights is not only to increase muscular strength, but to increase also the ability to do work anaerobically, to obtain greater strength with less fatigue, tolerate acid accumulation (in muscles) better, increase oxygen uptake, and to replace ATP quicker (Adenosine Tri Phosphate, a catalyst for energy production).

Fig. 14. Members of the Under 21 national Judo squad, under the direction of the author, doing a fitness obstacle race—carrying medicine balls!

Fig. 15. More Under 21 squad work; team races carrying logs—very toughening work

PULSE RATE

Is a reasonable indication of the degree of work being done. It is of course a very individual thing, and it is very hazardous to refer a general rate to an individual. Anyhow I use it here simply as an indication of how effort can be estimated.[23]

For example, it has been shown that young men, in a laying down position before getting up in the morning, have a rate of about 64 beats per minute (although the range can be from 38–110!): for simply sitting down it is about 75 beats per minute, standing 83 beats per minute, and hard work (but not exhaustive work) it is about 150–180 beats per minute. It has been found that during very strenuous randori sessions (of national team members) that pulse rate goes up to 220–230 beats per minute! (This makes judo one of the most strenuous activities of all! No doubt it is because of the type of gross-muscular activity involved.) Therefore for the individual to get beneficial training effect, work rate should be between 60–100% of his maximum. To ascertain that, take his awakening pulse-rate (in the morning) say 64: his maximum rate – found in very hard training sessions-say 220 beats per minute, and then 60% of his effort would be

$$\left\{\frac{60}{100} \times (220 - 64)\right\} + 64$$
$$= 158 \text{ beats per min. approx.}$$

This means that if the man is to get an improvement in FITNESS, his working pulse rate (in training) must be more than 160 beats per minute.

Of course that does not mean that all of the training sessions should be of such a high rate. When skill training is being done, there is every chance that it will drop below that mark, that is how it should be – only if increase in fitness is being pursued should 160 beats per minute be topped!

PRECAUTION

When embarking on a fitness programme the work rate should be somewhere around 50% or less (say 120–150 beats per minute), only gradually will it be taken up to 60–70% maximum (women are on the average 10/20 beats per minute less than the equivalent man). Going back to training after illness, is another time to apply caution (perhaps after injury too); patience should be paired with graduation!

NOTE: STALENESS OR OVERTRAINING

Whether in or out of judo training, overtraining is something which must always be looked for. One of the problems in recognising it is that it is very similar to under-training, i.e. pulse rate too high, poor recovery, lassitude, lack of appetite, sleeping badly. Usually the main cause of this condition is boredom (with training), therefore change the variety of activity (even a complete break from training!) If after such a change the symptoms are still there, then a doctor could be consulted.

GENERAL ACTIVITIES

Although "measurable" fitness methods are very effective in producing results they can be – if not watched – tedious and boring. Therefore it is of value, if general games are introduced into the programme (i.e. football, basketball, squash etc.) the higher the work-demand of course the better. General factors can be catered for (i.e. speed, fast change of direction, body awareness, etc.) and a lot of fun and enjoyment can be achieved. (See figures 14 and 15.)

If more of a "rest" is required, that is more than just a change of activity (and a change is as good as a rest), then talks on care of injuries, tactics, and the like can be introduced.

Fitness Inside Judo Training

In my opinion, this is the least developed, specialist area in judo training. General fitness and fitness training is fine, and even in Japan – where there is an abundance of judo training opposition, there is a need (real or imagined) for supplementary physical training. But in the ultimate, it is agreed by all that the best training for judo is judo. As has already been mentioned, the greater part of judo clubs spend much of their time doing randori. It is assumed that that will, by itself, not only get them better (at all the skills) but will get them further – by and large true! But one of the greatest hazards of uncontrolled randori (when the players are just allowed to do what they like for an unspecified period of time), is the cultivation of the ability to "coast". If for example, a man knows he has a period of training, lasting approximately 2 hours, stretching in front of him, with only himself as motivator, he will "ration" his energy to last out that period. The result, is, that apart from one or two particular practices (with particular people) he will not be "overstressed" for the whole session. He will get so organised at "rationing" that seldom will he ever be taken over that pulse rate of 160/170 beats per minute mark, which will improve his stamina. Of course by doing even the haphazard approach long enough, he will improve – but it will take time! If he cannot afford such a timescale, something more organised will need to be done.

A Traditional Method

This is where the whole group is divided into two teams. They are lined up facing each other. The whistle is sounded (or whatever), they compete, each man with the man opposite, for a specific time. The whistle goes, they all return to their original position. One man at the end of one team moves along to the other end of his team; they all move down one and the whole thing is repeated, and repeated and repeated.

Such a system has several good points. For example, presumably the time of each man to man competition lasts as long as the contest time of the event to come (so getting all to recognise the contest time span), the continual non-stop aspect can improve stamina. The weaknesses are that it does not allow for skill or size. When the small man faces the big man, the big man is not (usually) worked hard; when the less skilled meets the skilled, he does not get a chance to do his "thing".

A More Contemporary Method

The total training group is divided into weight/size groups. (If there are not enough for all 5 weight groups, then into say three – light + light-middles; middles; and light heavies + heavies.) One man is selected from each group, for the duration of the specific contest time (i.e. 6 minutes) he will compete against the rest of the group. It is up to the members of the group to ensure that the "man-in-the-middle" has no "coasting"

periods. At the end of the time, another man takes the place of the other, and again the rest of the group come at him one after the other. The good things; the man-in-the-middle only deals with his own size/weight, he learns to fight for the contest time, he is really pushed hard (by the others in the group). The not-so-good things; too many of the group are not working, the man-in-the-middle may get very little opportunity to improve his skills (he could be so tired, that his concentration is to just stay on his feet!)

RESTRICTED OXYGENATION

One of the main factors in the development of fatigue in judo training and play, and one that therefore must have a major part in the judo fitness programme, is that of oxygen restriction. Judo, by the involvement of two people combatting against each other, produces very restrictive movements of an isometric or partially isometric type; the restriction of the chest movement, both in standing-play (by the use of arms) and in ground-play (by use of body weight), the interference with heart and lung rhythm by sudden changes in direction, pace, force, etc. will tend to reduce blood flow and hence oxygen supply to the working muscles.

The concept of oxygen restriction will manifest itself in two ways in the training programme:

1. The need for the improvement of the anaerobic power of the one man; to minimise the effect of oxygen restriction.

2. Improving ways of limiting even more the other man (the opponent's) ability to cope with oxygen restriction actions.

The Problem

And this seems to me to be the major un-answered problem in judo training at the moment, how are stamina and skill to be developed alongside each other? Stamina is fairly easy to cope with, on its own; technique or even freeplay skills are also – comparatively – easy to improve; but how to improve competitive skills under pressure?

I am afraid I have no complete answer. But I can make a few suggestions. It seems to me, that worrying about this problem when the trainee gets into the national squad (for example) is too late, and a waste of time. It must start from the very first day of training, the first day the novice first steps onto the judo mat. If from that time, the trainee learns about space, pace, direction, etc., etc., so that he can – to a greater or lesser extent – isolate these factors in movement, then when he gets to the competitive training situation he can simulate specific areas of the required conditions. This is, in other words, an extension of what I said earlier, a throw – to work – takes two people! Instead of spending all the training time on the thrower, just as much (and I sometimes think more) time should be given to the partner/opponent. For it is he who must reproduce the various conditions that the thrower has to learn to handle. If for exam-ple a throwing attack needs to be practised against a medium paced moving opponent, going backwards, in a half offensive crouch, with his right foot forward then not only ONE partner would need be able to reproduce these conditions, but EVERYBODY in the group should!

Only in this kind of way could ALL the trainees learn how to combat the many and various situations they will meet in actual contest (see Mutual Benefit). Of course, not every situation can be reproduced (but a surprisingly large number can!) Sometimes the fighter will have to learn from a one-off situation that he meets in the opening round of the European Championships. But that should not only have to apply to EVERY situation that he will/can meet (as is too often the case at the moment). Only if all (or most!) competitors fully under-stand all of the skill factors involved can simulated contests be set up. Only when this can be done – in all kinds of ways – will there be a quick hand-in-hand development of skill-under-pressure.

Miscellaneous

Diet, and Food Supplements

Diet is an aspect of training which is sometimes overlooked by the enthusiastic sportsman. For those who are only interested in sport as a recreation, it is not necessary to go into the business at all. A good all round eating habit is perfectly adequate; i.e. eating a variety of food, is usually enough to cover (obtain) the necessary vitamins and minerals. However, for those who train hard for championship events, diet can become important. Yet even the authorities are not sure in what way, or how, it is important, although agreeing that it is.

"It can be stated categorically:
1 that none of the ordinary foods eaten by man are either of special value or contra-indicated in athletic training;
2. that preparations of vitamins and minerals, given in addition to a good mixed diet, will not improve athletic performance;
3. that alcoholic drinks taken in small quantities by people accustomed to them have no effect on training."[24]
Some research work done by the Swedish Medical Association (similar enough to a British population to have some validity) — found that in general, the eating patterns of the bulk of persons had two characteristics — they were overfed but undernourished! The effects were largely the results of "wrong"

living habits, i.e. change in habits of food consumption and (lack of) physical activity. For example they found 60% of the present energy consumption (of the people investigated) came from fats and sugars, compared to less than 30% at the turn of the century. The more fat and sugar foodstuffs contain, the lower its content of important nutrients (e.g. protein, minerals and water-soluble vitamins).
The athlete is essentially concerned about the production of energy. His food can be divided into three categories; protein, carbohydrates, and lipids (a word used by the biochemists to cover only certain kinds of fat).
Energy equivalent of food is measured in kilocalories (or big "C", as it is sometimes called). Some research work done in Russia has tried to categorise sports into energy categories, for example gymnastics and fencing were calculated as being the same energy type, i.e. 65 Cal/Kgm body weight. By working along these very (apparent) scientific lines, the food intake of the athlete can be measured and made suitable for the job that needs to be done. (It is of interest to note that a gram of protein and carbohydrate produces 4.1 calories; whereas a gram of fat produces 9.3 calories.)
Most athletes have at least a rough idea of what the "Big 3" are for, i.e. protein, carbohydrate and fats. Just to give an idea of their respective importance in the body make-up here are some proportions based upon a 65 kg. man.

Protein 17%, Fat 13·8%, Carbohydrate 15%, Water 61·5%, Minerals 6·1%.
Protein replaces the continually wearing out body tissue, particularly in the (hard working) muscular section — which is of immediate interest to the athlete! Protein is also the only one of the three that produces nitrogen, a necessary element in the metabolic process. Carbohydrates provide the energy — in the form of various sugars and starches. By an involved chemical process glycogen is produced from these sugars and starches, and is then made available for "burning" by the muscular system. Fats also provide a source of energy, but if not "burnt off" by (hard) physical exercise, they are deposited in various convenient — or inconvenient — parts of the body.
Back to the Swedish paper. It goes on to speak about the various amino acids needed for the various chemical processes which bring about the results outlined above, i.e. reproduction of cells, supply of glycogen, etc., etc. Many of them are related to various (and essential) vitamins and minerals which are very unstable — unstable because they are drastically reduced in effectiveness or even eliminated by cooking or by "warming up" after cooking or by exposure to air. Among these vital ingredients are: Vitamin C, needed for healing wounds and for general well-being; found in citrus fruit, green vegetables and potatoes. Riboflavin (vitamin B_2) needed for oxidation of carbohydrates and of amino acids; found in liver, milk and eggs. Theomine (Vitamin B_1) needed for breaking down car-

bohydrates; found in cereal grain and certain other seeds. Pyridoxine (vitamin B_6) needed for breaking down amino acids, and hence indirectly of protein, found in a wide variety of foodstuffs.

Folic acid; needed to combat anaemia and found in various foodstuffs.

If, because of the type of food the athlete eats (i.e. lots of warmed-up food in works' canteens), it could be guessed that "something" was lacking from the athlete's performance (i.e. he showed lassitude in training), then perhaps some form of supplement could be taken which would contain the kind of vitamins listed above.

Another "diet hazard" that can threaten a performance, is the crash-diet undertaken by the over-weight competitor. The man who suddenly finds, just before the big day (either a week or a day before) that he is several pounds over his fighting weight limit. There are two common ways of solving the problem – dietwise. First, he doesn't drink! The hazard here is that the man can become dehydrated and suffer a dramatic drop in performance; there can be a salt loss, which can bring on various degrees of cramp (ranging from fingers tightening up, to severe stomach cramp), which can be very disabling. Taking salt tablets can offset this danger. The second way, is about a week before the event carbohydrates are not eaten (i.e. bread and potatoes). The hazard here is that if training is maintained (and it usually is), the usual supply of energy is curtailed (through this omission of

carbohydrates from the diet) the body begins to draw upon its energy store, and runs on that. Comes the big event at the end of the week or so, not only has the day-to-day running supply gone, but also has the body-store been largely used up. The result is that frequently the man gets through the first round and even the second, but then feels completely exhausted. He cannot understand it because he has been going well all week; so the total situation (especially if he also gets cramps as well, which does happen!) thoroughly depresses him. His chance of winning goes as low as his depression!

CONCLUSION

As far as diet is concerned, the most important thing is to maintain a varied and regular diet. A varied food supply is usually enough. However, sometimes, for various reasons, it is advantageous to add food supplements, in which case the following possibilities should be kept in mind.

MENTAL 1. Food is very often as much psychological as it is physical. If the Japanese does not have his rice, or the Englishman his fish and chips, he can feel as if he is undernourished; if he feels it hard enough, then he is!

The big steak before the match is quite superfluous as far as a contribution to the fight performance goes (generally we eat too much protein anyway!), but if he wants it badly enough, the boosting of confidence may outweigh the disadvantages of over-eating!!

2. Taking pills of any kind (and food supplements are often in pill form) can be very depressing for some as well as stimulating for others.)

3. Taking food supplements may make a great improvement in performance; whether it is real (which it certainly can be) or whether it is imagined (which it also can be) does not matter, as long as there is improvement.

4. Diet should not become a fad if possible, there are enough training problems without adding to the list. Eat what you like, and like what you eat is a good rule!

WEIGHT CONTROL

Any kind of "crash dieting" to get down to a weight should be avoided wherever possible. It can have both long and short term ill effects. If weight control is necessary it should be spread over a long period, so that the right kind of food intake can be ensured, with no damage done to the body. If it is found that drastic measures are needed to keep weight down, then mature consideration should be given to the matter of going up into the next weight category. I know some fighters will argue, "Ah, but it is 'easier' in the lighter weight, there are not so many tough boys there", which is a difficult argument to refute – particularly if it is true! But nevertheless for long term body health, I would still recommend the individual moves up a weight.

Ritual, Myth and Magic

As has been mentioned earlier, there are a number of escalating skills contained within the total ability to perform at a high standard of judo — "dolls within dolls". There are many factors which go to make up that total skill, some are more rational than others. For example, it is fairly easy to comprehend that a fighter must be fit, even if the principle is not an agreeable one, but to accept that the order the performer undresses or dresses in is relevant to that total skill may take some swallowing. The fact, however, remains that if the performer is disturbed by having changed in the "wrong order" and it affects his performance/skill for better or worse, than for practical purposes, the ritual of changing is a part of the total skill.

Certainly throughout the whole range of sport practice, from preparation, through training of all kinds, to competition, ritual, myth and magic can be found in one form or another. Sometimes it is so implicit and accepted that it is not recognised as such (i.e. the "right" clothes "have" to be worn, the "right" language has to be used). Other times it is so obvious that some observers will just laugh (i.e. at rabbit's feet etc.). Here I just want to introduce the subject and mention briefly some of the ways that skill, in all its ramifications, can be affected by ritual, myth and magic, and make the point that all should be given considerate attention by both performer and coach.

The occult, in all its forms, has been in the weave and weft of human society since the dawn of time. Frazer says that mythology was the philosophy of primitive man. Over the last couple of hundred years or so (since the Age of Reason!) the occult has been denigrated as the pathetic plaything of the savage primitive, a mixture of stupid ignorance and rampant superstition. However, over the last couple of decades or so the occult has been getting its fair share of reappraisal and a lot more tolerance is being shown towards it. Jung[25] for instance claims that much of contemporary man's trouble, ranging from vague apprehensions to the insatiable need for drugs, alcohol and tobacco — to say nothing of a big sackful of neurosis — is because he has ignored the "mystical" side of his nature. Until he, man, can get back to a sympathetic relationship to this side of his being, things will not improve.

RITUAL

Hook[26] says the origins of ritual can be seen "as an attempt to control the unpredictable element in human affairs." Certainly it has played an enormous part in man's development and takes many forms — both in scale and complexity, from inconsequential signs and gestures to religious actions that shook the world. Is ritual different from luck? I think so, to me there is an essential and critical difference. Luck is a "one-off" happening, which favours or not a particular happening or incident. It can of course be evoked by charms and talismans, but that does not guarantee that luck is on the side of the talisman. Luck is chance, is random selection. Ritual is different; it is a sequence of movements, a pattern of performance, which if done in the correct and proper order, will achieve a desired end. Each stage or step is stipulated precisely, and if strictly adhered to will — inevitably — bring about the specified result. If, however, there is any deviation, however slight, however unintentional, then results will decline in efficiency, usually in relation to the size of the deviation. Perhaps it could be said that for practical purposes ritual is the same as luck, for perhaps both are finalised by a whim of fate. But true? For ritual is a part of play and play can be seen as the great sculptor of culture. [27] Mumford[28] suggests that ritual is the first move towards self-control and discipline; if so the final product is more controlled than luck and is also the first definite step towards communication through the media of language. Henderson[29] (a Jungian) in his own way supports this view, and his is a fascinating description of the developing ego, certainly in terms of ritual and it can be seen in many sporting situations.

Henderson sees a kind of grand ritual of rituals; a fundamental ritual that steers our lives (as distinct from the common, everyday ritual of going about our business), the object of which is to free the ego from the fetters of the senses (much like the objectives of Zen). All four stages do not have to be passed through, some can be omitted (but most people do go through some, and certainly the last freedom stage is not achieved by many). In brief the stages are:

1. THE HERO MYTH

The "Hero" is common to all ages and societies from Gilgamesh to St. George down to Billy the Kid.[30] He symbolises all that is expected of a great leader — and more — as defined by the group that utilises the myth. (Taylor[31] defines such a group as a "network of interpersonal relationship and emotional investments.") A common feature of all the Hero myths is that he always has a big fight or battle with the forces of evil — whatever form they take, dragon or over-zealous law-man. This seems to offer a sympathetic point of contact for the combat sports; many fighters visualise themselves, as do others — particularly spectators — as battlers against "evil". But the aspiring sports hero-figure (for it is usually a self-elected role) has to conform to the ritual of the emerging champion/hero figure; the displays and sequential patterns of that ritual are mainly specified by the group or team of which he is an emerging part.

2. THE INITIATION RITUAL

Another very common ritual, signifying generally the breaking away from the small family or pseudo-family group (where protection of the individual was the principle rule) in order to join the larger group, symbolising both society at large and adulthood. In a sports context, this may mean the initiate is "forced" to adopt the same training methods as the others within the group (they will not allow him to stick to his own methods), he will be expected to behave in certain ways, and even wear certain kinds of clothes. If he does not do that, and each stage is dictated by the group, he will not be accepted by the group. To enhance the power of the group, as a group, they will generally have a group totem e.g. a teddy-bear "mascot" for one team, a club badge for another, a flag or picture for another — some may use the Hero symbol itself! The ritual itself may be quite loose i.e. conforming to sequential demands, or it may be quite specific i.e. national trials for entering into national squads; whatever the form is at base it comes out as a "trial of strength"; by accepting the challenge of the "trial" and by going through it and out the other side the initiate proves that he is bigger, stronger, faster, braver (and sometimes more obnoxious) than anyone else in the group.*

3. THE RITUAL OF COMMUNION

This particular ritual is usually symbolised in the form of drinking from a common bowl or cup. It purports to show the absorption of the group's spirit or psyche by the individual — the circulating bowl is the fountainhead of the spirit, its spirit being imbibed by the genuflecting neophytes. Perhaps in these more contemporary days of ritualism the source of the drink is not always the one cup but the one pub!

4. THE LONG JOURNEY

This is the long search for knowledge (as Christian in Pilgrim's Progress), the emancipation of the individual from the restrictions of the group — enlightenment! The group does not really appreciate or accept the man who becomes the Hero (why the myth is preferred). The man as Hero only highlights the group's own weakness and faults, so they quickly give him a medal (or a knife in the back) shake his hand and send him on his way. The destination is immaterial — oblivion or fame. Sometimes if the Hero is too much of a hero, the group will sacrifice the Hero (literally or symbolically, depending on circumstances!) Whatever his fate, one thing is certain, the Hero as man cannot stay with the group he came up in! His excellence has proved he is no longer a part of that group. Mediocrity is the pass-key for group participation (see Shiai page 64), he must move on to other forms of achievement.

If freedom is, or can be, the result of such a series of progressive rituals, then the participation in them is worthwhile — even if it does take several years, and such a process inevitably does! From quite a different approach Sir Kenneth Clark [32] when speaking about great movements in art, likens them to

---

* I would suggest there has been a great mistake of evolving civilisation to do away with the initiating ceremony of youth into manhood, for without it youth (with little empirical confidence anyway) does not "know" when he is a "man", because he does not "know", he must "prove" it — generally by being anti-social. These "initiations" showed him clearly — for all to see — that he was a man, so he did not (as he does now) need to "prove" it.

revolutions and says about 15 years is the longest either lasts.* Or put another way, fifteen years is about as long as the individual can maintain his dedication to one objective – or is allowed to dedicate himself for! After that, for one reason or the other, he or they will need to change their objective (after all a Movement or revolution will only last as long as the people who drive it).

Ritual does not of course need to be as purposeful as Henderson suggests; for example Sir Kenneth Clark is quite sure it can be very trivial, and in another part of his book says, "The late antique world was full of meaningless rituals, mystery religions that destroyed self-confidence." It is this type of ritual that the perspicacious coach must watch for and avoid. If ritual enhances performance, so well and good, it can be encouraged; if not dispense with it as any time-wasting training aid would be discarded, for though some may want ritual to help their performances, others may not.

MYTH

In the language of the 19th century, myth was anything opposed to reality, but now it too is being revalued and Eliade[33] for example talks about it being "sacred history", a transhuman revelation of what happened at the dawn of the Great Time! Because it is "real" and sacred, it is eminently respectable, and therefore serves as a perennial model for all subsequent occasions. A model, which if not absolutely perfect, is at least the best known!

(I expect the reader can hear all this being said about "kata".) All strive to achieve the standard of that model – through imitation with the support of ritual. Again all that remains is to ensure the myth, in judo terms anyhow, is real and did exist, and is not just "opposed to reality", for falseness and hypocracy can lead to stagnation. Wilson[34] is very concerned about this very point and says the chief problem of humanity is passivity; the excitement of living is being drowned in the triviality of everydayness. The mind coagulates, slows down and ossifies into a blob of insensitivity. Something very organised has to be arranged to wake things up, to generate curiosity, to enthuse the individual to get up and achieve and create something. Myth and ritual, if used with understanding, can be used to provide the spur to incite activity.

The Shaman

He's the fellow that stands between "them" or "it", (the gods etc.) and "us", the ordinary people. The Shaman interprets, he approves of the ritual used or judges that it is not being done correctly. It is to him and only him that the divine message is revealed. Does he sound familiar? He could do; he's the fellow in sporting circles who's called the coach! To bring in Eliade again to explain better than I "Shamans are specialists in ecstacy . . . he is recognised as such at the end of a two-fold instruction: first, of the ecstatic order (dreams, visions, trances, etc.) and second, of the traditional order (shamanic technique, names and func-

tions of the spirit, etc.)." By substituting weight-training, pressure training into the first bracket and technical skills and kata in the second, it describes the modern sports coach quite well.

Contemporary sport contains a plethora of ritual and myth, so a shaman is necessary if they are to function as they should. So it is yet another job for the "omniscient" coach to learn. He cannot afford to restrict himself just to the "business" of techniques and skills; he has to try and be all things to all men!

MAGIC – OF THE WORD!

As was mentioned above, one of the Shaman's important tasks is to interpret the word. He decides not only what the word means but also the status and power of the word. When the German mystic Eckhart tried to infer the total "unknowability" of God (note the Capital G) in one of his sermons, he could only say "God is without name" to suggest the enormity of the subject. Similarly the coach has to use words, not only for the transportation of meaning, but also for containing ideas and concepts. In these circumstances the word, in common parlance, becomes jargon. Jargon is inevitable when specialist

---

* Revolution should not be confused with evolution. Evolution is a process – in terms of man's development – which seems to be an escalating phenomena. What took centuries to develop only a hundred years ago, now seems to get done in a few years!

knowledge has to be moved from one person to another; all that is necessary is to ensure every attempt is made to make that jargon as succinct and understandable as possible (an excellent example of the opposite, obtuse jargon par excellence, is that of wine-making and wine-tasting!)

Words have a long tradition of being closely connected with magic. At the dawn of language, sounds were made to represent or symbolise objects. With the passing of time the sound or word began to take on the qualities of the thing it represented. The word became the thing. From then on words had a potency of their own and frequently took a major part in the ritual of all kinds. Perhaps poetry is one of the better examples of how words – and their rhythms – have become an important part in ritual. The magic of the word can frequently be seen in a judo coaching session, especially a "traditional" kata one! Words like tsukuri, tsugi-ashi are passed from mouth to mouth with HOLY respect, few if any knowing what they really mean, but each word carries its own aura of transubstantiation – and it is not to be questioned!

It can also work in reverse of course; in antique Roman times, a slave could not have a legal name, for legally he did not exist. So in teaching, if the ability not to land on the back does not have a name it does not exist. Give it a name, as Kano did to the nebulous business of losing control of stance, i.e. kuzushi and it becomes tangible and a part of the teaching vocabulary.

Some readers may feel that word-magic is not a part – or only a small part – of contemporary sophisticated society ("We don't fall for that rubbish!") But pause to think of the great increase of logography in advertising (a giant modern ritual, of world-wide proportions) a clear indication that words or sounds are still valued as controllers of attitudes.

It is generally accepted that primitive vocabularies tend to split major concepts into smaller, separate, ideas because abstract ideas or all-embracing concepts are difficult for the primitive mind to grasp (see page 12 "Gestalt" – another view on the same point). Cassirer[35] discusses at some length, language and its influence on man's development. He suggests that myth and words mould thinking, and it is this combination (of myth and words) that takes the thinking process from the primitive (the momentary experience) to the sophisticated (the enduring conception). Zen, on the contrary is extremely wary about putting concepts into words[36] for it claims that by doing so the original essence of the concept can be lost. The basic tenet of Zen begins by saying, "There is a special tradition (of achieving enlightenment) that is outside of (orthodox) teaching, and does not stand (depend) upon words." Also of course there are other ways to transport ideas and concepts from one person to others, i.e. music and painting and these too must be recognised as legitimate means of communication.

The coach has certainly got to put words to concepts and ideas; it is the most convenient way to communicate to his trainees (other ways are films etc.) but the risks are many. He can bewilder as easily as he can clarify. The meaning he has of a word is not necessarily the same meaning that class members have. By implication, the minds of the trainees are not so sophisticated (not in terms of judo anyway), so like the other primitives before them, they will tend to reduce the size of the ideas down to what they can cope with/ understand, which could invalidate the whole explanation! Or again, because the word is poorly explained, but is obviously an important part of the coaching ethos it takes on a magic quality of its own and becomes something of a totem; in judo such a word was/is ukemi – only if you can "ukemi" (whatever that means) can you throw! The coach's job – and difficulty – is the achieving of Cassirer's objective; by using words and myths advantageously, the trainees' mind – and performance – is taken upwards towards the realm of enduring conception!

Imitation and Tradition

Imitation is no doubt an essential part of a learning process, for it can be a form of stimulation as well as a medium for discipline. As such it can take its place among the subsidiary processes of "art" and do what Solzhenitsyn asked of art in the opening quotation in this book. As long as it does extend one man's appreciation of another man's achievements, and does not stultify it (as it so easily can) then imitation is fine, and can be incorporated into the training programme. Imitation has already been mentioned briefly in relation to the myth of the model derived from the dawn of the Great Time ("it wasn't like that in the good old days!") And certainly in judo, imitation has loomed large in the matter of "getting better". One of the most frequently heard pieces of advice was to copy. I can remember being told to imitate the champions, especially while I was in Japan, which of course I did conscientiously! The implication was, as I understood it, that if I could succeed in copying a particular champion precisely (granted the one I chose to copy) then I would become as good a champion as he – nothing was said about being better! Perhaps it was taken for granted by the "shaman" that by going through the discipline of copying I would inadvertently – and eventually – acquire a superior skill to that of the champion I was imitating.

If so, he never told me, and I wish he had for it may have made the business more congenial and purposeful. For let's face it, the advice to imitate can be and often is, a substitute for teaching, if there is not enough knowledge available to make the business of teaching possible.

To put it another way, is imitation a means or an end? As a means, it is a type of training I would accept. Copying can be a discipline and can develop a disciplined approach to the acquiring of a skill, providing the implication is to SURPASS what is being copied! If the disciple does not finish better than the teacher, then one or both has failed the other. If imitation is only to equal that which is being copied, then indeed it is a sore waste of time! For such punitive ambition does never, ever, achieve the object being aimed at; it always falls far below it. It also smacks strongly of the "self-taught" claim to success; which Constable, the painter summed up well when he said, "If a man claims he is self-taught, he must have studied under a very ignorant teacher!"

Imitation is of course very closely linked with tradition, for tradition frequently dictates or defines that which is to be imitated. But tradition appears to be of two kinds, long-standing and short-standing. The long-standing has a patina of integrity, whereas short-standing tradition has the polish of the fashionable newly made. T. S. Eliot[37] for example wrote: "Yet if the only form of tradition, of handing down, consisted in following the ways of the immediate generation behind us in a blind or timid adherence to its successes, tradition should be positively discouraged."

But then later on he said, "It (tradition) cannot be inherited, and if you want it you must obtain it with great labour".

By possessing the very capability of lasting a long time, a "way of doing something" seems to prove its reliability and in turn produce its own integrity of purpose. Newton (the falling apple man) put it in a different way again – a very charming way – "If I have been able to see further than others, it is because I stood on the shoulders of giants."

Tradition of the short time type does not only appear to have had no time to prove its worth, but also has not had time to discard its faults. I remember my coach warning me about people who copied my judo style – "they will only copy your bad faults".

Tradition to last a long time, to be worthwhile, must have an integrity of its own. In order to have that integrity it must be made NOW of the right kind of stuff. For tradition is being created now, although it will not have "matured in the barrel" for some years to come. But unless it is done right now, future generations will have no traditions worthy of the name.

To imitate the ideal, contained in the long established tradition, can provide the "spur" to go on and produce original work and higher standards. To imitate the short lived, untried tradition of yesterday is to court the superficial and become the mediocre.

Mutual Benefit and Sportsmanship

Kano, the founder of judo, was very concerned about sport and its place in society, both as a professional educationalist and as an amateur humanist. Although the individual, and the development of that individual was the most important thing as far as he was concerned, he realised that sport could play a part in that development and help the individual to coexist congenially with society at large. Kano of course realised that everyone had to find their own way to their own goal. Some through their intellectual ability, others through the medium of the arts, others again through industry and commerce. He wrote much on this theme, in the form of papers to various societies and associations, and apparently lectured on it extensively. It is a pity that, by and large (in Britain anyway) his views on individual development *vis-à-vis* society, are given very little recognition.

Judo is manifestly and ostensibly competitive. It is a continual striving of one man trying to beat another. Or is it? Kano was very concerned that winning, *sine qua non*, would not become the sole and dominating aspect of judo training. Apart from the moral and ethical consideration (mentioned elsewhere in the book) the stresses produced by a highly charged competitive training scheme could produce long term damage to the body. It certainly is true that many retired national class fighters do suffer much from long lasting injuries.

It is true too that in Europe, especially since the war judo has been seen by the fighters – by and large – only and entirely as a competitive sport. True, from time to time, there have been waves of high-flown mysticism pushed out alongside the promulgation of the competitive image; but fighting and winning has been the steadily mounting climax of all training. The sports media has, over the recent past, made its contribution to this development too (the "sports media" is a euphemism for a small group of writers and commentators whose job is to put something in at the second place that wasn't there in the first place). Together, the sports own P.R.O. people and the sports media have manufactured the contemporary ideology that winning is the ultimate accolade of participation.

Having said that, it should be realised that the understanding of competition and winning is quite different in the East from that in the West. The whole concept of sport, and competition is a product of European culture, and English culture in particular, and even then only·from the end of the 19th century onwards. Sport before that time referred to hunting and killing (a carthartic definition of sport I heard once was, "any kind of fight or competition where blood is spilt; and war is the greatest sport of all!") Competition (as understood now!) is not a "natural" part of the oriental "think tank." It is something they have had to work at, in order to understand and absorb. As I have tried to show elsewhere, Japan has made great efforts to emulate the West in many ways; and of course "competition"

came within that span of concepts to swallow, but it was not, and is not easy.

There are many stories illustrating this aspect of incomprehension by the Japanese mind of the Western ideas on sport. For example, an American champion archer was watching the Kyudo (archery) Master; the old boy, full of Zen and with sublime confidence in doing it "right" slowly and painstakingly put arrow after arrow in the target-centre. The American gets impatient with the slowness, "Gees, I could put six in the gold whilst you are getting an arrow out!" The old man nods sweetly in agreement, and replies, "Let us stand 20 paces apart and shoot at one another; we shall then see who is the best archer". It is said the American did not accept the challenge.

In judo too, the feeling that competition is not all important, is still struggling to survive in a welter of ambivilence. Whilst at the Olympic Games, I suggested to a famous Japanese judo coach, that the rules of the sport should be drastically changed to make it more appealing to the spectators. His reply to my purposefully provocative statement was, such changes were not necessary because judo was not a sport! I then asked him why he and his team were here at the Olympic Games? He became confused and did not answer.

The Japanese character, at heart, seems to prefer a decision made – like a spark from two pieces of flint striking (to quote a famous Zen analogy). The Japanese do not appear to go for protracted confrontations; everything they do – providing they have control of it – seems to work this way. Sumo, the most popular "sport" in Japan, has matches which last for about 30 seconds or less!; whether judo or jujitsu in 1887 should get the official stamp of approval (by the State) for future adoption into the national physical training scheme, was decided by one match (not the qualities of each); Japan entered the last world war by a "throw of the dice" at Pearl Harbour. So the examples could be extended, to all spheres of Japanese participation. If there is a competitive streak in the Japanese, it is quite different from that in the Westerner. The occidental seems to prefer his competition to start slowly and then build up gradually; attitudes like, give him another chance, cheer for the "under-dog", he who fights and runs away, lives to fight another day, become apparent in the total make-up of competition. But these are attitudes totally foreign to the Japanese. How many Japanese soldiers are still hiding in the jungles of S.E. Asia, because once committed to soldiery always committed to soldiery? Similarly with the kamikaze pilot, his whole life was synthesised into one supreme act of commitment. So in judo. The Japanese at heart, are not interested in seeing a long rational, tactical exchange of skills, they just want to see one big bang explosion of spontaneous ability. It is not really a question of seeing who is the better man — in terms of utilisation of a wide skill range — but who can sum up his life's training in one moment of total commitment. He is the man who earns the respect of the Japanese spectator.

There have been a few concessions by the Japanese (for they still largely control the international administration of the sport), minor attacking efforts are now scored, a public score-board has very recently been designed (but it is still far from clear), a broader edge round the fighting area has been defined; but all these are only very much secondary issues. For judo to appeal to a Western sports audience, it must contain the following ingredients:

1. The fighters to be clearly marked and differentiated.
2. The fighters must be able to make a running score (i.e. giving more than one chance).
3. The time has to be fixed, and the fight goes to the end of that limit — unless there is a specified difference in scoring which would indicate the dangerous inability of one man to stand up against the other.
4. Making a scoring system, and a scoring board that is easily comprehensible to all, so that all know what is happening at any one time.

If this could be done, then watching judo could be a really exciting affair, for make no mistake, judo can be very exciting — providing the rules of competition allow it to be so!

But what's all that got to do with mutual benefit? Well, the type of match dictates or controls the type of training to be done. As things are, with the one-point, one throw, sudden-death, terminating score contest there is no incentive for the fighters to broaden their skill range. Because the result of

a match will frequently depend, not on the most skilled man, but on the man who first makes a mistake, defence and negative tension takes the dominating role in the behaviour of the competitor. He gets screwed-up tight, so as not to make a mistake — not to make a positive winning move. The training he undergoes simply reinforces that approach. If he practises anything positive at all (most unlikely!) it will only be a "big bang" attacking action; but by and large he will simply practise how to stand there and make as few moves as possible so that the mistakes are as few as possible! Not the most exciting way of spending an evening!

If, however, he could score by several big throwing attacks, in addition to several other subtle ways of establishing his superiority, then he would HAVE to broaden his training and include all the other skills. In turn, training requirements dictate how other club members, team or squad members treat one another. As things are, no one wants much from anyone else. Providing there are adequate people to warrant the "senior" player practising his defence — with an occasional throwing of the inexperienced opposition — the training is considered worth while. There is little cause for anyone to help anyone to broaden the skill range, because it is a manifest waste of time. After all, all you have to do is stand there!

I have of course painted rather too black a picture (although nevertheless a true one). Of course most (judo) club members do help each other; by and large there is always a very friendly spirit abroad (a friend said to me once, "it is a bond of suffering that holds us together!"), but is that enough? The senior members do help the less-experienced members by "instructing" them, i.e. telling them not to put the hand there but there, but I think it needs more than that. If skill is to be broadened, as I want it to be, certain competitive situations need to be simulated in training, which in turn should mean that trainees must have the ability to reproduce quite specific conditions in order to help others to experience and learn from these conditions. For example, each individual should have learnt what technique, space and pace means — in terms of skill performance — therefore by putting these factors together in a particular but different way (specified by either a coach or the player himself) he can reproduce a very good facsimile of a certain situation. In other words, EVERY PLAYER HAS TO LEARN TO DO SKILLS AND MOVEMENTS, which DO NOT IN ANY DIRECT WAY BENEFIT HIS OWN PERFORMANCE! They are for the improvement of others, which in turn and only indirectly helps him.

For a competitor, a man mainly interested in his own improvement, such generous, altruistic behaviour may seem an unreasonable ideal. He will say (with some justification) that he has too little time to train his own skills, let alone train in skills which he will never use in competition. But unless that man is a part of a big club situation (which means having several HUNDRED high standard players) he will never meet the range of different situations that he will have to cope with in competition. Therefore somehow those situations must be reproduced. It is hardly fair (or even possible) to expect a small group of players to train just to be an "opposition group" for an even smaller group of egocentric would-be champions (although I have seen the "set up" imposed upon certain gullible people). ALL have to learn the many skills necessary for each one to benefit — only a small part is for the individual's own fighting repertoire.

The matter of training and "mutual benefit" is further complicated by the average judo personality type. The generally accepted judo archtype personality is a man who is sociable, optimistic, adaptable, confident and aggressive — in short an "extrovert". Whereas, along all the years I have known judo people of all levels and many nationalities, I have frequently found them much the opposite! In my experience, the general run of judo player (and it goes without saying there are many deviations on both sides of my "norm") is unsociable, pessimistic, rigid in his adherence to the status quo, very insecure and uncertain of himself in most situations (even in his own well-known judo one!), and is very much a pacifist to boot! In short an "introvert". To reiterate this is only my observation over the years, although it was somewhat supported by research material obtained from a few selected judo men some years ago who were in various international competitions. A further complication is, that society generally prefers the "extrovert", or at least that is the preferred image of the socially integrated personality, therefore many judo "introverts" put on the cloak of the "extrovert" in order to get approval. They act the part; even to the extent of fooling themselves. Sometimes they do think they are brash, confident, adaptable, and they will prove it by wearing gaudy clothes, strutting postures, loud talk. (Because such behaviour is artificial it is frequently objectionable.) But when the pressure is on, just before the big event, when they are faced with a training alternative to improve skill, at a moment when they must decide whether to help others at the cost of their own self-constructed images, their true form emerges. The big event throws them into stubborn antipathy, and helping the up-and-comer produces an apprehensive indifference. Sometimes the training undergone does help to make the personality characteristics positive not negative, although of course the "basics" can not be changed. To give but two examples, assertiveness can become either bullying or kindness, reservation can become cringing fear of any situation or complacent humility. (It was probably this kind of developmental alternative that caused some physical educationalists to become cynical pessimists and attack the well established, *mens sana in corpore sano*!)

Anyhow this underlying common characteristic among judo people, of being uncertain of themselves, does not help in the club situation, where they need to help others. The "natural" reaction of such people is to withdraw into themselves and/or form small cliques so that the newcomer is left on his own. To overcome this fault, they will of course need to be EDUCATED! They must be educated out of this attitude so that benefit can be felt by everyone. That is a big job for the leader!

SPORTSMANSHIP

It is easy to step from the ground covered above to sportsmanship. For a time, somewhere about a decade after World War II at about the same time as the adage *mens sana in corpore sano* was taking a rather surreptitious bashing (for the amorphous "they" claimed that the healthy body did not necessarily produce a healthy mind); sportsmanship tended to be included somehow along with "mind" and suffered consequently a dereliction of useage. It became the smart thing to cheat honestly. But just as it was realised that in spite of everything, in spite of the many flaws in the biased sportsman's self-congratulatory philosophy "you may think I am a sporting bone-head, but because I have a healthy body, I have a healthy mind", there was some truth in it – if only sport were done "right". In the same way sportsmanship was re-seen as being essential if playing games were to have

any long term benefit, or to have a worthwhile place in society.

The road back is always hard! It is easier to knock down than to build up. It had become established that the thing to think was that to win was the only worthwhile reason for taking part in sport! You were a mug if you thought any differently. The whole uncomfortable moral and ethical dilemma is parcelled up in dope. Do you or don't you take drugs? If winning is all important, then – providing there is no danger to health – (and even that is not always a prerequisite) then drugs are taken. Why not? It's all right to use special equipment (i.e. glass-fibre vaulting poles) why not dope, it's only a different form of "equipment"? If however, taking part, fair play, consideration for the other competitor, is important, then dope is not taken. So with sportsmanship as a whole, it may appear to be an unreasonable ideal, but in the long term it's the only basic thing that makes playing sport worthwhile. Again the individual leader (player, coach, manager, sports-caster, etc.) tends to set the tone, fix the standard. If he condones or turns a "blind eye" to drugs, then O.K. winning is the name of the game. If he condemns, then he is for the game itself.

Me, I am for the game! Sure, win if you can; you owe it to yourself to make every effort to win – right up to the limits of the rules, but don't go through them! A great (Japanese) friend of mind, Daigo (twice all-Japan Champion) broke his wrist in training. In order not to stop training (in case it healed in time for him

to fight in the Tokyo Championships), he had it splinted and strapped up very tightly and carried on. Come the Championship it was still far from healed, but he entered anyway. Talking to him just before he went on for his first match, I noticed he did not have the wrist strapped up. I asked him why not? He replied it might put his opponents off! He did not get far in the event!

That's playing the game for the game's sake! That, to me, is what it's all about! Let me quote a piece[38] which I feel sums up the larger issue very well.

"Sport, like every other invention of man, can be used for good or evil. The spirit of sportsmanship, genuine admiration for a champion, regardless of colour or creed, may help us to shed our prejudices. If international contests between individuals or teams are treated as involving national prestige or as proving racial or national superiority, then they may serve only as an additional cause of international misunderstanding. And yet, in a world that has no common religion or political philosophy to share, perhaps the field of sport and the universality of the ideal of sportsmanship may provide a meeting ground where co-operation and understanding, a respect for the rules, and a sense of fair play will prevail."

In 1964 an international committee was set up (*Comité Francais pour le Fair play*), in order to try in every conceivable way to encourage the spread of sportsmanship and fair play (is it not significant that in a French title for a committee, the English words Fair Play have to be used??) It has published a booklet on the aims and objectives of the organisation and lists some of the winners of the International Fair Play Trophy since the foundation in 1964. (I will look forward to the day when a judo man wins that prize.)

The British Association of National Coaches is a group of full-time coaches and between them they cover 29 sports. After the Olympic Games of 1972 these coaches who went to the Games were very concerned about the whole field of sportsmanship displayed at Munich. A special conference was called and the following statement was released to the press and the B.O.C. and the I.O.C.

"Doping and Sport.

1. Sport without fair play is not sport and honours won without fair play can have no real value.

2. Methods of enforcement of doping laws must be given priority. Long before steroid detection tests had been devised it was possible for international federations to decide upon methods of enforcement. Their failure to do so must cast serious doubt on their will to rigorously apply whatever tests are ultimately devised. Punishment must be immediate and severe if doping is not to become a way of life in international sport."

The fact that such a statement had to be made and committees like the French Fair Play need to be organised, shows how some standards of sportsmanship have declined recently. A great pity. Sport is only really worth doing, if it is done with joy and unselfishness. Let me finish this Part with the summing up of Fair Play by the French Committee:

"It is a form of self-respect shown by: straightforwardness, a spirit of fairness; respect for the opponent, whether winning or losing, respect for the referee and the officials, and a steadfast spirit of collaboration with them: sportsmanship without ostentation: a firm and dignified attitude when the opponent or the public does not play fair, modesty in victory, equanimity in defeat."

An Exercise in Comparison

To conclude this part, let me try something which has not been done before.

There is a value in comparing authoritative versions of well known techniques, in order to see if there are any points of identity between them, and if there are differences. Noting the "sames" and the "not sames" can tell much about the technique (and much about the author). I have selected five recognised experts in the field of judo theory; four are written in Japanese, one in English. I have included mostly Japanese because few readers will have the opportunity to read the originals. Harai-goshi was quite an arbitrary choice (I could have chosen almost any one), although it does offer an excellent range of performance. I have made no value judgement on the descriptions, that is left to the reader; all I will say is that it is interesting to note that no-one mentions pace of performance or range of opportunity.

INTRODUCTORY NOTE:

Tori is the Japanese jargon word for the attacker, or the one who is doing the technique; uke, is the opponent, or the one who is getting the technique done to him! Note that in Japanese the surname is first. The translations are mine.

Comparison of Harai-Goshi

1. **KANO JIGORO.** The originator of the sport of judo, and because he was, he had no grade, i.e. he was not a black belt.

Uke and tori begin by facing each other, then both move into right (foot forward) natural position. The first one or two things to do, especially regarding the pull forward (of tori) is similar to hiza-guruma and sasai-tsurikomi-ashi and very much like uki-goshi, including the starting position of uki-goshi, where the (right hand) of tori is thrust forward under uke's (left) armpit, which is the same as for harai-goshi. As uke is pulled forward he raises his right leg in order to escape (by stepping round tori's hip). In order to stop that from happening (tori) brings his right leg forward so that the outside back of the thigh sweeps (back) against the front outside of uke's right leg. Completion is done as in uki-goshi.[39]

2. **YAMASHITA.** One of the early "greats"; first man to be awarded a 10th Dan black belt; travelled to America in the early days of this century.

Uke by moving his right foot forward takes up the right (foot forward) normal position. Tori also moves his right foot forward to adopt the same position; tori then pulls forward moving his left foot back slightly (to reinforce the pull), turning slightly as he does so. Tori's right leg now swings through and back against the right leg of uke with a feeling of lift as well as sweeping. By leaning slightly to his left, tori completes the throw.[40]

3. **KOIZUMI GUNJI.** 8th Dan. Did much for the spreading of judo in Britain, particularly just after World War II.

This throw is suitable against the opponent who keeps his body rather upright and moves his right foot to his front or to his right.
Tsukuri: Following uke's move, tori with the weight of his body, takes his left foot to the position that forms the letter T with uke's right foot. At the same time, tori curves his body forward and presses the right side of his chest hard against that of uke's, balancing himself on his straight left leg, making uke do the same, but on the outer edge of his right foot, the left hand holding uke's right arm across his chest; the right hand embracing uke's body.
Kake: Tori with a combined swinging action of the outstretched right leg and hips sweeps uke's hips to the right back corner, throwing uke over his right hip. In effecting these actions, tori should be careful not to take the weight of uke's body on to himself, for it would hinder his action and also endanger his capability.[41] (Acknowledgements to W. Foulsham & Co. Ltd.)

4. **ODA JOIN.** 9th Dan. A great fighter in his youth and a recognised specialist in ne-waza. My opponent and I stand in right (foot forward) normal position. He has much the same grip as I; we both hold the other's right outer middle sleeve with our left hands, but my right hand is thrust forward under his left armpit, with the palm strongly placed against the upper part of his left shoulder (his right hand is holding my collar). I pull with my left hand to his right front corner, whilst my right hand "floats" him up (making him "ride" high); as he comes up onto his toes, I put the

whole of my (right) side, from armpit to stomach up tight against the front of his chest and stomach – so we are "glued" together. That is kuzushi. I now move my left foot back to the inside of his left foot, in line with his toes. My left leg is now carrying his weight, my right leg floats into a position where the back, outside of my right thigh is going to strike the front outside of his right thigh. I sweep strongly upwards, at the same time pulling my left hand down towards my right hip and my right hand drives down towards the lower part of the opponent's abdomen.[42]

A NOTE: Oda, under the heading of harai-goshi does repeat the tale of how it can be used against an opponent who jumps over uki-goshi, but he does not credit Kano with it.

5. JUDO KOZA. A 5 volume tome produced by tne All Japan Judo Association and written by MIFUNE 10th Dan, KUDO 9th Dan and MATSUMOTO 8th Dan.

Tsukuri.
Both are in right (foot forward) normal position. With your right hand pull strongly on his left lapel, so that he steps forward with his left foot. As you make this pull step well back with your right foot. Pull sideways and forwards with your left hand, pulling him off balance to his right front corner. Just as his left foot is about to touch the mat, quickly shift your left foot to just inside his left foot. Keep the pull going with your left hand, and push with your right.

Fig. 16. Kikomu-nage (clothes-throw) Kake.
Trying to recover his balance, the opponent moves his right foot forward. At that instant pull more with your left hand putting him more off balance to his right front corner, pivot on the left foot and turn strongly to the left, then bring the right hip through in front of his left leg. Stretch your right leg and apply the back of the thigh to the front of his thighs. Make a springing up action with the left leg as the right leg sweeps up with a sort of scooping action. Twist the head and shoulders strongly to the left to throw him.[43]

CONCLUSION:
It should be realised, that not all Japanese sources of judo information are infallible or expert. An illuminating example is figure 16, taken from *Judo Gokui Kyohon* (Judo Basic Principles) (1952).

SHIAI

"Exercise and recreation are as necessary as reading; I will say rather more necessary, because health is worth more than learning. A strong body makes the mind strong. As to the species of exercise, I advise the gun. While this gives a moderate exercise to the body, it gives boldness, enterprise and independence to the mind. Games played with the ball, and others of that nature are too violent for the body, and stamp no character on the mind . . . I would advise you to take your exercise in the afternoon; not because it is the best time for exercise, but because it is the best time to spare from your studies."

T. JEFFERSON
Third president of the United States.

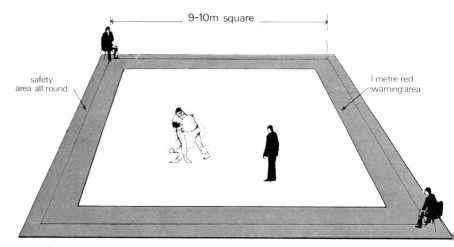

Fig. 17. Contest area

A Definition

Shiai is a match, a game, a competition; "shi" means a test and "ai" is a meeting – a "test meeting". Too often it is translated as "contest", but the word "shiai" is not really "strong" enough for that. A contest would really be "shobu". The first character is victory, the second defeat, which obviously tastes much more like contest than shiai. However, be that as it may, shiai or shobu is the time in judo when a man's skill is matched directly against another man's, to see which of them is better. A set of rules, formulated by a central organisation is accepted by both men before the match starts and these rules are

seen to be observed by three officials – a referee and two judges. The judges sit at opposite corners of the competitive area, whilst the referee is in the area moving around with the fighters, making close observation of the two contestants. (See figure 17.)

These officials are – or should be – trained in how to apply the rules. They will know what constitutes winning and losing, how to score, how to penalise, and by applying all the rules conscientiously at the end of the match the referee or all three will decide who wins.

Of course the best man does not always win! This is of course the objective, but the rules are defective, the officials have frailties, the competitors have guile and cunning. Any kind of combination of these factors cannot combine into a perfect or even near perfect system. That is why there must be sportsmanship; the ability to accept mistakes with equanimity and faults with tolerance. In the end, it is the game that's worth playing, not just the "winning".

Strategy and Tactics

The planning needed for winning a match comes under the two main headings:

strategy and tactics.

Because I intend to deal with some aspects of tactics later, here I will only briefly deal with strategy factors. However, that does not mean strategy should be undervalued – as indeed it has been up till now in the judo world. Strategy, as will be seen by the following notes, covers a lot of ground, and to do the subject justice would need a book of its own. However, here is the kind of thing that would go to make up a strategic campaign.[19]

Strategic Planning

Strategic planning would cover four main areas:

1. Style development.
2. Reports on matches and players.
3. Scouts and personal reports.
4. Visual records.

Elaborating on each area we find:

1. STYLE DEVELOPMENT

By studying and observing closely the contemporary style of competitive fighting, the perspicacious coach or player attempts to forcast how that style is to develop in the near future.
It is not easy. It needs a lot of knowledge in order to see what is happening now, and more knowledge still to see how it will grow. But if it can be done, it has great value for the training of a team. For it means that instead of training to catch up with the present style, which is a forlorn hope anyway (it needs too much work to even stand still!) the effort is put into training to anticipate the coming skills. This is the mark of a true champion – to get out in front of the "mob" and stay there!
To some extent I did this in my book *Anatomy of Judo* where I anticipated a development in sutemi-waza which materialised several years later in European Championships (i.e. the across the body tomoe-nage). At first, attempting to "fortune-tell" may appear too difficult, but with practice and application it can be done. Like most other activities, judo skills are subject to fashion changes. There is a minor cycle every 2–3 years (i.e. change of primary skills, say uchimata this year, ippon-seoi next year) and a major cycle every 5 to 7 years (i.e. a style change – from a very "mixing" style, where legs are being grabbed etc. to a very "clean" style, where both stand away and blast-off from time to time). If the present pattern can be ascertained, then prognostication is possible.

2. REPORTS

In this area, record sheets can be devised which can take down the history of any match. The user must of course be reasonably knowledgeable about judo (but by no means a profound follower of the game). It is the sheet which does the greater bulk of the work. It will be so devised that it can easily register such things as:

1. type of throw, direction of throw.
2. scoring value of attack.
3. where it took place in the area.
4. time (in the match) when the score was made.
5. direct or linked attacks.
6. ground skill standards and skills used.
7. variation of, or standard of, pace.

All such information would be pooled and used to help towards building a training scheme. By and large, teams of any sort (providing they came from roughly the same place) will have a certain style that covers all in that team. There will of course be differences within the style, but each group will have a recognisable pattern. So again, the strengths and weaknesses of such a style could be built into the training plan.

3. SCOUTS – OR SPIES

These will be knowledgeable judo people who watch and observe very carefully the possible or potential opposition, and then they bring back that comprehensive information to the training centre. Such a person could also be able to add personality assessments to this technical reporting. For example, does the "enemy" individual like fast or slow starts, does he like big or little crowds, is he a "loner" or does he like a crowd around him? All such information would have an effect upon the training devised.

If such "spy" records cannot be acquired, then an alternative (although an expensive one) is to have "friendly" matches or tours against some of the future opposition in order to make on the spot assessments. If care is taken over such tours several advantages can be achieved. For example if some of the opposition (not all of it) is chosen for their weakness, as others are for their strengths, then much confidence can be obtained from the results – which should be largely wins! The West of England Judo Association toured a part of Germany just before the 1974 British National Team Championships. They won every match in Germany – and got to the finals of the British Championships. It was the best they ever did. Hardly a coincidence!

GENERAL COMMENTS

Such strategical planning as I have outlined above would need a lot of organising. At something like club level competition, it may not be worthwhile, but at – say – regional level and upwards, such arrangements could be critical. After all, most of the well-organised sports (i.e. football, swimming, athletics) do have this kind of "spy system" operating. Why not judo too!

4. VISUAL AIDS

Of course if there are films or video-tape of the opposition great use can be made of them. Although again intelligent and knowledgeable "translation" is essential, for two-dimensional pictures (even when moving) are not the same as 3-D eyeball to eyeball observation.

Care must be taken too, that the opposition is not made to look too good on pre-view films. If it does, such a film could have a back-lash effect (see page 73).

Some Tactical Considerations

Tactical Planning

Strategy is what goes on, in general terms, preparing for a series of battles or matches. Tactics is getting down to the "nitty-gritty" of what to do in actual battles or matches. There are two areas that have to be worked on:

1. Personality: How, in all its ramifications, does it impinge on and affect skill performance.
2. Technical appreciation: Both in terms of tactical as well as technical understanding, and how factors like physical size and flexibility affect performance.

Some of these factors, (in fact many) can be, and are sorted out long before the match turns up. But some, for various reasons and in spite of the care taken, turn up again on the day of the event – but in an enlarged form – and something must be done about them there and then. For the sake of the book, I shall treat these aspects as if they just manifested themselves on the day of the big match (heaven forbid!). It does show of course, how impossible it is to really untangle randori from shiai and shiai from kata, and kata from randori. On what day of the year does spring begin?!!
What sort of "baggage" does the fighter bring to the edge of the fighting area? Let me outline some of them!

TECHNICAL ABILITY

1. Is he flexible or inflexible? Which means what sort of skill has he got? Does the man use mainly Rollers or Drivers?
2. Does he appreciate pace? Is he a "one pace" man, or can he play several paces? – say 4 or 5?
3. Does he mainly use one technique or many?
4. Is his standard of katame-waza the same as his nage-waza? If not, which is stronger?
5. Can he use linked-attacks? What's his stamina like?
6. Can he fight from the back and front? Which means, can he change his fighting style to suit changing conditions – or is he a one-style fighter?

TEMPERAMENT

1. Does his general behaviour stay much the same from training conditions through to competitive events? If not how does it change? Is he more or less stable in his attitude?
2. Does he like performing in front of a big or a small crowd? It is one thing to win in front of a few hundred people in the home-town, something else again to fight in front of thousands at the World Games in Pocomoco!!
3. Does he start slowly, carefully assessing his opponent, or does he start with a bang! Letting his opponent do all the assessing – of him!

4. Does he like attacking first or second? The obvious risk with attacking second is that the man may never get the chance to attack – the opponent having beaten him with the first attack! But on the other hand, if the other man's first attack IS stopped, the psychological advantage is great. It really is a question of taste (I for one liked to attack second).
5. Does he fight the whole match at one pace, or does he vary it? In other words, does he like consistency or variation?
6. Does he take a long time to "get going"? Are the first couple of minutes (or even couple of matches!) very much under par? If so, perhaps he could be taken to a supplementary training area (there usually is one at a big tournament) and given a bout with one of the team's reserves – to start him off. Does he start with a "big bang" everything going – attacks coming from all directions? If he does, then his fitness must be such that, not only can he keep up that starting pace, but he must be able TO INCREASE IT! Only in this way will he avoid having to slow down and so lose his grip on the match.
7. Can he take advice from the side of the mat? In most matches, even the World Championships, a competitor is allowed to have a "supporter" – a coach or a team member – on the side of the mat. Now this "supporter" cannot keep up a running commentary on what his fighter should or should not be doing (a waste of time anyway), but he is allowed to make a few remarks from time to time, in the "natural breaks". There is of course no point in

telling the fighter to do things he has never done before. Which may sound too obvious to mention, but I do remember several British Team Managers who have told the fighter how to solve a particular problem by saying for example "as he crouches down, whack him with uchi-mata". The poor recipient didn't know one end of an uchi-mata from the other, but through part loyalty and part knowing that if he didn't try he would not get picked for the next British team, he tried it! Result? The opponent buried him with some great thundering counter!!!

Advice offered from the mat-edge mid-contest can only be the form of reminder. In the heat of "battle" it is quite possible for the fighter to forget, temporarily, some very relevent piece of skill that he has learnt during his training time. The coach, or the knowledgeable "supporter" sees how the match is going, realises there has been an omission, and reminds the man what has to be done, i.e. change the pace, cancel out the opponent's collar-hand, open the side-spaces. Such advice can be very brief, and can even be given in code, both for brevity of communication and also so that the opposition does not understand. (Perhaps that's why the Japanese used "fancy" names for their throws.)

Personality

Judo style and skill is largely a reflection or projection of the fighter's personality. It is no good, for example, to expect the taciturn, dour player to exhibit a very ostentatious series of combination attacks. What the man does is, after all, a part of himself. So much so that I would now judge a man by his performance on the judo mat.

If, for example, his skill was "dishonest" (e.g. he would pretend to try, but did not really try), then I would consider he would be dishonest in other facets of life too. That is, the personality of the man would lead him "naturally" into certain areas of skill and skill development. Which does not necessarily mean that he cannot acquire specialist skills in the other less "attractive" areas. It only means that, in order to accomplish any kind of success in these other areas, he will have to work very hard indeed (and of course they will never be up to the standard of his own "natural" skills). Many of course will just not bother to venture into those other areas; it would necessitate too much work and diligence, and they just cannot be bothered. They will excuse themselves by saying, for example, those other skills are not necessary; doing your own thing best is the only way of doing anything. But of course the truth is, the more skill areas the individual can cover, the better chance he has of bewildering, and therefore, beating his opponent. For example, he can start the match off in one of his secondary "unnatural" areas of skill or style; the opponent, thinking this is

the "real" or constant style will adjust his actions to suit; thereupon the man changes style completely, going into his "natural" form, and causing complete devastation.

Here, for convenience, I have put the various types into two main groups (contrary to what may appear to be the case, there are very few "types" that reach top judo competitive levels). It is something of an oversimplification, but it makes my point, I hope, that personality has to be given full consideration when training performance of any kind, particularly of the top-class competitor.

THE CONSCIENTIOUS TYPE

He sees judo as a personal challenge to himself. He works very hard in order to satisfy his own private ambitions and to achieve the high standards he sets himself. He is seldom interested in the approbation of other people. He is usually taciturn and is probably very shy (he may try to cover that up by being very "extroverted"). Yet in spite of being generally withdrawn from those around him, he is very aware of the need to help others (sometimes he can be found helping, for instance, in youth clubs, or the like, unknown to the rest of his judo fraternity).

Because he works hard, and complies to the group "rules and regs.", not so much for his own sake, but because he thinks by so doing, he will help everybody else in the group, he assumes everybody else is doing the same. If he discovers this is not true, he can become very upset (sometimes even to the point of leaving the team or even the sport). By expecting others to have the same high standards as himself, he can be storing up a lot of problems for himself. Because he is withdrawn and concerned very much about his own performance, he can give an impression to the others in his team, that he is "stand-offish", or a "snob", which can upset them. He will acquire nicknames, or will acquire appellations like "the silent fellow", or "he's a mean guy", or the "iron man". Although the team will afford him much respect and admiration they will seldom feel "at ease" with him, the few friends that he does have will usually reinforce this "divorced" feeling by telling others how self-sufficient he is.

The coach's job can be a difficult one, when handling this type. It starts when (and if) he begins to admire "the silent fellow" too much (a very easy thing to do) and then he extols his virtues to the other team members. That only makes the team members more "jealous" of "the loner". The coach must be absolutely honest with the "loner" and fair. Because of the high general standards of the "conscientious" type, if the coach starts double-standards or is hypocritical (summed up in such phrases as "WE made a good win", instead of "the TEAM made a good win"), then the conscientious type will quickly lose faith in that coach and move totally outside of his influence.

The judo done by the conscientious type would be as expected; very honest, direct. This sort of man will go mainly for single, direct, attacks, and although he may acquire the ability to do combination attacks — especially if pressured to do so by his coach — he will always have a sneaking suspicion that they are "unfair". He will be very methodical (that does not necessarily mean that he plans — although if he doesn't he should), he is very consistent and goes about the business of winning in a very workmanlike way. His range of skills may be quite small (only having as few as 2 or 3), but they will be very good. The same will apply in both throwing and grappling work. His skills are not spectacular and will therefore be generally underestimated. Few will take the trouble to see past the veneer of a "job well done" to the very effective skill underneath that veneer. The coach's job will be mainly to ensure that his skill range does not get too small (and hence inefficient because of its predictability — not because of itself). The conscientious man may have to be forced to broaden his skill range (that will have to be done very diplomatically!) but if sound arguments for this are put to him, he will readily accept them, and get down to the job of doing just that. Such a man is a great asset to any team. He is a tower of strength; someone on whom the others can lean — if he has been positioned correctly in the team by the coach or leader of the group.

THE IMPULSIVE TYPE

There is much in the man that is opposite to the "conscientious type". He is a man who is often afraid of his own performance. This makes him very erratic; he's very good this week, very bad next. He likes being in the top rank of the group, but not head man. He appears to be a very confident man, sure of himself in all situations, but actually underneath it all he may be very insecure and unsure of himself.

Because of this basic insecurity he may feel the need to dominate his immediate environment, in order to prove to himself that he is not insecure. Some (of this type) will dominate like a Sherman tank, crashing and smashing all opposition by their views and opinions. Others are more subtle and will use guile and cunning to get their way with the people they are with. To make the person more discernable I list below some of the typical signs of such impulsive (or possibly immature) types. Perhaps you will recognise some people you know — I certainly do!

He may want to train at different times from the rest of the group or team, and will probably need special privileges; demands attention, and can be jealous of other team members: may not accept the team's "rules and regs" (regarding behaviour, punctuality, etc.); has his own training schedule, but is disorganised and his private life can be shambolic; has his own moral and ethical standards (which are different, and sometimes lower than other people's); has difficulty in forming deep emotional ties with others; often avoids learning from his own mistakes.

The judo this man does is first of all erratic; having said that he will prefer to have several skills (as many as 5 or more), none of them really exceptional, but the success he gets (when he gets any) is by being able to use one or two effectively when the others are not suitable (and so can look very spectacular). He will be able to do the "physical" part of combinations well enough, but will seldom have the tenacity to learn them fully. In fact the man's biggest problem is that he will tend to diffuse outwards, getting more and more "skills", each being less and less effective. The coach's job is to try and limit his skill range, without fundamentally changing it, so that it stays effective (and then offering advice for improvement, when it is needed).

A difficult man to have on a team. His erratic behaviour will have a very disturbing effect on his team mates. He is a very good "actor" and usually shows to the world a very affable face (for he wants the world's support and acclaim). The world accepts this face, and imagines that he is like that at all times, and therefore must be a great fellow to have in the team. The insecurity is not known, and therefore the world does not appreciate some of his problems. For example, how jealous and vindictive this type CAN become in a group or team, if he is not treated "right" – and if he's a bad case, then even if he IS treated "right"!!

COMMENTS

As with all attempts at classifying human capabilities and attributes, the trap must not be fallen into, which says or implies that there are clear cut lines of demarcation between them. So with the above two types. In practice of course, there will be many people who overlap from one into the other; there will be some men who have many skills and are reliable, and mature types, just as there will be the one-throw men who are impulsive. In short, there is a type-continuum running from the one extreme – the mature man – right through to the other extreme, the impulsive man. But in my experience it is a beneficial rule-of-thumb to see the trainees as one or other of the two basic types.

The category into which they fall, will largely influence the type of training they undergo, and the type of performance they will produce in competition.

Problem Characters

Emerging from these two general types, will be specific characteristics which can give a coach some headaches. Here are some of the ones I have found most frequently during my contact with national teams.

THE NATURAL LOSER

This is one of the toughest problems for a coach to deal with. I only became aware of this enigma comparatively recently (about 5/6 years ago), although I had been subconscious-ly aware of it a long time before that. Because it struck at the very roots of all I thought about competitive play, I refused to recognise the problem. It was the reading of Ogilvie and Tutko's book[44] which had a carthartic effect upon my thinking in regard to this matter and from then on I realised how true the problem was. What is the problem? The man who WANTS to lose!

It can happen at any level of competition, from club performer right up to World Championships team member; somewhere along the line of ability to win, the individual will (subconsciously) decide now is the time for OUT! Up to that point, he will have tried to win, and generally has won; for example he has won the British Championships, but when the time comes to win the European Championships he pulls back and loses.

Of course he never admits this – even to himself. If asked, of course, he would say "fancy asking such a stupid question, what do you think I've been training for all these weeks/months/years, if I didn't want to win?" But nevertheless, for various reasons, come the key match, and he will be seen to make that tiny, critical error that ensures defeat. He will delay that split second before turning on to his side, to avoid a pinning attack, he will twist out of a throw after he has landed, not before (showing that he tried, but just could not make it), he attacks hard, but relaxes just that fraction before the throwing effort and is countered. Only the most experienced coach or observer will be able to see these tiny deliberate mistakes, and the question is of course, why? At first it seems crazy, many coaches I have spoken to about it, at first refuse to accept it, for it is so obviously irrational nonsense, but after consideration they begin to realise it is the only explanation to cover many past puzzling situations they have experienced, but could not explain. What are some of the reasons that make a man want to lose in spite of himself and in spite of all the hard work he has put into the training? What is it, that in spite of his real ability to win a gold medal, makes him covertly pull down his skill, so that he does not win? Here are a few of the more common ones.

A CHAMPION'S RESPONSIBILITY

Many things are implicitly expected from a champion. Not only in terms of actual performance (i.e. dedication, consistency, altruism etc.) but also in behaviour and the approach to life in general. They are expected to be morally and ethically sound, to live a "good" life, to be an exemplary example to others. Many competitors are not prepared to accept that responsibility. They will claim they want to be "free" to be their own man. Being tied to a champion's title, to be expected to win and win again, would destroy that "freedom". It is usually – but not always – a sign of immaturity, for being "free" with no purpose or control is really anarchy; and in terms of personal development – disaster!

PROGRESS EVER UPWARDS

Once a gold medal is won, there is only one direction to go – down! A certain type of immaturity leads certain individuals to see sport as a bolt-hole from life. Whilst they are training every day and all day (in order to win that coveted gold medal) they do not have to think of getting a (permanent) job, being educated, or to think about the future, because the only future there is, is winning that gold medal. Once the gold medal is possessed, the excuse for dodging life is gone; they will then have to get down to the miserable business of thinking where they are going! By not winning that gold medal they can keep putting off that day when they have to tackle the problem that really frightens them.

Another common form of "not winning" is the bloke who fights just to get into the team. He will often be so "guilty" about his weakness (not wanting to win) that he will try and bluster it out with everybody, himself included, by telling everyone (but NOT the team manager or the coach!) that he has only come along for the ride! He's never been to Rome or Wigan Pier, so he thought he would make the trip on the expense account of someone else.

LOSER'S APPROBATION

Sometimes it happens that a man gets more adulation as a loser than he does as a winner! His friends turn up at the match in large numbers, to cheer him on. He makes great efforts, but just doesn't quite make it. His followers crowd around him, "next time you'll make it!" Next time, they are all there again, cheering him on. The man feels (possibly with some justification) that once he wins, they won't cheer him on so much, indeed they may move off and find some other "under dog" to support. Such a man would only see winning as losing!

THE COMFORT OF THE COACH

A common characteristic of a top-class sportsman is that he is very coachable. Or to put it in broader terms, he is very easily influenced by other people. That is to say, he likes other people (and often that means the coach) to make decisions for him. This provides the trainee with a great feeling of security (which he often lacks) and providing the coach's behaviour and standards are consistent, and known, the man gets great comfort from the decision-free atmosphere.

If he wins, the trainee can visualise that perhaps the coach will leave him, or at least will not be so attentive to him again (no doubt with some justification), for the coach may then want to spend more time with other up-and-comers. In such a case the man may lose the protection and care of the coach, and will be thrown back – to a greater or lesser extent – on his own resources. Again it is enough for him to ensure that he loses!

THE PARENTS

Many of these characteristics are produced or affected by the parents, particularly if they are instrumental in launching the boy into the sport in the first place. A common problem is when the parents take over the organising of the boy's (not the man's) training time. They pay for the coaching, they see that he's at the right place at the right time, and indeed even make sure that he trains hard. The lad is no doubt very appreciative – or is he? Because at the same time he realises that he is missing out on the "good" things of life, when he wants to go to the pictures or out with the "boys" he has to go training. So he grows up with an ambivalence towards authority; he likes it for the protection it gives him, but hates it for the restriction it puts on him.

The coach can then easily become an extension of, or a substitute for, the parents.* The lad, who by now has turned into a man, sees the coach-dominated situation as just another form of the earlier parent-child situation, and so maintains the same degree of ambivalence towards it.

So the parents can do much for the youth who is just starting out on the long road to sports top-performance. Not only do they help in the "here and now", but build patterns and structures that will almost certainly last for as long as the lad is in sport (and even longer!). It is their responsibility to give the whole matter of encouragement – which is very important for a budding champion – full and mature consideration, so they can do the very best, long-term benefit for their child.

* I am reminded of the story of the gymnast who was asked why he lost, "Well," he said, "it's my coach, he reminds me of my father – and I hate the pair of them!"

Some More Personality Complications

The Coach

goes without saying that the personality of the coach also has a great effect upon both the training and competitive situation. Although there are of course many sub-types of coach, the research done on coach personality does seem to indicate one general type, whose common characteristics are:

Highly dominating; they always want to be on top, very organised; like to plan ahead; are conscientious and sympathetic with general social values; are emotionally stable when under stress; they are trusting to people who are not too defensive in their attitude towards them; they score highly in most leadership qualities; they accept blame readily and do not pass blame on to others; they are very tenacious in all they do.

Somewhat on the negative side, in terms of that part of the coach's job to help others, are the following two characteristics: generally they show very little interest in the dependency needs of others, which does NOT mean they cannot help others, they certainly can — that's their essence. What it does mean is they have difficulty in helping people who can't help themselves! Because he is largely self-sufficient, the coach does have difficulty in appreciating that others do need support and

aid, especially if that aid is needed to patch up personality weaknesses rather than to improve performance.

Generally the good coach is inflexible or rigid in the adoption of new methods of teaching or coaching. Again usually a result of his own confidence (his enemies would call it conceit!), he feels that his ideas and methods are the best anyway. He may not actually SAY that, but that's what he means, so why use anybody else's?

COMMENT

It is the reaction of these three people to each other — trainee, parent and coach, that can help or hinder the training and the competitive situation. Certainly the coach should not omit, if possible, the influence of the parent from his training programme.

Some Other Problems

Having looked fairly closely at the possible problems intrinsic in personality and its related influences, let's spread our attention a little farther and recognise some other, more peripheral — but none the less important — influences, on the business of skill development.

SUPERIOR AND INFERIOR OPPONENTS

Some competitors have an "inferiority-trick" of turning some individual opposition into permanent "bogey-men". They credit certain fighters with real or imagined superior skills, which are far superior to their own; so superior

that it makes the beating of them — in the two words of Sam Goldwyn — Im Possible!
Usually in order to make the superior's skill even more superior, the "builders" have to denigrate their own performance. They have to say how awkward and clumsy their efforts are, how little they know in terms of techniques and tactics — and anyway "he's been to Japan"!

The superiority of this "bogey-man" is seldom real, or even if it is, it is so by such a small margin that if an extra effort were produced (by say the stimulus of the event itself) it would more than eliminate it. Too often, it is just another excuse for the inventor of the "bogey-man" not to win. In this case however, it is usually simply a case of not enough confidence. If the coach can manage to boost confidence, then usually the "bogey-man" disappears.

There is then of course the opposite case, where a competitor tries (and often succeeds) to "psyche out" the opposition. By "proving" to the opposition, just before, or even during the event (if it's long enough), that the guy is so superior that the others have no chance. There's the story of Herb Elliot, when on the last bend of the mile race and when all were bunched up together all bursting their hearts to keep up with him — he'd shout — "O.K. let's start running!" and kick into a soul-shattering burst. Geesink (the Olympic Judo Champion) told me the story of how he found out when and where the Japanese trained in the mornings (during the week before the Olympic judo event); and then arranged it so that he passed them as they went OUT to training, and as he was coming IN all sweaty and hard. He "proved" to them what a "monster" of fitness they were going to have to take on! Tricks like these can have a very valuable place in the "psychological warfare" branch of competition!

THE INJURY

In this section there is no intention of speaking about injury as a defect in the body total — only as it is used in competition!

Of course injury as injury is important. For example it should go without saying that prevention is better than cure. In this context it means that the vulnerable parts of the body should be well padded BEFORE injury occurs! I find too often, in the judo world that elbows, knees, ankles, etc. are ONLY wrapped up AFTER they have been injured! As necessary as that might be, it is rather late. Yet very few bother to wrap up before the injury and therefore protect the body part. Another "it goes without saying" is that competitors should ease off severity of training three or four days before the big event, so that injury risk is minimised and the body allowed to recoup from the strains put on its energy resources.

No, here it is injury as one of the psychological props, that is being discussed. These injuries, sometimes real, sometimes psychosomatic, are used for two main objectives.

1. It is an excellent excuse for slackening the contest pace, so moving into the range of the opponent — the injury loses! Because he is injured he is in no way a traitor to his team-mates!

2. It gets plenty of sympathy from his supporters. By carrying on, in spite of the injury he becomes a martyr to success, the spectators feel sorry for him, and sympathise when he finally (inevitably) loses. Such maternal sympathy for losing is sometimes preferred to the paternal acclamation of winning.

The coach can do little for such real or imagined injury (and in practice it doesn't really matter which it is); all he can do, is to decide how much time he wants to waste on the man and his injury. If it is a symbol only of a confidence lack, something is possible (i.e. put him on a programme of ego-boosting); if it is a continuous excuse for slacking in training, lack of result in critical competition (because performance in non-critical matches will be unimpaired), then perhaps the man will have to be thrown out of the team or squad. A difficult choice for the coach to make!

Another, but a more real problem, arises, when a competitor is free of injury for a long time. He goes for years with no real injury, undoubtedly he has the odd bruise and the like, but no injury of any consequence. He feels he is somehow immune, he has a charmed life, the gods are looking after him. Bang! Suddenly he is injured, a bad one! His feeling of immunity is shattered and his nerve is shattered.

He can now be too frightened to go back onto the mat. The coach may have to be very gentle with him for a considerable time, in order that he is nursed back through this traumatic experience.

NERVES AND FEAR

This ingredient of a skilled performance could have been put under the heading of "Personality", but I have put it here because it is not a consistent factor. Nerves, the degree of nerves, can vary depending upon the size of the event and the size of the opponent (not always physical size either), hence why I've put it among "some other problems".

All athletes suffer from pre-competition nerves, therefore the novice competitor need not worry about being any different from the "others", or having a handicap that the champion does not. Of course the experienced fighter may be very good at covering up his nerves (after all he's had them often enough before!) He may indeed use the act of "no-nerves" as a weapon to destroy the confidence of his more inexperienced opponent, but rest assured under that facade of "I don't care" lies a very nervous competitor.

As always with such a basic natural reaction to an environmental situation, the nerves have to be controlled. "Nerves" are tied in with the reaction of "flight or fight", the person who has them has got to try and learn how to steer them into the right channel of attack or defence, but at the same time, not to let them go too far along those channels. Too far along the defence (flight) channel will produce terrorised inactivity, too far along the attack (fight), channel will produce frantic, useless, scrabbling physical movement, with no result.

Nerves, when used as they should be, should tighten the body up ready for the big effort to come. The adrenalin will get pumped round the body system, the pulse-rate goes up, increasing blood-flow to muscles, the brain will shift into top-gear ready for instantaneous decision making. All that and more, is important in preparation for the big "do". Indeed I remember some Japanese teachers advising their more soporofic, or dull trainees (and the latter are the only ones who might not suffer from "nerves") to go along to the zoo the day before the match and watch the big cats and try to imitate ("drink") their pacific-aggression ready for their own performance the next day (more ritual and magic!). In other words if nature doesn't make you nervous enough, then find ways of producing your own nerves!

For I can also remember, the few times I was not nervous before a match, my performance was always very sub-standard. Nerves are necessary for a great performance, providing a check can be kept on them and some control.

Sometimes "nerves" can lay dormant, apparently well under control, then something happens — bang! the clamp that held them down snaps, and the man falls apart in front of your eyes. It can be the sight of his pet "bogey-man" long before he has to fight him,

or it is his best friend beaten (who he thought would do well), or he sees a bad injury, almost anything can break the dam.

In such cases "nerves" can very easily turn into real fear; any problems there were are now greatly enlarged. After all judo can be dangerous. It is possible to get very badly injured, even killed (very unlikely), but the hyper-nervous type will begin to see these possible hazards. When he does he can easily slide from just nerves into fear. I have seen British judo team members reduced to a totally immobile lump, not even capable of properly holding the jacket of the opponent. They simply stood still and waited for the inevitable. Not a pretty sight to see.

Can anything be done? Well, there are signs which give some indication that the man is being wound up to such a dangerous pitch. One of them is the long "warm up". Long before there is any real need, the man will start jerking and twitching, calling it "warm up". Lord Moran makes some more general points in his book on courage.[45] "Moods expose the workings of the conscious mind, as dreams lay bare what has hitherto been hidden in the unconscious . . . Where there is lavish display of feeling, the mind is not at peace; it is divided against itself." I expect we all know the fellow who begins to speak louder before a contest, than he generally does, or the fellow who starts waving his arms about, and moves around a lot more than he usually does. These, and similar, are the signs to look for, they will indicate when the man is coming up to that

critical state, when, with some little silly aggravation he can "blow"!

The Americans have a good word for it, they say the man "chokes"; his body seizes up, and he produces a very poor performance. Keep him "this" side of the choke and nerves will stimulate his performance; let him pass to the "other" side, and failure is the result. Can anything be done? Well it would appear as if there are two main ways of handling it:

1. INDIVIDUAL

If the individual has gone beyond the "normal" state of nerves, then the causes can be looked for. For example, one of the commonest is a "high expectancy performance" load. That is the man is being expected to put in a very high level performance (i.e. win the gold medal), the man begins to worry whether he can live up to this expectancy. OR perhaps the other team members are continually "pulling his leg"; this shatters his confidence. I remember seeing a "coloured" team member, the butt of a lot of "non-racial" jokes, having his performance shattered by them. The continual use of the "can't you take a joke" line visibly decreased his confidence and composure.

Whatever form the extra-loading takes, it is up to the team captain or coach to discover what it is and try to eliminate or alleviate it as much as possible. It needs a careful but very diplomatic eye kept on all individuals.

2. GROUPS

Group activity is frequently used to circumvent "nerves". Such activity frequently takes on the form of ritual. The commonest is "warm up". Whole teams will "warm up" together, the exercises invariably having a strong numerical base, i.e. everyone counts in unison. Doing exercise in this way, complying with a very set kind of pattern takes the mind off the nerves or off what the nerves are about! Such "warm up" comes very close to the "mind-numbing" drills of the soldier, which was to take his mind off death (see page 97).

The Japanese use this approach more than anyone. But then of course they are from a very group-orientated society. There sport, commerce, industry, politics, education are all permeated and impregnated with the importance of the "group concept" (even the language recognises group relationships).[46] Batsu is Japanese for group, so there can be found the zaibatsu, business group; kambatsu, the bureaucratic group; gakubatsu, the university group – and so on. Sport is not exempt. Certainly not judo!

In it will be found the "in" group and the "out" group (in and out of favour with the "establishment"); the "teachers" group, and the "fighters" group; there will be the Kodokan group and the "others" group. What there is not, is a place for the individual! Be that at your peril! So before the World Championships (or whatever the major championships is) the Japanese will always move around in one massive group, the "coaches" group encircling the "fighters" group. In such

a situation, the nervous competitor can get much comfort and solace from the tightness of the group. All will hold each other up with equanimity. There will be no "picking on" individuals by the greater part of the group – leastways, not till AFTER the event! The "seniors" too, the coaches, will also protect them all from anything that looks as if it will threaten the inner group.

It should be remembered however that such a group solution to nerves (bordering on the methods of group-therapy) is an extension of the national social pattern.[47] To try and apply it with no modification to a different socio-cultural group could be disastrous. I remember for example seeing a British trainer (who had trained in Japan) try to impose this kind of Japanese team warm-up on the British contingent, and nearly destroyed it. One of the best members, who was very much a "conscientious-type" player walked away from the group, and lost "contact" with the rest of the team for the duration of the whole event. Many of the others were alienated to a greater or lesser degree (depending upon their toleration level), from the trainer and from each other for a long time after that.
So again it is a matter of looking closely at every situation, and then trying to find specific solutions for specific situations.

GENERAL COMMENT

What has gone before represents a complex situation to face, and the match has not even started yet! But as I said at the start, skill, total skill, is not just a question of whether the man can do uchi-mata – or whatever – it is the effective use of the TOTAL person, which is important. Can all the qualities that he possesses – the bad as well as the good – be rallied into one whole coordinating piece of intent?

The integrating and interacting of all these many factors and ingredients are bound to produce difficulties and problems, but the solving of them is the challenge that makes participation in sport worthwhile. By laying them out as I have done, by putting name tags on some of them, I hope it has made at least the ingredients of the problem easier to recognise and hence understand. Of course they certainly do not occur in the simple way I have described them, each staying in their own little pigeon-hole, waiting to be recognised and dealt with. Some individuals will be found who have very few of them, others – poor creatures – will have most, if not all of them! With them, the coach will hardly know where to start! But start he will have to, if a skilful performance is to be dragged out of them on the big day!

Some Technical Considerations

Tactical Factors

Again, by definition, it is virtually impossible to list all the factors and ingredients contained in a tactical alphabet. Every player and coach will have their own set, but nevertheless, let me try and put down some, that perhaps not everyone has thought of, and therefore will act as a stimulant to add more on to their own lists.

For a bit of fun I have tried to list the factors in some kind of chronological order; how they come up in a contest, but of course it is really only guessing. In practice they could come up in any order. But what I have done, is to audaciously call them "basic fighting factors".

1. DRIVING LEG

Which is the opponent's driving or rudder leg? This is important to know because
(a) ATTACKING: it will tell which leg should be attacked and why; it will indicate the direction of the throw and – to some extent – the type of throw.
(b) DEFENSIVE: it will indicate which side the opponent will throw on; it will also tell how to counter and with what type of counter. Generally it can be discovered very early, on the bow in fact – the one which starts a contest. A man will bow, straighten up, and step forward – OFF his driving foot! That is, if his driving leg is the right, he will step forward

with his left foot. If he is aware of how important the knowledge of this leg is (for example, after he has read this book!) he may try to camouflage it. He may practise to step off with his driver. If there is any doubt, finding out will have to be left till the match actually starts. Normally a fighter will stand and hold with his driving leg back. However, again if he is astute he may try to camouflage it, for as long as he can anyway. Spin-turners are cases in point. They stand with their driving foot in front, ready to cross and spin. Exploratory probes should be used with care. Pressurise each leg in turn, and it will soon become evident which leg is which, and then what will need to be done.

2. DIRECTION

Does he, the opponent, come straight forward, or move sideways — to his left or right? Forward is usually aggressive, sideways caution. Joined with the knowledge of the driving leg, moving sideways can tell if he is to attack on open or closed side spaces.

3. SHAPE

Does he come in "big" or "small"? Is he crouched, with hands up, down, or level? Is he standing up straight with hands up down or level? If he is straight with hands high, he may be after pulling the opponent's head and shoulders down, ready for back or side attacks. It is an approach used by a very experienced – or inexperienced – man. It can give a lot of opportunity for the other man to

get in under the arms quickly and launch attacks from "inside" the man's defence. But it is a very dominating start, because it makes the big man look very much bigger (Geesink used it a lot).

Body straight, arms in front or down, shows aggression but caution also. The man is ready to cover the lower spaces from any form of quick opening attack. He will possibly use mainly driver type of attack, but more specific information would depend upon grips.

If the shape is crouching, is it aggressive or defensive? Aggressive, then attacks will possibly be rollers, very much to the front, but again grips will decide. Probably there is a preference for sudden explosive attacks; grip will indicate one or both sides. Defensive crouches of course usually indicate a counterer, but can also mean "trick" attacks (leg grabs etc.) and/or a preference for ne-waza.

4. GRIPS

Critical this from any viewpoint. Generally vastly underestimated. There are so many ways of catching hold of the opponent, they cannot all be listed. Again I have tried to give general groupings, so that variations can be fitted into one of these major groups.

(a) The cross hold.
Very cautious. The right hand goes out first and catches RIGHT sleeve of opponent. Very cautiously, the sleeve is passed to the LEFT hand, the right then moves onto the collar.

Fig. 18. The above throwing style is very aggressive, throwing hard downwards and only turning the (opponent's) body at the last moment

(b) Right hand goes straight to opponent's left collar, but with left hand –and side – kept well back.

The right hand keeps pulling down and forward, trying to keep space small (attacking opportunity small, for opponent). The left hand is ready to protect the internal space (stop the opponent's hips swinging through for example), until ready to grip (opponent's) right sleeve. If he's crouched as well, rollers are usually the favourites, but now the range of direction is greater.

(c) It can be the opposite, the left hand goes out first, holds the (opponent's) right sleeve, with the right hand protecting space, eventually moving to and holding onto the collar. Drivers can be the usual attack in this situation.

Occasionally both hands are put forward together. This is not common because it commits the man to a specific shape and position. However, sometimes the experienced man does use it, in which case it can be an example of the very ordinary, when used by the super-craftsman, becoming extraordinary. It can mean attacks to both sides, left and right. However, once the grips start the hands should hold firmly but not with tension. Elbows should be kept down, covering the attacking space. Shoulders should be able to move independent of feet position, and if possible at a different pace and rhythm.

5. WEIGHT DISPOSITION

Is the weight to go forward with the leading hand, or stay back on the back foot? Again the type of person and the attack to be used will decide. Weight forward can mean throws to the (opponent's) front; weight back, can mean throws to the (opponent's) back/rear. Weight distribution will of course vary with grips. If the man prefers a very variable grip, with the hands changing almost continually (moving from sleeve to armpit to chest, to collar, to neck, to belt, to back) then the weight too will be moving continuously from one foot to the other to both. Variation of grip, usually variation of attack. If a constant grip is preferred, the hands staying more or less in the one place, wherever that may be, then the weight too usually stays in the one place. Consistency of grip, usually means limited range of attack.

6. DOMINATION

Who dominates the other? Another critical factor. The way the grip is made, the weight displaced and the shape formed, will usually clearly indicate who's in charge. The dominator then begins to impose rhythm and pace on his opponent, now it is only a matter of time before he wins. (See figure 18.)

If the dominated allows himself to be manoeuvred around like a hypnotised rabbit, he has no future. He must fight back and try to regain the initiative. The dominator will be controlling space all the time; this is where the other man must try for his comeback. He must try and threaten and break up the spaces that are being controlled. He must not of course move carelessly into the intervening space, even with just a hand or foot, for the dominator can seize that uncommitted purposeless part and use it to beat the careless fighter with; by using the total body mass, in an aggressive, coordinated and governed manner, large slabs of the inter-connecting space can be pressured and threatened – by the dominated – without actually moving forward into the space. By varying the threatening pressure on different areas of space (at shoulder, chest, hip level) perhaps the dominated can make the dominator relax his grip and hence his control over the space between the bodies.

Once even the smallest of inroads is made on space control the pace can begin to be varied. Change of pace, either up or down, can affect space. Perhaps the hands/grips themselves can be pressured (they cannot be hit as it is against the rules), elbows can be used to push them off the clothes, body twists to wrench clothes free of grips. Many "dodges" can be used to get the grips loosened or get rid of them altogether. Perhaps the opponent can be so exasperated

by the continual pressurising of his grips, that he makes a mistake. Submission to domination must not be meek and passive. Once domination begins, and it will begin even before the fight starts!, the "victim" must fight back to rebalance the situation.

Of course, "rebalance" can also go out of control, and put the man in even deeper trouble. A comment I wrote about some of the British players in the European Championships of 1974 is relevant here. "The 'snatch' hold (where the hand is 'punched' forward, grabs, then is immediately released, so that another grab and snatch can be made elsewhere) seems to be used to the extent of being a fault, for this grip is being used so quickly on and off that it produces weaknesses immediately before and after contact is made!" By that I meant just immediately before and after a grip is made there is no control over the space it should be covering. A quick, responsive opponent can be in with an attack before control is gained. Changing grips quickly as described above, continually punching them in, can be very tiring (for the opponent – and somewhat ache-making) and is usually used as part of delaying methods.

LINKED ATTACKS

Having sorted out some of the basic fighting factors, the fighter can mentally add this to the information he already has (if any!) and start

sorting out his tactical plan – if he hasn't already!

Is it going to revolve around mainly direct attacks or linked? Let me reiterate quickly the factors which will influence the answers and the scheme devised.

1. Which is the driving leg? Is the throwing to be done on the sleeve or collar side – or both?
2. Grips. Is the grip constant or variable? Is the grip mainly for rollers or drivers?
3. What kind of spaces are being fought for? Lateral or vertical? Whichever is chosen will indicate type of attack to be used. Is the opposition organised or "by guess and by god"!
4. Shapes. Crouched or straight? Defensive or offensive?
5. What sort of movers are they? Erratic, jerky or smooth and silky? Do they vary the pace, or is it mainly constant?
6. How do they move? In straight lines, or curves? Do they attack going forwards, backwards, or sideways?

All the information is quickly put through the tactical computer in the fighter's head and in seconds a plan ought to begin to emerge. Much of course has already been done. Personality type, the skill pattern that has been evolved (in training) depending on body flexibility or inflexibility, have already been coordinated (we hope!) all that is needed now is the integration of all this information with what has been found out about the particular opponent in order to beat him.

Let me now try and inject a touch of realism and introduce a few of the notes I took down while watching some of the major world class championships over the past few years.

Real Match Observations

THE 1965 EUROPEAN CHAMPIONSHIPS

"The skill standard shown by many of the competitors was not as high as the fitness standard. If the skill standard is below or out of proportion to the fitness standard the competitor's overall ability will decline.

The Russians were the most impressive contingent of the lot. In general all their competitors showed skill and originality, and many of their wins were the result of the unexpected and the unconventional. There is a high standard of sportsmanship amongst the Russians; they play very hard but fair. They attack continuosly but with purpose; they are ready to seize any opportunity, whether it is "right" or "wrong". They very seldom resort to negative or delaying methods, but usually concern themselves only with a match that is both entertaining and worthwhile."

THE 1972 OLYMPICS

Because each participating country was only allowed to enter one man in each of the six classes, the general standard of skill quickly sorted itself out into two main groups, Europe and Japan then the Rest. There were excep-

tions: Korea of course is strong and countries that have big Japanese immigration groups, like Brazil, also have good individuals, but by and large, the big fights were among the Europeans and the Japanese.

In the extracts I have included here from my reports, I have kept to the heavier weights (the light-heavy and heavies), for I found them, generally, more satisfying than the lighter weights. Among the lighter weights the Japanese did tend to dominate, and too much domination can be boring. In the heavies however, the talent was spread out much wider, and some very fascinating matches were the result.

BRONDANI (France about 200 lbs.) v
ONASHVILLI (U.S.S.R. about 300 lbs.)
The Frenchman had a plan. He constantly attacked the back driving leg of Onashvilli and got several good "knock-downs" (these score points) but not a terminal score. The strain of moving such a big man began to tell; after 4 minutes he began to slow down and lessen the pressure of attacks. The Russian then began to take the pace up, maintained a continual barrage of throwing attacks. The Russians won by the officials' verdict. (Note: An obvious instance of where fitness decided the loser.)

GLAHN (West Germany) v
ONASHVILLI (U.S.S.R.)
The Soviet fighter, instead of holding the collar with his right hand, went right over the shoulder and down the back, and held the belt

(such a grip gives excellent control of the opponent's head and shoulders). Within seconds he jumped in under the German and threw with harai-makikomi. To make doubly sure — but unnecessary — he went straight for a hon-kesa-gatame and got it. The Referee calls ippon. Onashvilli jumps up in the air waving his arms in victory — a great win over one of the hot favourites, within seconds of starting. But wait — the judges object. They talk to the Referee; he changes his mind! He gives only a wazari (7 points); they can continue. Glahn jumps up, rushes at Onashvilli like a pepped up tiger, knocks him down with ouchi-gake (over the driver-leg) for wazari, pins for another wazari. He took as long to beat the Russian as the Russian took to beat him!

NOTE: It is very interesting to note that frequently when a score is made (not a terminal) the loser does jump up and returns the score within seconds. It would appear as if the original scorer frequently loses his concentration for a short period after his success.

NISHIMURA (Japan) v
ONASHVILLI (U.S.S.R.)
Onashvilli right from the start hit the Japanese with everything he had. Nothing scored over 5 points, but the Japanese just could not control the storm; he was swept from one side of the fighting area to another. He had to lose. He did!

Fig. 19. A typical "uncommitted weight" uchi-mata. The attacker was a "one-throw" man, and used the "lifting" action (as shown) almost solely. His success rate was high, but often, as here, the opponent could "lay-out" and prevent rotation; the attacker will have to put him back on his feet!

NISHIMURA (Japan) v
BRONDANI (France)
The Frenchman's best throw is a right sided osoto-gake. Nishimura attacked with right osotogari. Even though Brondani was not up to the general skill standard of the Japanese, he could counter such a foolish attack. It was only Nishimura's experience which allowed him to twist in the air and only lose the minimal score. Attacking the "action leg" (NOT the driver) is a very hazardous undertaking, unless the person concerned knows exactly what he is doing.

RUSKA (Holland) v
NISHIMURA (Japan)
Nishimura started the attacking with several lifting uchi-matas. By continually opening the top space Ruska blocked these every time. Ruska then started to use yoko-gakes (as Drivers); every time he scored at least a "knockdown". Nishimura did not appear to understand these flank attacks, because at no stage did he modify his stance (relative to Ruska) or pace at any time. Ruska won.

Comment
Nishimura preferred a very slow, constant pace (to get his lifting uchi-mata); all very well when he could dominate the match, but when he could not, it was obviously the wrong thing to do. (Both Ruska and Onashvilli beat him on that one factor.) (See figure 19.)

CHOCHOSHVILLI (U.S.S.R.) v
SASAHARA (Japan)
The Russian was right handed (a left driving
leg); the Japanese left handed (a right driving
leg). Sasahara began strongly with his left
uchi-mata, which meant it was hitting the "action leg" of Chochoshvilli. The throw made no
effect at all. Chochoshvilli began to gain in confidence. They broke apart at the edge of the
mat; as they re-took-hold, the Russian threw
with a shoulder-roller for a full ippon.

Comment

As Sasahara's uchi-mata failed again and
again, he began to look very worried.
However, it appeared as if he did not understand why it was failing, for he made no
attempt to modify any point of the attack. As
his confidence went into decline his opponent's went up. This always happens. If a
man starts off dominating and his opening attacks have little or no effect, then the domination can very quickly swing around. Therefore
for several reasons a fighter should not keep
"banging away" with an attack if it shows it is
having little or no effect. Perhaps it would
have been better for Sasahara to have
changed and attacked the "rudder-leg" of
Chochoshvilli.

THE WORLD JUDO CHAMPIONSHIPS SWITZERLAND 1973

I will change the pattern now. Instead of
describing individual fights, I will just put
down general comments on the event which I
made at the time. I have expanded the notes
slightly when I feel it helps the description.

FITNESS

It is now accepted by most of the top countries that fitness is a prerequisite of skill
development. Without it, long-range effectiveness goes. The best example of this was
the Americans, who frequently started well
enough but just "ran out of steam" towards
the end of their matches.

FIGHTING SKILLS

Too many still try and win with a direct attack
(making little attempt to prepare the opponent). The hope seems to be that the gods
are kind and the attack "clicks" and the thing
happens. (Needless to say, "clicks" seldom
happen, only "bonks", as the bolt is shot and
they disintegrate with frustration, bewilderment and counter-attack.) The best have a
plan, but even that it appears to last only to the
making of the first score. After that it is usually
back to "by guess and by god!"
There is a big increase in the two-feet-on-the-
ground attacks. Due to the intrinsic instability
of one-leg-in-the-air attacks, an increasing
number are going for this less spectacular but
safer form of attack.
Active players are going more for change of
pace attacks. Although the techniques are
poor, because the change (of pace) is done
with confidence, it works. The lesser
experienced countries were very susceptible
to this form of attack.
There is a gradual but very recognisable increase in the number who are using "multi-
bite" attacks. When used with purpose they
were very successful. (This is when an attack
is made, the opponent blocks it, but instead of
the attacker retreating — as is expected — he
adjusts slightly and repeats the throwing action.) The "bites" (attempts) can be done more
than twice — indeed as many as needed!
Usually the attack is initiated as a series of
bites — ending with a big score. That is, it is
seldom the result of a failed terminal attack,
which is then repeated without retreating.
Too few, even of the top players, appreciate
which leg to attack and how. Too many still
simply attack the nearest leg to them, because
it IS the nearest leg. They seldom realise that
usually it is the FURTHEST leg which is best to
attack,because (usually) that is the "driving
leg" and is therefore the hardest to move (for
the opponent).
Some of the strongest fighters realise that
they can win on "attacks only" (not even
scoring a knock-down). They are very
good/wily at it; struggle to the edge, make an
attack (where they are comparatively safe
from counters), break up, back to the middle.
Repeat as long as necessary. Inexperienced
fighters seldom have a solution for this
negative approach to winning.

GENERAL COMMENTS

Notice I have said nothing about newaza. This is undoubtedly because although it is very important that every fighter must be very competent in ground-fighting, the wars are invariably won by the throwing battles. Of course it is not always so. The finals of the Olympic lightweight class was won in 42 seconds (and 30 seconds of that was taken up by a pin!) but even that could be discredited as a statistical factor when the loser was disqualified anyway for taking drugs! However, newaza can be, and often is used as a "fatigue-maker". By "grinding" a man heavily in ground play, by lying on his chest and thereby limiting his breathing, it is easy to make him tired, (restricted oxygenation). When they stand up the defender can be so exhausted that he is comparatively easy to throw. It can also work the opposite way! I remember when Starbrook (Britain) was fighting a Russian in the World Championships of 1971 (the Russian was that year's European Champion), the Russian got himself into a very strong attacking position for juji-gatame (his favourite newaza winning arm-lock), both legs across Starbrook's body, arms fully entangled ready to pull it out straight. AFTER ONE AND A HALF MINUTES (I timed it!) the Russian had still not got the arm out straight! He had used every trick in the book, and still the Englishman's arm was bent. The Russian gave up fatigued and disgusted. As they joined grips standing, Starbrook felt the fatigue and threw the Russian for a terminating ippon! Of course Starbrook is very strong, exceptionally so, but the point I hope is made!

TACTICS TOWARDS THE END OF A MATCH

Having given, I hope, some indication of the things that can happen at the start of a match. What about halfway through? or towards the end? There are many things to be considered; let me give a few. The most important one is the ability to change the fighting style if a score has been made. What I call back and front fighting.

FRONT FIGHTING

This refers to the style of fighting that happens when a competitor has made a score. Naturally he wants to retain his position in front. He could of course go completely negative, close up all the possible attacking spaces and "coast along" to the final bell. The only snag with that kind of scheme is that he would probably be penalised for "passivity" (negative play; see I.J.F. Contest Rules) and lose anyway. So the first thing the "front fighter" has to be good at is "acting"! He has to learn how to make good attacks, that satisfy the contest officials that he is really trying, yet at the same time to give nothing away in terms of opportunity.

The most common way of doing this is to keep opening the spaces, particularly by letting go with the hands; doing drop-down shoulder throws – which have no hope of ever working!

– near the edge of the mat, so "break" has to be ordered. On returning to the centre of the fighting area, the same kind of attack starts again. Of course the referee does have the power to stop this kind of thing, but very few have the courage of their convictions to use that power. The "old timers" of course are very good at wasting time, but because these methods are not "recognised" (because they are not quite the thing to do) somehow these dodges are not seen as a necessary part of a training plan. Very few fighters actually learn how to beat these well known delaying tricks.

POSITIVE TIME-WASTERS

The using of a whole series of linked attacks wastes a lot of time. None of the attacks are intended to score, but they are strong enough for the opponent to have to respond to them. Because there is no intent to score, weight commitment is minimal and the situation is (fairly) safe. Who knows, perhaps in the attacking series there may be an opportunity created for a real scoring attack!

Body-throw attacks (sutemi-waza) can also waste a lot of time (providing the man is not dull enough to just fall down and lay on his back inviting his opponent to pin him down!) Grappling too is a great place for actively doing nothing. I have known many fighters who could waste "hours" down there, and although the poor referee has a strong suspicion he is being "conned", he can't really prove it and make them stand up.

NEGATIVE TIME-WASTING

Some fighters are very good at getting their belt to fall off just at the right moment. (Everything has to stop whilst they tie it up again.) Others will get "injured"; doctors will have to be called, checks made. The referee should (and usually does) add some of this time on to the overall time, but he does not add it ALL on. Some time does get "lost" in spite of even the most conscientious referee. I expect some of the "establishment" will not approve of me writing about this "unseemly" aspect of judo competition! It is not the "done" thing. I too don't like these negative ways of "killing" matches, but it's no good the fighters or the coaches — particularly — burying their heads in the sand and pretending the stuff doesn't exist. It's there! The fighter will, sooner or later, meet it. He will have to know how to cope with it. The only way that can be done is to include it in the training scheme! The only way negative or nasty tricks will die out is when they are proved to be ineffective!

BACK FIGHTING

The opposite situation to the above. Here the man has lost a score and he has to get it back. It is a much tougher job than "front fighting"; first because the "behind man" has lost the psychological advantage as well as the scoring advantage. Secondly, now he has to make all the "running" (that takes courage as well as skill). Thirdly he has got to dominate a match, which almost by definition he has not done since it started. Well, what to do?

1. A fast about turn. If the "loser" gets up very quickly and attacks very quickly (within seconds of losing the score) it is surprising how often it works (see Olympic reports). It appears that for some obscure reason for a brief moment after scoring the scorer is unstable. Perhaps because he momentarily relaxes physically and/or mentally e.g. "ah! I've got him!" That's the time to "hit" him!!!

2. If that does not work, then a battle of attrition must begin. The "loser" must tighten up his attacking spaces, and force the opponent to move at a pace which he does not like (it may even have to be at a pace the "loser" does not like either!) But he must try and force the opponent to make a mistake. To do that the "loser" has got to know precisely what he is doing (he could have learnt that from kata). The attacks have got to keep the opponent's head down, and they must be strong enough to force the opponent to respond — move — to them. What the "loser" must avoid at all costs is panic and frantic movement.

In the European Championships of 1974 the Russian' Gogolauri was beaten in the early rounds of the middle-weight category. However, his life was renewed when he came back into the repêchage system. His first opponent was an Englishman.
Gogolauri just had to win, it was essential if he was to get a medal. He started fast (too fast!); he lost a small score! He now went beserk! The splashing of arms and legs was frightening! But nothing was organised. All

the Englishman had to do — and he knew it — was to weather the storm. It grew more and more violent, but less and less effective. The final bell sounded, the Russian had lost! Perhaps if he had settled down, thought what he had to do and got on and done it, he may have won, but no, he assumed that frantic activity would carry him through. It didn't!

SET PIECES

There are times, moments, in a match when the number of variables are minimal. These times are the best times for going after big scores. For instance when fighters catch hold of the opponent's jacket, at that moment they are frequently quite static. Therefore such situations could be exploited, but practice time would have to be given to them.
Other "set pieces" can either be created or recognised. For example, fighting on the edge of the mat can be a recognised set piece. The edge itself limits what can be done, so sets could be organised. Does the man involved have his back to the edge, or is he facing the edge, or is he sideways to it? All these relationships provide a set-piece for the development of a special skill.
By gripping the opponent's jacket in certain ways, combined with a particular stance, certain set pieces can be created. By holding over the opponent's arms in a certain way, the movement of those arms can be restricted. If the arms are restricted, quite often the feet are too, partially. Another created set piece. The good fighter, the winning fighter, must be able

to attack both in fluid and fixed situations. He must learn how to create and utilise both.

PLAYING THE OFFICIALS

Another area of competition which is often overlooked, because the "establishment" will not admit that it exists, is the prejudice of the contest officials. The "system" claims that the officials know the rules thoroughly and that they will apply them without fear or favour and without racial prejudice. The fighter knows that is not true! He knows the officials are only human after all; they have many weaknesses; they are prejudiced; they don't always know the rules, and they are frightened of some people (either in ones – the fighters, or in groups – the spectators). The fighter will play on these weaknesses. It may not be an admirable thing to do, but it is a part of the facts of life, so they might just as well be recognised – "warts and all"!!

1. Some experienced fighters will try to bully the officials. If they throw for say a score of 3 or 5, they will jump up in the air, waving their arms, as if they had scored a terminal ten. At the same time, they will look understandingly at the referee with the unspoken compliment "we both know it's a good one, so just for the benefit of the public, stick your arm up and call "ippon". It works far too often!

2. Sometimes a fighter knows he's the favourite of a particular referee. So he puts on a big display, both to impress the spectators and possibly the other competitors he will have to fight later.

3. If the fighter thinks the referee is "weak", he will start quoting rules at the referee in the nicest way, at a difficult juncture in the match. If he has been fighting very defensively all through the match (and therefore may have made a bad impression on the referee) for the last minute or so, he will set up a cracking pace, and hope that impression will eradicate the earlier one.

The inexperienced fighter can of course be easily beaten by these tricks of the "old hands", so they should be prepared for them. The coach should simulate some of them in a training session. Just so that he is prepared for all, or most, eventualities.

THE END OF THE MATCH

So there are lots of ways that the best man can be stopped from winning the match. Some ways will be accidental, others will be intentional, some will be fair – tough, but fair – others will be very unfair. All that matters is that both winner and loser take the result in good spirits, and show all – both spectators and players – that in spite of everything they can be sportsmen.

CONCLUSION

It is of course easy enough to say that contests must be planned, but the reader may well ask, if it is so important why, even now, do so few fighters do it? As always there is not a simple answer; complexity is the order of things.

Too often the lack of planning is simply the result of lack of knowledge. The fighter or his coach, just does not know enough to plan with. They know a little bit of technique and that's all; factors like pace, space, direction, etc., are completely unknown to them, so how can they plan? To cover this abysmal lack of knowledge many will say planning is not necessary, it's superfluous, how can you plan when everything is unknown? As far as I am concerned all these are only excuses.

Of course if the opponent is totally unknown (which is very seldom) then planning can only be minimal, but even now many skeleton plans can be made before the match starts, so that as the match is progressing, these skeleton plans can be filled in with the information (of the opponent) as it becomes known. Skeleton plans would consist of how to change pace and direction, what kind of link-attack to use, etc., etc.

If the opponent is known (complete with films of him and reports) then a lot of planning can be done. Methods of negating his favourite gambits, ways of frustrating his best hold/grip; the best kind of link attack to beat him; all this and more could be comparatively easily planned and trained for. Even so the plan against a known opponent would still not be fixed or rigid. It would be flexible, able to absorb any unexpected or unknown variation in the opponent's performance.

Judo, like so many other sports, is becoming more and more professional (I mean that strictly in its financial implications). Results are becoming very important, if only by winning there is more money available, so that more winning can be done in order to get more money in order to win more! Therefore consistency will sooner or later become one of the top priorities in training. Judo, being an "open" skill sport, will never be as consistent, in terms of performance, as say running or swimming, but it could be a lot better than it is at the moment. Planning and organisation is essential if any kind of consistency is being sort for. There is enough information available now in judo for such planning to take place. I can only hope it will!

PART THE THIRD

KATA

"Those who fall in love with practise, but without science are like a sailor who enters a ship without helm or compass, and who never can be certain whither he is going."
LEONARDO DA VINCI

A Philosophic History

A definition: kata is one of the most profound words in the terminology of judo. It is only equalled by the ju of ju-no-kata and judo itself. In the Kenkyusha dictionary (the Japanese equivalent of the Oxford English Dictionary) kata is defined as form, shape; pattern or design. In simple, practical terms, kata is a contrived movement pattern, which is intended to improve skills by increasing accuracy, through the medium of discipline, that the repetition of the sequence (of movement) imposes on the participants.

Although kata has come to have a flavour of judo and judo only about it, the "movement pattern" defined above, can be found in all sports training. In other words, it will not of course be called kata, it may have the more mundane name of pressure training, skill-drill, etc.; but whenever one aspect of a total skill is isolated from that total and put under some form of stress – in terms of physical or mental rehearsal – then it can be called kata.

It would be beneficial if an attempt were made to track down the origins – and hence the meaning – of the ideograph, kata. Why? Why can't kata just be done? Why does the origin

have to be known? The short answer is of course, the origins do not HAVE to be known. The fact that Beethoven was deaf when he wrote his glorious 9th Symphony does not have to be known to enjoy the music. The poetry of the Imagists – Pound, Eliot, Lawrence – can be enjoyed without knowing the poets were influenced by Japanese Haiku and Tanka, and Chinese calligraphy. No, it does not HAVE to be known, but the longer answer is that "background" does help tremendously to improve the total realisation of the final product. So with kata, I feel that knowing something of its origins, helps to increase the total flavour/understanding of the whole.

To pursue kata back to its possible origins is a monumental task. There is very little to go on, and speculation is the only possible vehicle anyway. However, philosophical genealogy is seldom indulged in in judo circles, so I have taken it upon myself to indulge! Of course what follows is only a thumbnail sketch, for I have not the armoury or the training to do a really thorough job. However, perhaps it will incite someone else, who is capable, to do a better job.

It means of course jumping right into the whirlpool of Chinese philosophy, and that can only be exciting, because of the enormous wide range of thinking that has gone on in that country over the past centuries. To track down the source of an idea in such a maze of intellectual activity, reminds me of Josephine Tey and her book "Daughter of Time" – a

detective story trying to discover what Richard III was really like. However, the starting point is clear enough! That must be Jigoro Kano! But immediately it must be realised that he was standing in a spaghetti junction of history. Yet not only did he have the equipment to recognise where he was standing and to know which roads were from where, but he had the perspicacity of an educational utilitarian to take advantage of all of them! That is, as an educationalist (and that was his vocation in life) he knew what he wanted for the people he was influencing, and was prepared to use any means to achieve his ends. And his ends? I think they could be summed up in his two famous maxims Ji ta kyo ei and Sei ryoku zen yo. (More about these later!)

Back to the spaghetti junction! The routes from the East came from Confucism, Taoism, Buddhism (in general), Zen (in particular), Shintoism, samurai ethics; from the West came the new industrial ethics of Europe – the Graeco-Roman culture and the logico-rationalism of the Kantian line of thought. What a mind-boggling array of intellectual gigaws!

If the period 1880–90 is taken as being the approximate time when Kano's thought processes were undergoing their first major transition, I think it would be fair to take as the two main influences, the samurai ethical tradition (Bushido) because of its domination over Japanese past cultural development, and the European educational ethic – because of the obvious effect it was having over the future technological development in Japan. The type of language Kano used in his writing would seem to substantiate that speculation. His physical training jargon was drawn largely from traditional samurai training methods, whereas his intellectual training vocabulary (educational and political) was from the democratic West.

Samurai training and thought was dominated by Zen philosophy. It is not difficult to understand why. Zen taught basically that enlightenment (the ability to see life as it is, devoid of hypocrisy, sentimentalism and the delegation of responsibility to any others than oneself) is achievable without academic learning; add this to a hyper-developed sense of feudal loyalty, an indifference to physical comfort, to a degree where even death is treated with disdain (a very useful asset for a man who can be called upon at any moment to die for the most trivial of reasons, if told to do so by his feudal lord), and there is a supreme fighting philosophy.

Zen offered simple rules, for simple people. It did not indulge in complex metaphysical speculation; it did not ask its adherents to dilectically discuss morality[48] either in major terms of life and death, or in terms of fair treatment for the underprivileged (why if he did, he may even get to thinking that perhaps dying was not the ultimate act of living!) Provided he kept his sword clean and sharp, his mind opened to the beautiful in life, and had singleness of purpose, his standing as a fully functional feudal warrior was guaranteed.

In spite of the claims of Suzuki and other authorities, Zen seems easy to understand; enlightenment is comprehensible. Having said that I suppose I am morally bound to say what is Zen. I must fly into the teeth of the pundits and define the undefinable! But just as the conscientious sports coach must analyse and define the nebulosity that comprises a physical skill (even if he knows it is to be – at the moment – inadequate), in order to help his trainee to achieve their objectives; so with Zen, in order to help people assess and value Zen, an attempt must be made to analyse and define it so that "explorers" can participate or not. So what is Zen?

Zen literally means "meditation" (from the Indian word dhyana), therefore by extension it is the training required – and very hard training – to free the inner self of superfluous, hypercritical or crippling inhibitions; by so doing the person is able to react spontaneously and sincerely to his own external and internal needs. It goes without saying that Zen is not the only training available for this kind of achievement, indeed some may consider that "training" is rather an incongruous word to use when considering Zen and its purpose, but "training" to me means the organised striving towards self-imposed objectives. Others may advise and help in achieving those objectives (be they coach or priest), but in the end it is the individual's own contribution, in terms of effort and intent, which is critical. For that, I call Zen, essentially, training.

There are illuminating similarities between

the kind of erratic (and sometimes acrimonious) development of Zen[49] and judo. Both have suffered schisms, not only in Japan, but in Europe and America too. But unlike many who see division as a weakness, I see it as a strength – providing each new offshoot is tolerated by the others. There are many many people who want to do judo, as I have tried to show in the previous part of the book; they are all different; a single method, a single "school" cannot possibly cater for all of them. The more different ways there are of teaching and doing judo, the more people will be accommodated. That can only be good for the sport.

Bernard Shaw said he would modify that one of the ten Commandments which says "Love thy neighbour" to "Tolerate thy neighbour". I feel he had a good point!

Back to history. "Thinking" being largely a reflection of the times, when life stabilised and war (virtually) disappeared, culture was allowed to develop, "thinking" began to reflect that stability too. The Sung (1127–1279) was one of the great periods of Chinese civilisation, and as well as producing a fabulous standard in all the art forms, certainly threw up a new strain of thinker. A new look was given to Taoism, the pessimism and austerity of the early creed was no longer acceptable.

Life was seen as fuller and richer; the new thinking had to reflect that. Shao-Yung (1011–1077 A.D.) was one of the most important leaders of the new wave. He was nicknamed "The Master of Tranquil Delight" (his poetry had much in common with Omar

Khayam). Shao did not accept the passivity or the withdrawal from life, advocated by early Taoism and Zen; perhaps that is why he is called a neo-Confucist! He went into life full-blooded! He wrote this about his idea of man:

"He does not flatter the Ch'an (Zen) masters;
He does not praise the man of occult arts.
He does not leave his home.
Yet he is one with Heaven and Earth."

Shao worked out a life-structure that had a dominant influence on the succeeding centuries. First, he called the "supreme ultimate" Tao*; from there he devised a number system through which Tao acted in order to produce form – that is kata! (Some Western authorities say this number-system of Shao's is very similar to Leibniz's binary system.[50]) These forms or kata are then filled with matter. Tao is then sub-divided into two main forms "Motion" and "Rest"; each of these are again divided into two sub-divisions. Under "Motion" is the yin (the dark side of all creativity) and the Yang (the light side of all creativity). Under "Rest" is "ju" (the variability of life) and "go" (the constancy of life). "Earth" then becomes a mixture, an interaction of "ju" and "go" (the "softness" and the "hardness") and "heaven" becomes an interaction of Yin and Yang (the "female" and the "male"). Each of these four factors in turn can have a strong or weak version; by permutating these eight factors, Shao claimed that any known phenomenon could be produced.[51] Indeed the whole concept was put forward with such con-fidence and profundity that the whole subsequent line of neo-Confucists accepted it as a basis for a life-bearing structure.

Shao also wrote another very influential, although imaginary dialogue between a woodcutter and a fisherman. They discuss the finiteness of form (kata) and the infinity of matter (matter in the sense of fundamental essence, in Japanese it is called "ki" and can be found in such logograms as Aiki and Kiai). This concept of form (kata) was picked up by other contemporary and subsequent neo-Confucists and used in several ways. For instance, the Ch'ang brothers ("second generation" philosophers after Shao) developed the idea of RI, which was a cosmic principle that is above kata, and therefore kata would be shaped or moulded by the cosmic principle RI.

There is too an interesting divergence by comparing Shao's kata with Plato's form, discussed by him in both the Republic and the Phaedo. There is a remarkable similarity and when considered together, give an excellent "taster" as to what is "form". A quite different approach, but one well worth trying is to read Scholes' essay on Form in the Oxford Companion to Music.

Zen came to China in the T'ang period (618–922 A.D.) a time when China was imperialistically expanding outside her then home confines, and obviously bringing in to her culture all kinds of foreign influences, during the expansion. Indeed T'ang is said to be the golden age of Zen.[52] Its second best time was the Sung, and it was at that time it got itself transplanted into Japan by such masters as Dogen and Eisai (Soto and Rinzai respectively). To compare the parallel times of the Sung and that of Japan again has intriguing inferences. In Japan it was the time of the Kamakura period (1192–1333) when the feudalism and the samurai skills dominated the four islands. The neo-Confucists of the Sung did a great job of synthesising Confucism, Taoism and Buddhism† (as Shao himself did), so the Japanese must have got quite a barrage of liberal education as they studied in China, in readiness to return to Japan! As always they would have extracted whatever they needed – the beauty of the simple thing (Zen), the loyalty to the clan (Confucist), the training of the mind through the body (Taoism – in Taoism can be found the roots of kung-fu and tai-chi). It is sometimes easy to forget how frequently people did travel in the days of yore.

Because we have been "spoilt" by jet-planes, we sometimes think that before those terrors of the conservationists, people tended to stay in the one place. It is not true of course! Needham[54] talks of several contacts between

---

* Here is an excellent opportunity to see how the idea Tao is used more as a convenience than as an exactitude. Cheng-Pin, a colleague of Shao called the essence of matter Tao. Indeed most Chinese thinkers – Confucists, Buddhists, as well as Taoists – all used the word "Tao"; what they meant by it, depended upon their prejudice.
† Very much in the same way that Thomas Acquinus[53] synthesised Aristotolian and Christian philosophies. Again it is an intriguing coincidence on the time scale that each was doing much the same job at much the same time, but in their own cultures.

the Romans and Chinese, and these spasmodic foreign contacts continued through the centuries; and certainly the flow of people and goods between China and Japan was very consistent and regular; at least up to the time of the Tokugawa (1603), when it was cut off due to an attempt to shut off Japan from the rest of the world.

So I would like to suggest it was in this line of development, Chinese thought through Japanese action, that Kano developed his own idea of kata, kata as concerning itself with the wholeness of things. Indeed it is interesting to note that Needham[50] does in fact equate Hsing (the Chinese reading of the ideograph called kata by the Japanese) with "gestalt" in the Germanic psychological sense. That is, the concept of kata or form is concerned with totality and NOT with PARTS of that form. If parts are extrapolated or dissected from that whole form, then by definition that form is destroyed.

I make the last point, somewhat heavily, because many judo players "read" kata as being "basic" or fundamental! This, I would suggest, could be extremely misleading. For by seeing kata as "basic", the intellectual line of vision can become restricted and limited to parts, the parts that make up that "basis". For what are "basics"? Who's to decide? What's to decide? What part of the whole is more important than any other part of the whole? By getting involved with such trivia, the total form can be lost sight of, and it is, after all, the form as a whole which is so important. As

Shao said, "form is finite, matter – that which makes up form – is infinite". If the form is delineated by name, i.e. nage throwing, it is finite – limited by the very name of the title. If anything other than "throwing" is incorporated, then that nage-no-kata is immediately destroyed. As Plato says in the Phaedo, "Evenness is incompatible to the form of three."[55]

But once the finite form is established, then the constituents of that form are infinite. Or to put it in a different but a practical way, the details, what throw, how to throw, directions to move in, holds to take, etc., etc., can be varied indefinitely. This must be so, if through the contrived patterns of kata, the performer is to get the true feel, the "taste", the understanding, of what a total skill is. For the learner to learn, he must be able to get "inside" the skill, to learn it from the inside. Everyone uses their own different words, trying to express the inexpressible, but it is quite clear what they mean.

Bowie[56] when discussing the art of Japanese calligraphy speaks about "kokoro-mochi". "Kokoro-mochi" is the living moment, it being, so to say, the transfusion into the work of the felt nature of the thing to be painted." Yagyu[67] the Japanese fencing master speaks about "being at one with the sword". Stanislavski[58] tells how the actor must BE the part, and when it comes to writing poetry for the first time,[59] the advice is "to flow" or what has sometimes been called "talk with the pen". Contemporary learning jargon uses

phrases like "mental rehearsal", "behavioural loops". All point towards the essential empathy with what has to be learnt. It is the "flow" (being an integral part of that experience), it is being completely identifiable with the total form, that is so important in kata training.

So much for the "long range" influences on Kano, which seems likely enough, for no other source than the one I have mentioned, speaks about, for example ju and go, in the very way that Kano tries to use them in his kata. There is, of course, the possibility that he dredged the whole concept out of his own head, with no recourse to external sources, but unlikely I think, particularly when the "short range" influences are looked at also.

THE SHORT-RANGE INFLUENCE

In 1878 Kano entered Tokyo University to read literature, therefore if only for his chosen subject he would need to have read and spoken English well. More than that, English was the academic language – the lingua franca – of higher education. Japanese, as well as foreign lecturers spoke in English, and the whole campus pulsated with virile, intellectual activity – discussed largely in English – and stimulated largely by European thought.[60] Kano would have been particularly suited to absorb the new knowledge that had permeated throughout the University. By 1881 Kano had graduated; in 1882 he founded his Kodokan (to promulgate his judo). He also obtained a lectureship at the

Gakushuin, the Peers School. It must have been quite a couple of years! The Peers School was an elite college for the elite. It educated, or it could be said indoctrinated, most of the future political leaders of Japan. (The Emperor Hirohito entered the college in 1908.) By 1888 Kano was acting Principal of the College. Quite an achievement. By 1898 his ability had taken him on to the head of Education Department in the Ministry of Education. So although without doubt he must have been greatly influenced by the anglophilic teaching of Tokyo University, he in his turn must have done a considerable amount of influencing!

Japan was awakening from a 250 year Rip Van Winkle sleep of torpid feudalism. She had been rudely awakened from that sleep by Perry, the American Prince Charming, who had shoved a cannon between her eyes and said, "Awake and join us, or we blow you to the other side of the Pacific Ocean!" The awakening was traumatic. Seven hundred years of European development had to be concertinaed into decades. It took four! Japan proved her membership of the international mugging society by slapping China into a state of political malleability in 1894.[61] It must have been one of the most exciting periods to have lived in at any time in history. For a young, intellectually awake man like Kano, it must have been so indeed. Let me try and briefly show how, yet at the same time keeping everything as close to Kano's position as I can.

There was a starving man's hunger for all and any foreign knowledge, especially European. From the 1860s European literature – especially English – began to flood into Japan. Translations ranged from Spencer's *First Principle* and *The Charge of the Light Brigade*, across to Gray's *Elegy.* Books like Samuel Smiles' *Self Help* (a Victorian tome telling true stories of men's heroic qualities) and Mill's *On Liberty* were top of the literary pops for years on end.[62] And the centre of this Anglophilia? Tokyo University!

Tokyo University for many years, up to the 1890's, the only University in Japan, trained most of the teachers for the country's educational system, and so had an enormous influence on all leaders of learning.

Nishi, called the father of Japanese philosophy (1829–1897) dominated that University from the early 1860's. In 1862 he was sent abroad to study in Europe and brought back the works of men like Compte, Mill, Cousin, Montesquieu and Hegel (to say nothing of books by Dumas and Verne!). All these became compulsory reading for philosophy and education students in about 1870. Nishi was a great enthusiast for Mill, and much of his work was dominated by the Englishman. In 1877 he translated *Utilitarianism* and later produced a book on the logic of Mill. Because of his influential position, Nishi really stamped English Utilitarianism* on the Japanese educational development.

The other great leader of the "thinkers" of this time was Hirogaki, President of Tokyo Univer-

sity from 1881–1900. (He it was who insisted English should be the academic language of both staff and students – the staff were expected to speak English in the "staff room" and on all other possible occasions.) He travelled with Nishi and was imbued with many of the same ideas and enthusiasms. He was the great – and continual – advocator for the need to shed Japanese servility, so that the people could be free! Free anyway in the Western political sense.

Many foreigners, especially English, were employed at Tokyo University to teach philosophy, education and Western ethics in general. Men like Syle, professor of logic in 1877, Professor Cooper, who in 1890 introduced German philosophy into the curriculum, to say nothing of that great Englishman, Basil Chamberlain, who was professor of Japanese and Philology, from the late 1880's onwards. Kano lived and breathed in this heady atmosphere of the "newest is the best" (Just like the contemporary "the biggest is the best" – and can be just as wrong!). He must have come in for a big slice of this influence. Towards the end of his life Nishi produced his magnum opus – a great philosophic dictionary which tried to synthesise Chinese terminology, Western

* At the risk of being audaciously brief, I would summarise 19th century Utilitarianism as being essentially hedonistic, solemnised by a heavy doseage of morality and social service.

thought processes and Japanese spirit. Yet another clear indication that syncretism was congenial to, and incarnate in, the times. And remember only abstract cultural influences have been dealt with so far. Let's now look briefly at the "real" political scene. (Kano had graduated in literature *and* politics.) Here in politics was the concrete, the practical pressure. The starting point is an effete feudal society, ready to disintegrate at the first blow of challenge, (very much like the Empire of Montezuma when the Conquistadores arrived). Perry's gunboat in 1854 was that blow. The filigree structure shattered. For forty years there was a mad scrabble to survive, an example of Darwinism in the raw! To follow the many weaving strains of political, educational, sociological patterns is an impossible task, and would require a tome of its own, but I will try and indicate the confusion, the idealism, the conscientiousness that tied the many events together.

The essence of any feudalism was the warrior and he of course dominated the total situation. In Japan it was the samurai; a tag which can cover the whole range from the Shogun (a kind of generalissimo) who ruled the nation, (by permission of the Emperor – even though the knife at his throat was held by the Shogun), the Daimyo, the feudal clan chiefs (a status ranging from "baron" to "squire"), but although these were the "supreme" samurai (who did after all come from Samurai stock) the tag normally referred to the class of warrior that went from affluent aristocrat at

one extreme to poverty-struck part-farmer part-bandit at the other. They cannot be forgotten at any time when discussing this incredible period of transition.

From the time Perry gave the ultimatum in 1853, to either join the happy band of imperialists or their ancestors, some individuals within the upper echelons of the Samurai class, realised that if they were to survive they would have to "get with it"– in terms of measuring up to the trend-setting Westerner, and quickly. So a handful of these young men tackled the job of ruling the country. They set balls rolling in all kinds of directions; some they lost control of almost as soon as they set them off, others ended up in places where they had no intention of them ending up. But if they didn't score very high on control, they certainly got top marks for trying.

In 1868 they formalised a Charter that could be seen as the first attempt at a Constitution. The objects were: to abolish the base customs of former times, give freedom of expression to the individual, to provide some form of dialectical government, to seek knowledge from all quarters of the world – in return, the State would expect devotion from the people to that national policy. What it did not do was to try and get rid of class distinction, or offer any form of elective government. Although it underwent several modifications over the next 30 years, the government did try to do two main fundamental jobs – keep the samurai "happy" and give hope to the masses, both with only some success. A part of the general deal between the

new government and the old feudal leaders was that the Daimyo should give their feudal territory to the central government. In 1871 this was in turn given back to local government, as a basis for administrative prefectures. As compensation, the Daimyo and their dependent hierarchy of samurai were pensioned off. But two major snags immediately showed themselves; it produced a class of social parasites overnight (samurai traditionally despised work and the pension gave them no cause to change their view) and the country couldn't afford it! The whole economic situation was extremely sensitive, taxes could not be raised any more – it would have been disastrous, so there was only one choice left.[63] The pensions, after a very short time were drastically cut. It caused much hardship and bitterness. A cry for "the good old days" began to be heard. In 1870 a conscription law was passed, but the army was not formed till 1873 (based largely on the Prussian model). In 1871 a choice was officially given, whether swords were worn or not. (The first step to cut the samurai down to size.) The bushi began to get very restless, his status and future was at great risk; he was having great difficulty in "changing his spots"; he began to get frustrated. The obvious way to cure frustration – a fight! The ruling junta recognised the signs, and gave the samurai a nice little war in Formosa (this had already been squared with the Chinese main land), but it had little effect. Then the official toleration of Christianity gave the xenophobic streak in the bushi another opportunity to express dissatisfaction and added to the general disillusionment. The same year of the Formosa war, saw the first of the samurai revolts. In 1876 came the banning of sword-wearing, the grand symbol of the samurai's dominant position in society (very much like the belt system in judo). It was the last straw. The recurring small revolts since the first one of 1874 crescendoed in the big one of 1877 – the Satsuma Rebellion (led by Saigo). It was stamped out, after a bitter battle, by the conscripted army of 1873. It was, for all practical purposes, the end of the samurai. The battle "proved" that hard-trained plebians could beat life-long trained professionals. (Another example of the characteristic of the Japanese to stand or fall by one throw of the dice.) The samurai's image took a considerable beating; he was now seen as – to quote a modern phrase – a fascist reactionary, holding the nation back from its glorious destiny.

But it was only the pendulum swinging. However, occurring at that time it must have had its effect upon Kano* and made him realise that perhaps he should disassociate himself from the "albatross image" of the anachronistic samurai figure.

"Whatever you do, don't expatiate in the presence of Japanese of the new school, on those quaint, and beautiful things Japanese, which rouse your genuine admiration. . . . Speaking generally the educated Japanese have done with their past. They want to be somebody else and something else than what they have been and still partly are."

Basil Hall Chamberlain.
Professor of Japanese and Philology in the Imperial University of Tokyo (written in 1890).[64]

Also emerging from the charter of 1868 was the opportunity to establish political parties. Not so easy to do of course. Before 1868 the people of Japan, even the well-educated, had very little idea of political liberty. Indeed it was not until 1874 that the first party was actually formed. It was called the Risshisha, and although ostensibly formed to spread liberal ideals, i.e. life, liberty and the pursuit of happiness, it was largely for the care of destitute ex-samurai, and proclaiming the morality expressed in Samuel Smiles' book *Self Help.* (Note the title of the book in Japanese was "Risshi Ken"). Again there is a perceivable link from here to Kano!

Much of the early organising enthusiasm for these political parties came from the more capable ex-samurai (for it was a medium for their ambitions as well as their complaints), but as the years slipped by and change became more and more drastic, even they had to concentrate fully on survival. The movement for "people's rights" (i.e. political franchise etc.) went from their hands to those of the rural aristocracy (remember Kano was a "country boy", born in Mikage, three to four hundred miles away from Tokyo). By 1882 socialism was percolating into Japan due to the writings of Marx. In that year was launched "The Oriental Socialist Party" and the short-lived semi-union party called the Shakai To (for all rikusha pullers!) Parties of all kinds were quickly made and quickly destroyed with the same enthusiastic dedication, but then we must remember the backcloth was very different to what we, Westerners, are used to. In England, for example, Parliament was made before parties; in Japan the opposite was true – parties before Parliament. (The Japanese Parliament, the Diet, was not opened till 1890.) Liberal organisations in Europe (like the Chartists in England) were usually produced from urban society and could therefore count on the money of the cities (i.e. the Guilds), but in Japan they came from the rural communities, and there was very little finance there to call upon. But if money was short, ardour was not, and the parties that did survive made considerable progress. As frequently happens

* Judo is sometimes classed in with budo (the method, or way of war, of the samurai). This I feel is very unfair to both judo and Kano! Not only was judo launched, chronologically several years after the end of the samurai era (i.e. 1877 and 1882) but in terms of morality, ethical and educational content, it was centuries after budo and bushido. Most, if not all, feudal codes of knightly conduct were only camouflage for, or the covering up of, brutal and savage behaviour that had to be suffered by the weak and unprotected. Bushido and samurai were no exceptions to that rule! There is a proverb found in a very famous Japanese story about samurai gallantry, called the Chushingura (the Loyal 47), which says, "Slaughter and rapine, the samurai's daily deeds."

with radical, hard-working, political groups, they soon become an embarrassment to the establishment, so – in 1864 parties were allowed, in 1884 all parties were disallowed! After 1890 political parties were again allowed, but this time they were very tightly controlled by the State. Any kind of anti-establishment view was discouraged – very emphatically! But there were many men who wanted their opinions heard. How? Well they had to join the establishment and try to speak (and reform) from inside. But it took a lot of courage. For back into new fashion came the Japanese old-fashioned panacea for all political troubles – assassination! A man who spoke up against the establishment could expect, within hours or at most days, the knife, the sword, the gun or bomb! (It is by no means a thing of the past even now!!!)

Ike[65] suggests that because the intellectual climate of the 1880's period was so dominated by foreign (European) thought the Japanese did not have the opportunity, and hence the ability, to create an adequate indigenous counter-symbolism to offset the, long-standing, "right-facing" symbolism, i.e. the Emperor and national polity. The "pioneers" of political freedom allowed an abstract, impersonal, totalitarian, ideal – Kokutai-no-hongi – to blot out all considera-tion for the individual. Kokutai-no-hongi was a complex nationalistic slogan, meaning linguistically something like the "national es-sence", but in practice meant anything the state wanted it to mean! It was this inability of

the liberal intellectuals to provide a long, lasting democratic structure, which gave the fascist element its first toehold on the future of Japan. For although the intention of the Constitution of 1889 was to limit the power of the growing military faction, it did in fact have the opposite effect. It is easy for us, with hind-sight, to see where the mistake was made, but at the time the attempt was genuine enough. The idea, was to allow only one military voice on the inner cabinet, then the other out-numbering voices could easily persuade a change – if that one voice was disagreeing with the rest. What was not realised, was that if the military man decided not to co-operate with his colleagues in the Cabinet, he could withdraw and bring the whole government down! If he withdrew he would take the whole nation's military service with him – no Government could stand without the support of its fighting service, certainly not Japan! So once the above was in the Constitution, it heralded the return of the warrior to Japan – after a very short absence! A different sort though from the one tossed out in 1877; no longer armed with a sword, he now held a machine-gun! Worse still he no longer had a long established tradition to stand him in good stead when he had critical decisions to make (i.e. to shoot or not to shoot!) But the un-derlying attitude was much the same as the old warriors – might overcomes right! It was all epitomised in the China War of 1894 – the start of the long haul to Pearl Harbour and World War II.

Just as there was a large national pattern, showing how, after a short virile start the liberals of Japan lacked stamina and slowed up, became apathetic and then allowed the nation to slide into totalitarianism, so that pattern was duplicated – but on a much smaller scale – in judo. Kano started with great enthusiasm in the early 1880's, changed his dojo several times, each one bigger than the last one. Most, if not all of the kata were devised in the 1890's and then from about the turn of the century on, he seemed to let the care of judo slide away from him. Cer-tainly in the 1930's judo (as well as Kendo, and the other combat activities) were largely taken over by the military and used for its own totalitarian ends. Many of the feared Japanese secret societies (mostly assassination groups) were based upon or around the combat cen-tres.[66] Perhaps Kano was too busy with his work (he certainly did do a vast amount in the education section of government), or perhaps he had little choice in the matter. I know that for a long time Kano was under a lot of pressure from the State to accept a State sub-sidy (which meant Army money and hence Army control), but he kept on resisting and stopped the Army taking over the Kodokan until after the war had actually started. Then he had to give in. It was for mainly that reason the American Occupation allowed the Kodokan to start up again after the war, while still banning other judo centres for their pre-war political involvement. But it does again help to emphasise too two very important

points when scrutinising the origins of a sport.
1. How sport is a reflection of the society that
nurtured it and to understand a sport, that
society has to be looked at just as closely as
the sport itself.
2. That however well-intentioned the initial
ideals are, of any social organisation, they
must be watched carefully, conscientiously
and continually, to ensure that those ideals are
not prostituted or contorted; or, to put it
another way, pioneering is a very exciting time
with lots of challenges to be met, but con-
solidating can be a very dull affair – and that's
when it can go wrong!

The Standard (Traditional) Kata

Kata as Training (Drills and Ritual)

Above, by showing what I consider to be some of the origins of Kano's thinking and some of the influences he must have undergone, I hope I have indicated, in some small way, the possible profounder considerations that are available in the kind of physical training known as kata. But it is very much like a good learning-to-swim swimming pool — it is very deep at one end, and then gets shallower and shallower at the other end, till the water runs out and the swimmer is imperceptibly left facing hard tiles. So with kata, as the deep end is left, it gets to the much shallower part called ritual and eventually disappears in what is just drills. It is not really possible to say when one type of exercise starts and the other finishes, nor can one say the very shallow end is any less important than the deep end — the non-swimmer will be only too pleased to stay where he can sit in the water and enjoy his indolence, just as the experienced swimmer will prefer diving in and enjoying the depth of the deep end. As long as the objects and purpose of the varying depths are clearly understood, all is fine, it is only when the good swimmer is expected to swim in 6″ of water, or when the non-swimmer is tossed into the 12′ deep end, that trouble really begins.

However, any form of ritual or drill which has lost its meaning or objectivity, can become simply a waste of time*, the worst kind of aimless drifting around in a ship with no rudder or compass.

Uchikomi, or butsukari as it used to be called (the repetition of just the attacking action, without the throw, done in a static situation) is typical of a physical exercise which may have started out as true kata (the "form" being a very limited movement, contrived for a very specific purpose) but too often it has degenerated into an "objectiveless" drill As such it can be largely a waste of time (apart from some possibly fringe benefits in terms of stamina). But providing that purpose and intent are visible in movement, then it can have benefit.

In most indigenous arts and crafts of Japan, there is a very strong tradition of kata being a part of the training. Generally it is written or spoken about as being only ritual, but in practice the stress is often on the empathy in what is trying to be done. If I may be excused for introducing a couple of personal examples it may help to make the point. When I was learning Kendo (Japanese fencing) under Master Kono, he insisted that when kata was being done (and in the kata he taught me, there were 50 offensive actions, coupled to the response for each one of those 50), he insisted that I had to be aware of the imminence of death. In other words I had to see the swords as real and not as wooden ones. Once they were made of wood there was no "threat" and spiritual awareness became flaccid; any

benefit — if there was any — would be restricted only to physical fitness.

When studying aikido under Master Tomiki he would use the analogy of prayer. He would hold up both hands, about a foot apart and say, "here is you, and here is your opponent — or your god and you. Only when they have come together through the tension created in that space (and he would join his hands as if praying) and become one, can true mutual benefit, be achieved". By repeatedly going through a ritual performance — the object and purpose of which is fully understood — the discipline of "knowing thyself" can be achieved. Moving away from ritual and participating in drill is not so beneficial, but even so there can be value. Drill is a lower form of ritual, the best example of course being the army kind. Soldiers are drilled for two very good reasons, or is it three?

1. So that they can make the correct tactical manoeuvre when ordered to do so by their officers.
2. By involving the mind largely in the close proximity of sequential movements that MUST be done in the correct order, there is little mind left over to dwell on the slightly further off fear of death or maiming.

* I am reminded of that story when a foreign visiting general watched an army team very smartly unlimber a field-gun from a half-track, fire it, limber up and drive away, all with meticulous order. The officer in charge proudly asked the general what he thought of it. "Excellent", replied the visitor, "but please, tell me, what was that man for standing still, all on his own, doing nothing?" The officer, very embarrassed, did not know. He crept away, determined to find out. After much research he discovered that he was the man who held the horses!!!

3.(?) To give the stupid, something positive to do in time of stress, in case they just "choke" and do absolutely nothing. (Is that the same as 2? No, it can't really be, for that would mean all soldiers are stupid.)

The second reason is of course the most important of the two or three. Because death creates omnipresent fear which can prevent the soldier doing his real job of fighting, any way of surmounting it, even for a few moments, has a very valid place in the training of soldiers. But it also shows clearly the hazards of such an approach when used in a sporting context. Drill can take the mind away from the main issue, and lose it in a welter of triviality.

In the transmission of Kodokan Kata, I have found – too often in my experience – that they have been reduced to objectless drills. Occasionally there has been an improvement when it has been raised up to a ritual, but seldom (dare I say never!) have I seen it done as a total "form". Most places I have visited (dare I say all?) throughout the world, teaching and doing judo, do not have a comprehensive knowledge of what kata is and what it is for. Even authoritative Japanese text-books give very little indication of what the form is; most limit themselves to the ritualistic aspect, and simply specify where bits of the two bodies go.

For example, kata thinking has become so regimental that most judo players think the only kata there is is what is contained in the "official" Kodokan list of seven. (Perhaps if some were pressed they may hesitantly admit that perhaps it is not so.) Few seem to realise that when they practise a combination attack, say ouchi- into tai-otoshi, they are doing kata! It is this very reason, that kata can cover such a range of complexity – from a simple linked attack to a tactical pattern involving fifteen or more moves – which makes it such an important part of a skill training scheme.

The Standard Kata

At this point I want to briefly spell out what the seven standard kata are and what is the purpose of them. I do not intend to go into detail (that can be found in several judo text books – of varying standards of "know-how"). Here I want to discuss "form" and let the "matter" become the responsibility of the performer or coach.

NAGE-NO-KATA

The form of throwing: devised in about 1890. It consists of fifteen selected throws, attempting to illustrate a range of throwing actions. Each throwing action is done to the left and right, and the – now thirty – throws are separated into four groups. The aim of each group is to draw the attention (of the participants) to the use of a particular factor in the technique of throwing. (There are in fact two groups of "body weight" throws, making a total of five groups with three techniques in each.) It is how the factor is used, in different types of throwing action, which is important. (See figure 20.)

Since this kata was originally formed there have been several changes made in the techniques included, showing that Kano did to some degree anyway, try to improve his creation, for the first decade or so anyway. Alas! seldom is there any attempt at explaining why all are done alternately to the right and left, and even that is omitted in some "drill schools". It normally is said that it "teaches you to throw to both the left and right side". This I find very dubious reasoning. In all my years in judo, I have met very few (and offhand I cannot think of any!) who can throw with equal facility on both sides.

Oh yes, when some fellow is fighting a considerably weaker opponent he can throw with his "other side", but if the opposition is anything like equal, then he sticks to his strongest side.

The reason, I go for training to do a throw both sides, is because of some research Cratty[67] talks about, which briefly is: that when a skill is practised on the weaker side of the body, somehow there is a transference in the motor-part of the brain, which improves the skill on the strong side. My own experience supports this hypothesis, so that's the explanation I prefer – and after all, in the long run that is all it is, personal preference!

For more detail of this kata, I would like to suggest my other book[8] which is concerned solely with nage-no-kata.

NAGE-NO-KATA (Traditional)

All throws are done to uke's right and left side in that order (except No. 4, which is opposite)

Fig. 20

Set	Japanese Name	Translation	Opportunity	(Uke's) Direction of Movement	Pace	Gleeson Type (throw)	Specific Comments	General Comments
te-waza; the technique of how to use the hands	uki-otoshi	turning drop	foot forward	forward	very fast	driver	on the third tsugi-ashi step	The whole of this set is fast, but there will be a slight slowing down from first to last No. 2 is a special case, only a part of the uke's body is moving fast.
	ippon-seoi-nage	one-arm shoulder throw	foot forward	static		roller or lifter	uke makes a "blow", upper body moving lower body static	
	kata-guruma	shoulder rotation	foot forward	forward	fast	driver	on the third tsugi-ashi step	
koshi-waza; the technique of how to use the hips	uki-goshi	turning hip	foot forward	static		roller	uke makes a "blow", upper body only moving	The direction of the blow in this set is different from in the previous set. The variations of hand positions almost make this a hand-set, like the first one
	harai-goshi	sweeping hip	foot forward	forward	medium	driver	the "collar" hand is behind uke's back, pulling him tight in	
	tsurikomi-goshi	blocking hip	foot forward	forward	slow	rollar	collar hands of tori, well round uke's neck	

Set	Japanese Name	Translation	Opportunity	(Uke's) Direction of Movement	Pace	Gleeson Type (throw)	Specific Comments	General Comments
Ashi-waza; the technique of how to use the legs and feet	okuri-ashi-harai	two-foot-sweep	moving together sideways	sideways	very fast	driver	the third step of tsugi-ashi	The varying directions of movement add some very interesting points to the attacking movements
	sasai-tsurikomi-ashi	blocking foot	foot forward	forward	fast	roller	the third step of tsugi-ashi	
	uchi-mata	inside thigh	foot forward	circular	medium	driver	the third step of CIRCULAR tsugi-ashi; to close the "inside" space	
Ma-sutemi waza; the technique of how to use the body weight backwards	tomoe-nage		foot forward	backwards	fast	roller	on the third NORMAL steps back – starting with the BACK foot	the main variation is of course pace; it has many intriguing effects on attacking and throwing actions
	ura-nage		foot forward	static	medium	driver	another "blow" again the movement of the upper body is utilised	
	sumi-gaeshi		foot forward	forward	slow	roller	both are in jigotai	
Yoko-sutemi-waza; the technique of how to use the body weight side-ways	yoko-gake	side-block	foot forward	forward	medium	driver	on the third tsugi-ashi step	A powerful set this; everyone needs a great deal of power (especially the last one), but applied exactly so
	yoko-guruma	side-wheel	foot forward	forward	medium	roller	another "blow" Uke is thrown sideways	
	uki-waza	turning technique	foot forward	forward	slow	driver	both are in jigotai	

NOTE: Tsugi-ashi, is a peculiar step which retains the same opportunity throughout the movement (i.e. one foot forward ALL the time.) One foot is pushed forward, the other brought up to it (but not close) the first moves on. By eliminating alternating opportunity, confusion is minimised (or at least, that's the idea!)

KATAME-NO-KATA

The form of grappling. Devised about the same time as the nage-no-kata. It too consists of fifteen selected grappling techniques, selected to show the various types of pins, strangles and locks. For some never explained reason (and contrary to the nage-no-kata) the techniques are only applied to the right side of the partner/opponent, figure 22.

The criteria for each group are totally different from those in the nage-no-kata. The only concern is with type of technique (i.e. pin or lock) not with application of technical factors at all, therefore it is very superficial and does not have anything like the value of nage-no-kata. It is very ritualistic and its ritualism is emphasised by the excessive scrabbling about on one knee! There is no explanation for all the knee-walking (pointless drill?), the only explanation I can think of is that it was an attempt at a theatrical effect – which went wrong!*

The fact too that the partner has to lie perfectly still is another aspect which makes this kata particularly valueless. After I had studied nage-no-kata I found I had enough material to write a book on it (a lengthy one too), but I would find myself hard put to write a few hundred words on katame-no-kata – unless I described in detail, how the "knee walking" was done, where the hands and feet went, for every one of the fifteen techniques. To raise it to the standard of nage-no-kata would need a lot of revision. (I get the feeling that Kano had very little interest in this kata.) Two major alterations I would make – and have made – are as follows:

1. The techniques, whatever they are (and they could be changed, because, for example, the kata includes a leg-lock which is now banned in competition) should be done to both right and left. There has been a most unfortunate effect on the teaching of ne-waza, which stems mainly from this kata, that ground-play techniques have only been taught on one side. Such "prejudiced" teaching should be rectified.

2. The partner/opponent must move. I usually have them both kneeling (see figure 21). In this way the attacker (tori) can "throw"

Fig. 21

his partner over the weak side of the stance (the knee), and then apply the technique AS THEY ARE FALLING! This is a very important "rule" to learn when training in ne-waza, namely that ne-waza must start before the ground is reached! No doubt other ways can be devised to overcome this manifest fault in a learning situation.

Once these two "basic" teaching principles are built-in, then many progressive additions can be supplied. For example, the opponent can try to avoid the attacks – either before he reaches the ground, or after. He can be "thrown" over his strong side, so showing the attacker the kind of power and effort required to do it. The attacker can study linked attacks – go for the weak side and then switch to the strong – or vice versa. "Trick" attacks can be used to "feed into" the main technique, i.e. snatch one of the legs, trip him down with that, and so into ne-waza. Nage and katame-no-kata considered as a pair, are called in traditional books, randori-no-kata (presumably because between them they cover most of the techniques found in randori); it is fun to put the title into practice! Mix them up, the first throw into the first pin, etc.,

change the order. It is still not breaking Shao Yung's principle – the name specifies the finite form, but the contents are infinite!

Tackling katame-no-kata in this kind of way is not only so much more fun than the "housemaid's knee" variety, but can give so much more value in terms of learning and training.

* To claim that "theatre" has crept into sport may appear to be far-fetched to an English reader, but it is true to say that in Japan, theatre has made a very significant and noticeable contribution to everyday communication, in the form of vocabulary, gestures, stories, analogies, toys, personality archetypes, etc., etc.

KATAME-NO-KATA (traditional) All attacks are done only once; usually on uke's right side

Set	Japanese Name	Translation	Direction of Attack – to Uke	Pace	Specific Comments	General Comments
osae-komi-waza; pinning techniques	kuzure-kesa-gatame	variation of diagonal hold	on uke's right side	slow	sometimes shown as *hon* kesa-gatame	uke is "allowed" three attempts to escape from each pin (with no success of course). Tori should move around frustrating these attempts; however, at the end of each three, both must return to their original positions
	kata-gatame	shoulder-hold	on uke's right shoulder	slow	push uke's right arm tight against head	
	hon-kami-shiho-gatame	standard upper-body hold	uke's head end	slow	both tori's arms UNDER uke's arms	
	hon-yoko-shiho-gatame	standard side-body hold	on uke's right side	slow	tori's weight on uke's lower rib cage	
	kuzure-kami-shiho-gatame	variation of upper-body hold	uke's top and right side	slow	tori at uke's side– upper body	
Shime-waza; strangling techniques	kata-ju-ji-jime	opposite-hand-strangle	front of uke	medium	tori leans forward over uke's head	For techniques 2, 3, 4 uke sits up; for 1 and 5 he lies down
	hadaka jime	naked strangle	back of uke	medium	tori's right arm across uke's throat	
	okuri eri-jime	two-collar strangle	back of uke	medium	same as above– left hand on uke's right collar	
	kata-ha-jime	one-collar strangle	back of uke	medium	same as above– left hand round arm behind head	
	gyaku-ju-ji-jime	both palms up strangle	front of uke	medium	tori rolls uke over to apply strangle (to his right)	
Kan-setsu-waza; joint-locks	ude-garami	bent-arm entangled	from uke's right side	fast	lock on uke's LEFT arm	In the first three, uke attacks tori by pushing with the ultimate locked arm. No. 4 is done from kneeling position, and tori is the aggressor.
	ude-hishigi-ju-ji-gatame	arm-lock-cross-hold	from uke's right side	fast	lock on uke's RIGHT arm	
	ude-hishigi ude-gatame	arm-lock-arm-hold	from uke's right side	fast	lock on uke's LEFT arm	
	ude-hishigi-hiza-gatame	arm-lock-knee-hold	from uke's right side	fast	lock on uke's RIGHT arm	No. 5, is done from a STANDING position, but again tori is the aggressor
	ashi-garami	bent-leg entangled	uke's right leg	fast	lock on uke's right leg– from a standing position	

NOTE: Uke lies still throughout the attacking movement, only moving AFTER attack has been completed. At the end of each set both kneel-up and tidy their clothes

Fig. 22

KIME-NO-KATA

Usually referred to as a "self defence" kata; it shows superficially, squatting attacks (Japanese style) with bare hands and knives and then twelve attacks done in a standing position with the same weapons plus a sword! Again produced just before the end of the last century, all the attacks are in the form of an assassination (any relation to the times?); see figure 23.

Calling this kata "self defence" is something of a misnomer I feel, or at least it makes too much of the more superficial aspect of the sequence. If that were all indeed, I would have very little time for it; for example, having done a considerable amount of kendo personally, I would have very little faith in a system which tries to tell me that a killing downstroke of a samurai sword can be brushed aside by a simple side-step and parry. I think, to be fair, it attempts to go deeper than that. The name "kime" is from the verb kimeru, to decide (nothing to do with "self defence". (See later – Goshin jitsu.) No, it would seem to refer to the ability of responding spontaneously with decisiveness, to an attacking situation. Maruyama[11] speaks about it as being a "real fight" kata, so dangerous that it should not be done in randori (implying that in his time randori and kata training were very intermingled). He says it is not enough to train in just the nage and katame-no-kata, but kimi too is a must. What I presume he is saying is that kime trains response to attack action – which certainly is an important quality in competitive judo – certainly the attacks and counter-attacks in this kata are almost in the go-no-sen style, which means that the counter attack is ideally made BEFORE the initiating attack! Perhaps it would be of value to make a small diversion here, and talk a little about a go-no-sen-no-kata. There are several "unofficial" go-no-sen-no-kata i.e. not included in the Kodokan's standard list of seven, which are taught in different parts of the world. Very loosely these kata are translated as being "counter" throw – katas, but again there are, or can be, very misleading overtones about such a translation. The "go" means "before" (it is not, for example the "go" which is the opposite of "ju", or the "go" meaning five, i.e. gokyo) (See fig. 14). "Sen" is a "line" or "point", therefore it means "before the point of attack". The flavour therefore is very strongly Zen, for it means to counter before the attack is launched! In general judo parlance, countering refers to the action AFTER the attack is launched (which is of course kaeshi-waza) and therefore it is not really go-no-sen, for go-no-sen means countering BEFORE the attack is launched – a quality rarely found in judo players, but very desirable to have!

If kime-no-kata was intended as being purely self-defence, I presume it would now be superceded by the goshinjitsu-no-kata (published in 1958). The title here confirms that it is "protecting-body technique". (It is the same "go" as in "jigotai".) Also that the movements are a composite of judo and aikido movements specifically designed for the purpose of "self protection".

Aikido by the way is a combat system, one of the many included under the heading of jujit-su: the underlying principle of which is to fight, wherever possible, within the space between the fighters – where the "ki" ("spirit" or "essence" of the individuals) meet "ai". In practice it means painful techniques are used against the arms (of the opponent) which are protruding into that intervening space, rather than attacking the body directly.

KIME-NO-KATA (traditional)

Twenty attacks of various types, from various directions, with grabs, blows, punches, knives and swords.

Set	Attack	Response	General Comments	Set	Attack	Response	General Comments
Idori:. I is to dwell, by extension, to sit à la *Japonaise* on the heels; Tori "t" usually "hardens" into a "d" when after other syllables), here can be said to merely emphasise the first ideograph In short, all this set is done with both, uke and tori, sitting on their heels.	Ryote dori: holding both hands (wrists)	Knee kick to the solar plexus, straight arm-lock on (uke's) left arm	In the first seven attacks, uke and tori are sitting facing each other about 2–3 ft. apart. Uke attacks with his right hand, tori responds to that hand. In the eighth attack uke and tori are sitting side by side with tori on uke's left, so uke stabs across his body; tori parries with his left hand, pushing uke's right arm into the space between the bodies, thus allowing tori to punch with his right hand	Tachi-ai: standing confrontation. These are various standing attacks with fists, knives, swords, from front, side and back. Here, too, the main emphasis is on ritual rather than pragmatism.	Ryote-dori: both wrists grab, from the front	Kick to stomach, straight lock on left arm	With a lot of applied practice, the first ten could be made to look feasible
	Tsuki-kake: a right fist punch to the stomach	Parry with left hand, punch between the eyes, straight arm-lock on (uke's) right arm			Sode-tori: left sleeve grab from side (both facing same way.)	Kick to knee, osoto-gari	
	Suri-age: upward blow at forehead	(Right) foot kick to stomach, straight armlock on (uke's) right arm			Tsuki-kake: straight right to face	Parry with right hand, naked strangle from uke's rear	
	Yoko-uchi: side blow (with right fist)	Duck, grab head and arm, throw down, elbow blow to solar plexus			Tsuki-age: right upper-cut	Sway and avoid straight lock (waki-gatame) right arm	
	Ushiro-dori: hold from back (over both arms)	Shoulder-throw, over left shoulder; punch (with left fist) to testicles			Suri-age: heel of hand (right) blow at forehead	Parry, right punch to stomach, throw with o-goshi	
	Tsuki-komi: knife stab at stomach	Parry – punch to eyes – straight arm lock			Yoko-uchi: right-hand blow at side of head	Duck, okuri-eri-jime, with LEFT hand working	
	Kiri-komi: down cut with knife	Step aside, and straight arm lock knife arm			Ke-age: right foot kick to crutch	Catch, take outwards, kick to crutch – right foot	
	Yoko-tsuki: a knife stab from the side	Step aside, parry, punch to eyes			Ushiro-dori: grab from behind, over both arms	Ippon-seoi, chop to mouth, with right hand	
					Tsuki-komi: knife stab to stomach (right hand.)	Parry and avoid, straight arm lock on right arm	
					Kiri-komi: down cut to head, with knife	Duck and parry straight arm lock on right arm	
					Nuki-kake: trying to draw a sword	Before the sword is fully out kata ha-jime is applied	These last two "defences" come under the heading of fantasy!
					Kiri-oroshi: a downward cut with a sword	Parry and avoid; straight arm lock on right arm	

Fig. 23

103

Dr. J. Kano, with Mr. Yamashita, performing koshiki-no-kata

Fig. 24

KOSHIKI-NO-KATA

Literally the "old style" kata; a very weird affair. There are twenty one attacks plus the responses, fourteen to the "front" and seven to the "back". It is difficult to ascertain what the critical point is that decides what is a "front" or a "rear" attack. My immediate reaction is — or rather was — to toss the whole thing out as some kind of quaint, crazy sequence, maintained for nostalgic but outdated reasons; which summed up means "a waste of time" (which is what many judo players have indeed already done). However, I have too much respect for Kano to do that, I am sure that if he felt it was worth keeping, then it must have some value of some kind. So I tried to discover this value, figure 25.

Kano is said to have received much of his technical stimulation from the short time he studied in a couple of old jujitsu "schools" — the Tenshin Shinyo and the Kito. Because of this study he retained much respect for these "schools" and the Koshiki is a kata that he took on permanent loan from the Kito Ryu ("ryu" means "school") (figure 24). Whether he took it over just as it was or whether he modified it (to suit his own ideas) I have not been able to discover. He did claim that it showed throwing actions, which if studied, would benefit a judo player. On the surface that appears to be nonsense. When it is done "correctly" (or whenever I have seen it, either in England or Japan), the participants move like very stiff marionettes and fall over like those rotund kelly dolls that cannot be knocked down. The usual explanation for this

weird movement is that it is a hang-over from when the samurai wore armour in battle, and so being very heavy they had difficulty in moving. Such a statement is very bewildering because if books on Japanese armour are read[68] it will say — in effect — that one of the great advantages of Japanese armour was that it was so light (after all it was made mostly of bamboo and thin strips of metal). The warrior could run about in it and leap onto horses — almost without restriction! There seems to be a contradiction somewhere! Again I can only suppose that ritual has taken over largely from pragmatism! Certainly the essential ways of throwing shown in this kata — cleared of the marionette movement — are very useful to look at, for they show how throws can be made by not using the clothes. (One of the intrinsic restrictions in standard basic judo practice is that the performers must hold the clothes.) By grabbing the head, shoulders, a belt (if there is one), wrists, etc., throws can be made — and effectively too. (I like particularly No. 11, shikoro-dori). However, whether the "poor theatre" need be retained is something else, i.e. the puppet movement. No doubt the purists and the pragmatists will argue.

EXPLANATORY NOTES.

1. The names, like all jujitsu names of technique, are very allegoric and are of little utilitarian use — unless you happen to know, for example that shikoro is the part of the samurai's armour that protects his neck!
2. The histrionic ingredient is very strong in the kata (as anyone who has seen the chumbara films knows — the Japanese equivalent of cowboys and indians, i.e. goodie v baddie samurai.)
3. One of the intrinsic premises of these attacks and defences is that, the attacker will breathe in just prior to the attack (to strengthen his body with a sudden influx of oxygen). That is his greatest weakness! That is when the attacked attacks!
4. The two most used throwing actions are yoko-wakare (no. 35 in the gokyo) and hiza-otoshi — the thrower kneels behind the man with one knee up; the opponent is pulled backwards over the raised knee.

KOSHIKI-NO-KATA (traditional)

Name	Description
1st set.	Mae. The Front.
1. Tai means body or by extension readiness.	Uke moves to tori, and by holding the belt starts a hip-throw attack. Tori grabbing him by the shoulder and belt forces him to arch his back, by kneeling (with one knee) behind him, tori throws uke down.
2. Yume-no-uchi — in a dream!	The start is the same as above, but now uke resists the effort of tori to bend him backwards. Tori using that resistance to throw him forward with yoko-wakare.
3. Ryoku-hi — avoiding strength	Uke tries to grab tori's belt with both hands which are crossed. Avoiding, and seizing the top hand, tori gets behind uke and throws him by pulling him over a knee (as in No. 1 above.)
4. Miza-guruma — Water wheel	The same start as in No. 3, but uke now does not let tori get behind him. Tori throws with yoko-wakare.
5. Miza-nagara — water-flow	Uke thrusts at tori's eyes with LEFT hand; seizing this arm, tori throws with a one-arm uki-otoshi.
6. Hiki-otoshi — pull and drop	The same as No. 5, but here uke pushes with his RIGHT arm.
7. Koda-ore — (untranslatable!)	Tori attacks first, thrusting at uke's head with RIGHT arm; uke grabs the hand with his RIGHT hand and tries to manoeuvre into a hip throw; tori throws again by kneeling behind him.
8. Uchi-kudaki — hitting and smashing.	Tori again attacks first, but now with LEFT hand at uke's stomach. Again uke tries to throw with (right) hip-throw. Tori throws him down over LEFT knee.
9. Tani-otoshi — valley-drop	Uke, from behind tori, grabs him over the arms and tries to bend him forward. Tori appears to go with force, but actually comes up against it (an example of "go") and throws uke over the left knee.
10. Kuruma-daoshi — wheel-fall	Uke's attack is the same as in No. 9, as tori is bent forward he deliberately falls, twisting under uke and throws with yoko-wakare.
11. Shikoro-dori — neck-grab	Uke grabs tori's neck with his LEFT hand. Tori lifts his hand to the chin, the right hand to the back of the head — twists the head, kneels down, throwing uke down in the process.

Name	Description
12. Shikoro-gaeshi — neck-counter	Uke grabs tori's belt with left hand. Tori reaches forward grabs uke's neck with both hands, and throws with tani-otoshi.
13. Yu-dashi — shower (of rain)	Tori attacks first, grabs uke's collars with right hand. Uke tries to slip inside the arm for a (right) hip-throw. Tori grabs the arm and throws with uki-otoshi.
14. Taki-otoshi — waterfall drop	The start is the same as in No. 13, but again uke's response is now converted to utilise yoko-wakare instead of uki-otoshi.
2nd Set.	Ura. Behind.
15. Mi-kudaki — body-smashing.	The opening moves are the same as in No. 1, but uke's left arm is grabbed before it holds and that is used to apply yoko-wakare.
16. Kuruma-gaeshi — wheel-counter	Uke rushes at tori, aiming to push him in the chest. Tori parries the push and throws with yoko-wakare.
17. Mizu-ire — water-entering.	Uke rushes at tori, pushing with right hand only. Again tori seizing that arm, throws with yoko-wakare.
18. Ryu-setsu — Willow (and) snow.	Tori attacks, he feints a slap at uke's face, as uke turns his head to avoid this, tori grabs the belt (with both hands) and throws with yoko-wakare.
19. Saka-otoshi — oblique-drop	Uke thrusts at tori's stomach, as he is moving forward. Tori grabs the thrusting left hand, avoids, and throws by pulling down and forward (tori stays standing), a kind of hiki-otoshi.
20. Yuki-ore — snow-break	Uke grabs tori from behind over the arms, tori throws with ippon-seoi-nage.
21. Iwa-nami — wave breaking on rock.	Tori attacks uke, he flicks both hands in front of uke's face as a feint; using the "shock" of uke, tori grabs both lapels and throws with yoko-wakare.

CONCLUDING NOTES:
Throughout the last set, the pace is getting gradually faster. There are of course many histrionic aspects of the kata which have been omitted for the sake of brevity, but providing the above essential factors are appreciated, then the extras can be devised to suit the performers.

Fig. 25

ITSUTSU-NO-KATA

The form of (only) five (movements). A temporary title which became permanent. It was never completed; somewhat similar to, but on a lesser scale than the great "unfinished" Symphony of Schubert. It is an attempt to show, in physical rhythmic patterns, the play of forces in a cosmological combat situation: that is, Kano was trying to show that the same microcosmic forces contained in human confrontation are essentially the same as those macrocosmic forces contained in the creation of the universe. Looking at what he was trying to do, and realising the complexity of the task, it is no wonder it was never finished! Figure 26.

As a passing point of interest, this kata is not mentioned in Maruyama's book (all the others are). I wonder if that has any significance? It was started when Kano was very young (in his twenties), and it was ambitious indeed for a young man of that short experience to attempt to manifest physically cosmological forces. A slight case of biting off more than he could chew?

But again, I can visualise that the times he lived in, tended to tell him that he could do it. The teachings of Spencer and Huxley from England told him that science was all. Study science and all the answers would come. When he was ten years old he would have been lucky to see a horse-drawn cart (most "vehicle" transport was "mandraulic"). He may have seen an arbesque, but little else. Another ten years of time under the bridge, and he would have seen cannons, iron and steam ships and steam engines. Why could he not put cosmological forces into a rhythmic pattern of movement?!

ITSUTSU-NO-KATA (traditional)

There are five principles illustrated. Usually they are done in a continuous movement, with no break between. Pace, movement pattern, application are all stipulated, but are not really essential to the illustrations.

Name	Principle and Purpose
Ippon me: it means simply first point or principle	How force overcomes opposition. Tori places his right hand on uke's chest; alternatively he pushes with thumb and little finger side of the hand. Uke tries to contain (by stepping back with appropriate foot) and push back, but tori's power escalates with repetition, and finally throws him down.
Nipon me: second point or principle	Utilisation of force. As uke gets up, he makes a thrusting lunge (with his right hand) at tori. Tori side-steps, grabs the arm and throws uke down again. It shows how uncontrolled force can be made to serve the needs of what it is aimed at.
Sampon me: third point or principle	The uncontrollability of spiralling centrifugal force. (Shown clearly in pictures of spiral nebulae in the various galactic systems.) With all arms outstretched (sideways) the two spin round each other till they go out of control. It is shown symbolically by tori being on his back, and uke standing.
Yonpon me: fourth point or principle	The power of rhythmic or wave movement. Tori "sweeps" past uke (from behind, facing the same way as uke) he then runs backwards, with arms outstretched, knocking uke down, as he "crashes" into him. Rhythmic power, be it in terms of ocean or seasonal, takes on the pattern of waves, hence this illustration.
Go pon me: fifth point or principle	Accidental chance. The participants rush towards each other; as they are about to collide, tori falls down on his back (across the line of uke). Uke falls over him. There is no contact between them. Force can be the result of a chance conflict or circumstances.

Fig. 26

JU-NO-KATA

A sequence of fifteen movements (some with, some without throws), divided into three kyos (or sets, like the gokyo) of five. The object is to illustrate how the principle of "ju" can manifest itself in different ways in different situations. It is not quite so ambitious as the itsutsu-no-kata, although still ambitious enough. The attempt is a very brave one (again remembering the youth of Kano when he did it). I think it is not a very successful attempt (too often the principle gets lost in a welter of flurrying movement), but that does not mean it earns no respect. On the contrary, I for one have great respect for it. The first time for anything, because it is the first time, must deserve credit; when it is breaking new ground of this type then credit is truly deserved. (See figure 27.)

'Ju' is usually translated in the spirit of that concept contained in the Tao Te Ching:

The gentle way
Will overcome
The hard and strong.

Chapter 36.

I do not go along with this translation, for it is too restrictive.

I prefer the view of the neo-Confucists which puts ju in a context of being a part of a greater whole – which gives a wider choice of meaning. In my experience, when the earlier idea of "ju" is applied in practice, it can so easily lead to loss of control – and there is no possibility of assessing the situation.

These two factors: control of a situation and assessment of a situation are extremely important in my opinion, when dealing with competitive training. When the attacker launches his "force" in some form of attack, if the opponent is only concerned about "giving way", avoiding, or being flexible, he is liable to go out of control because he does not know how big the attacking force is when he does avoid. Therefore I feel it is essential that the first step of the opponent is to CONTAIN the attacking force (however momentarily) in order to ASSESS its magnitude and direction; having done that it can be avoided and a suitably sized force added to it – in the same direction – to bring about control of that initiating attacking force. It is for this interpretation of "ju" that I translate it as being the "utilisation of force".

Therefore when ju-no-kata is done, force must be shown by the initiating man (uke) in the various attacks. Even in the early Taoist concept of "ju", where water was the common analogy used, because it was seen as a "natural" combination of "softness" and "hardness", force was acknowledged as an intrinsic part of that total concept. If there is no force, there is no justification for avoiding it (let alone assessing it!) The body too must show clearly the part of the body in which the total force is being focussed – the whole body must be "aimed" into that part. The recipient of that force (tori) must pause and contain the force – for a moment, then his force is added to the attacker's; the required result is then achieved.

The movements before the actual attacks are made, should show a clear build-up to the culmination of the initiating primary force. That is there should be a pace change throughout that movement. Similarly with the defence, the containing and application of the secondary force, should be clearly indicated in the change of pace in the body movements. Too often, when ju-no-kata is done, all power is extracted from it, the pace is kept virtually constant and the movement is flaccid, stilted and "unnatural". Result – boring and reasonless action. (Every movement should be prefaced with the unspoken question "why"? and an answer ALWAYS illustrated.) This aspect of change of pace and direction – should be used with flair, in training. Let the participants move anywhere they wish, let them move very fast all the time, then very slow all the time. Can they retain the performance of "ju" in these different conditions? Shao said the form is finite, the content infinite!

Doing ju-no-kata in this way (even sometimes completing the throws!) can often offer something valuable in the way of a training contribution. Whether a sagacious coach or player could or should devise his own ju-no-kata which does the job better than the traditional one is again something for them to consider. Being able to contain, assess, counter-attack by using the opponent's strength is a very important part of a trainee's learning programme. Whether ju-no-kata, as is done, is the best way of doing that, is open to question.

JU-NO-KATA (traditional)

Fifteen illustrations, in the form of attacks, showing the application of the principle "ju".

Set	Attack	Response	Comment
Dai Ikkyo The first set	Tsuki-dashi, forward (right) hand thrust, fingers stretched	Two circular avoidances, finishing with a right shoulder lock	Uke attacks from the front
	Kata-oshi, (right hand) push of shoulders	Tori ducks the push, moves backwards, uke pokes at eyes (with left hand); finish with both shoulders locked	Uke attacks from behind
	Ryote-dori, grabbing at both (wrists) hands, from the front	Avoids, frees right hand, finishes with soto makikomi	
	Kata-mawashi, turning the shoulders — to the left	The twist away from the turn, is used to do ippon-seoi-nage	Uke attacks from the back of tori
	Ago-oshi (side) push against the chin	The completion is the same as No. 2	Uke attacks from the right side of tori
Dai Nikyo The second set	Kiri-oroshi, downward cut at the head — with the right hand	Avoids pushes right hand down, revolve as pair, right shoulder locked as No. 1	Uke is in front of tori
	Ryokata-oshi, pushing both shoulders (downward)	Tori ducks, goes forward. Uke blocks the movement; tori finishes with ushiro-goshi	
	Naname-uchi, diagonal blow with right hand	Parry with left hand, twist round, complete with ura-nage	
	Katate-dori, the right hand (wrist) is grabbed from the side	Tori snatches arm free turns into (left) ogoshi	Both are facing the same way at the start
	Katate-age (each person) raises the right arm vertically and "crashes" together	After the "crash", the bodies sway twice, the right shoulder is locked	Start several feet apart
Dai Sankyo The third set	Obi-tori, (both hands) try to grab the belt — from the front	The body is turned by the parrying LEFT hand; finish (left) ogoshi	Both facing each other
	Mune-oshi (one hand, right) push at chest — from the front	A counter chest-push is made, bodies rotate finish with osoto-otoshi	
	Tsuki-age, (right hand) upper cut	Avoid, bodies rotate; bent arm lock, and osoto-otoshi	Both facing each other
	Uchi-oroshi, downward blow (at head)	Avoid, bodies rotate; Tori finishes with hadake-jime	
	Ryogan-tsuki (a right hand) poke at both eyes	Parry, the bodies rotate, tori finishes with left ogoshi	Both facing each other

Fig. 27

SEI RYOKU ZENYO KOKUMIN TAIIKU-NO-KATA

A national training kata (for the development) of (the individual's) total abilities. It consists of twenty eight or sixteen individual exercises, depending on how they are counted (i.e. arm, leg, trunk, etc.) and ten pair exercises (done in the form of symbolic knife and sword attacks), enabling isometric as well as isotonic exercises to take place. The object is to develop body and mind simultaneously and to avoid the possible strain and heavy wear that can be the result of too much competitive training. It is a much neglected kata, and few judo enthusiasts realise that it is even one of the official seven kata. See figure 28. The solo exercises are very worthwhile studying.

This kata can be seen very much as a product of its time – the 1880's – and it can throw more light on Kano's early thinking, although again only as speculation.

Taoism, from its very early days, has always been concerned with physical health for it was realised that through bodily health, mental health can be achieved. There are many records showing this concern and giving practical assistance and guidance on how to achieve it, (in the shape of what form the exercises should take). There were remedial exercises, exercises to improve sexual performance, respiratory exercises, gymnastic exercises and many others. A small part of this whole area of "physical training" was that of the "fighting" skills, skills like kung-fu and tai-chi, which are not so much an organised system of fighting (like for example karate or aiki) but rather a training to harmonise the body and mind and which can, if necessary be adopted for fighting. Similarly, but on the other side of the coin, among these many roots of many physical skills can be found Kappo or Katsu ("ho" is a method, and when added to katsu becomes kappo – the meaning is the same "keeping (people) alive"). There are many forms, or methods; some are for resuscitation (striking specified nerve centres to produce "shock" recovery), some are for bone-setting and the repair of injuries, i.e. bruises and strains, etc. (I have experienced some strange happenings in this latter group – quite inexplicable in normal medical terms.) Many of the old-time judo men I met in Japan were full-time professionals and their professions covered "pain-curing" in many forms (i.e. bone setting, rheumatism, etc.) a kind of poor man's doctor, as well as teaching judo. Again as with many other discoveries of man, this knowledge of fundamental principles can be used for good or bad. The same knowledge of where to strike – for the curing of body malfunction – can be used to destroy body health. This aspect of the knowledge is covered by "atemi" (body hitting).

However, the vast fund of accumulated knowledge, amassed by succeeding generations of Taoists, has always intrigued a few "outsiders". Back in the 18th century a French Jesuit missionary J. J. M. Amist[50] studied some of these old texts and in 1779 he published a translation of them in Europe. It caused quite a stir in educational circles, and had a big influence on the work of P. H. Ling. In 1814 Ling had founded a gymnastic school in Stockholm which in turn exerted a great influence on physical education in Europe – especially in England. Through the work of men such as Roth, Ling's principles were gradually incorporated into the English school system [69] and by the 1850's and 60's were well established. It was the kind of training and theorising which got back to Japan by the 1870's and 80's. So Kano would have been getting a "buffetting of Health Through Physical Training" from both East and West! Over the past twenty years or so, the training of the mind (or personality) and especially any esoteric qualities, has come under a lot of cynical criticism from physical educationalists in general. And who can blame them?! One has only to look at the atrocities of the last war, done by superbly fit soldiers, to say nothing of the "strength through joy" incantations of the fascists, to realise they have a very valid point. Judo (as do some other sports) claims exceptional qualities by which it can improve a man's character. Well, with no further qualifications such claims are of course arrant nonsense! I have always conceded that if a man came to judo as an oaf, then partaking of only the physical side of judo (i.e. training) it would only make him a bigger oaf. But that must not blind us to the possibilities that there are mind-training capabilities in physical training, if the matter is treated conscientiously and sensibly.

EXPLANATORY NOTES:

1. For the convenience of the Western reader, I have sub-divided the exercises into sets, but I have in no way altered the exercises themselves.

2. "Blows" and "kicks" are talked about, but it should be realised this is only to put intent and tension into the movement. Without it, movement can become slack and "soulless".

3. All movements should be done slowly (and with tension); gentle but strong extension of both limbs and body is the purpose, a brief moment of hesitation at the extreme range of extension is worthwhile. At no time should the movement jerk into the extreme range.

To give an illustration, several years ago, acupuncture was considered to be just another Oriental "con", but recently it has become reluctantly recognised, by the Western medics, as having a legitimate place in the field of curative medicine. So with "mind training" through "physical training", if it were given the same scrutiny that general skills have been given, who knows what could be developed. That's what Kano attempted to do with his Sei Ryoku Zen Yo-Kata, to synthesise into one long contrived sequence of movements, Ling gymnastics, Kung Fu, principles of "Ju", the development of a moral conscience. Again whether or not he achieved his very ambitious object remains to be seen, but you have to admire him for his efforts!

4. The first section is called tandoku-renshu, which means solo-exercises; and the second part sotai-renshu, meaning pair exercises. The latter is again divided; the first sub-section called idori, exercises in the squatting position, and tachiai, exercises in the standing position.

Name	Description	Comments
1st Set	This works one side of the body alternatively	Each exercise can be repeated as often as required
1. Goho-ate – hitting in five directions	Slow "punching" with each hand up, down, forwards, backwards, sideways	
2. O-goho-ate – "big" hitting in five directions	The above is repeated, but now the body-weight is added to the blow, by moving the same side foot as hand	The eyes too should follow the "blows"
3. Goho-geri – kicking in five directions	Slow kicking with each leg up, down, forwards, backwards and sideways	The upward kick should be made as high as possible
2nd Set	Work on both sides of the body simultaneously	
4. kagami-biraki – mirror-polishing	Raise both elbows shoulder high, palms in front of chest, facing outwards. Make large circular sweeps, one way, then the other	The polishing means there is an outward pressure in the hands
5. Sayu-uchi – sideways blow	Cross arms in front of chest, "punch" sideways simultaneously with both hands	

Fig. 28

Name	Description	Comments
6. Zengo-tsuki – front and back blow	Punch forward with both fists, then backwards with elbows	
7. Ryote-ue-tsuki – upward punch, both hands	Both fists, simultaneously, "punch" upwards	
8. Oryote-ue-tsuki	The same as above, but now a small jump is added to the upward blow	To stretch, from finger to toe, in the jump is important
9. Sayu kogo-shita tsuki	Each fist is "punched" down alongside the leg alternately	
10. Ryote shita-tsuki	Both fists "punch" downwards; at the same time, the knees are bent till the buttocks touch the heels	
3rd Set	Work across the body; diagonal exercises	
11. Naname ue-uchi – diagonal upward blow	Starting from the opposite hip, the hand sweeps across the body, up and out. Repeat with each arm	
12. Naname shita-uchi	From the opposite shoulder, sweep down, out and wide, with each arm in turn	
13. Onaname ue-uchi	The same as No. 11, but now step to the side with the foot, and reach further behind with the "cutting" hand	The movement is a very big spiral from one foot to the opposite hand
14. Ushiro-sumi-tsuki – back-corner punch	The "punch" or thrust is in front of the body, then aimed at the heel of the foot on the same side as the hand	The twist is to the front of the body
15. Ushiro-uchi	The "punch" goes directly behind the body, aiming at the heel of the opposite foot	The twist is behind the body
4th Set	Work along the length of the body	
16. Ushiro-tsuki	Both fists aim up over the head to the target BEHIND the head, then stretch up "punch" down to the feet, touching the feet if possible!	Only one exercise here

Name	Description	Comments
I-DORI	Exercises while squatting Japanese style •	These would be of little benefit to the Westerner
17. Ryote-dori – both hands grab	Both face each other. Tori steps across the body, freeing his hands	
18. Furi-hanashi – shaking-free	Similar to No. 17, but now tori steps back, so breaking the grip of uke	
19. Gyakute-dori	Uke holds with both hands, thumbs outwards, palms downwards. Tori pulls both backwards to free grips	
20. Tsuki-kake – Stomach-thrust	Uke thrusts at Tori's stomach, tori avoids and arm-locks the thrusting arm	
21. Kiri-kake – downward cut with knife	Uki makes a downward blow with a knife, tori avoids, and locks the falling arm	
TACHI-AI Exercises done in the standing position		These exercises are not nearly as utilitarian as the tandoku set. The movement is too restrictive
22. Tsuki-age – upward-thrust	The blow is parried, and a return blow to the stomach is made	
23. Yoko-uchi – side-blow – at head	The "blow" is parried and a return "blow" is made with the other hand to the nose	
24. Ushiro-dori – grab from rear	Uke holds over both tori's arms. By raising both arms, tori frees his grip; hips are moved sideways and a blow is made to the stomach with the elbow	
25. Naname-uchi – diagonal blow	Uke makes a downward blow with a knife. Tori parries, counter punches with the other hand. Picks knife-arm, and puts on a lock from the rear	A complicated movement, very similar to a movement in ju-no-kata
26. Kiri-oroshi – down-cut	Uke using a wooden-sword makes a down cut. Tori side-steps, arm-locks uke's right arm.	Note: All these attacks should be repeated on the other side (of the body).

Fig. 28

Fig. 29. The author with the Takasaki family

GENERAL COMMENTS

It is interesting to note that all the standard kata were devised roughly at the same time, just before the turn of the century. Kano was in his 30's, a young age for setting long-lasting standards. In a biographical essay by Maekawa and Hasegawa[70] (a couple of "educationalists") they suggest that Kano's age of maturity as a thinker was between 1916–28; that is when he was between 56 and 68 years old. What a pity that he did not create some new kata during that period! We may really have had something worth inheriting! The fact that he made modifications to the standard kata during the early years of the century shows that he was not totally satisfied with them, but how much more beneficial therefore if he had initiated something new when he was older. But because he did seem to taper off from judo construction in his middle-age (in terms of "theory" that is), does it indicate in anyway that he was disillusioned with the sport as a whole? How enlightening it would have been if he had only written a book, to sum up his life's experience in judo! The various articles he wrote in his later years were largely polemical and dealt with didactic expositions on the importance of the moral maturity and social responsibility. A some what turgid subject some may think. But then look at the political scenes of the 1920's onwards: the choking of freedom, the rise of fascism; none of it could have encouraged those liberal ideas born in his youth. In 1898

Kano became Head of the Education Department in the Ministry of Education. In 1901 Kano was made Japan's representative to the I.O.C. He held the position till his death. (He died on the journey back from an I.O.C. meeting in 1938.) As a member of the I.O.C. he attended the Games of 1936 in Berlin. That jingoistic display of sport being used for the benefit of a gang of national gangsters, could not have done much for his ideals.

There are many more enigmas regarding Kano we shall never have answers for. Certainly he was a great humanitarian and his ability as an educationalist cannot be questioned. (He introduced sport and physical education into the

Japanese school structure.) But was he too far ahead of his time? During the three years I lived with Kano's son-in-law, Mr. Takasaki, (see figure 29) we often talked about Kano; in his opinion there was no doubt that Kano was years ahead of his time. As too often happens with such protagonists of improvement for all, their lesser achievements tend to be applauded at the expense of their major work. It is ignored because it is not understood or because it is feared (because it inevitably attacks the status quo of ignorance) – or both! So in judo, lip service is sometimes given to Kano's moral and ethical teachings, but more often attention is paid to the heave and push of "fighting judo". Kano's two sayings: Ji ta kyo ei – by helping (developing) oneself, society benefits; and sei ryoku sen-yo, the right (moral) uses of one's own (total) ability; are far too frequently relegated to the back page of "How I became a Champion". Seldom is the more profound implication of the maxims discussed, for example take ji ta kyo ei. The concept of ji ta was (and still largely is) way outside the general limitations of social thinking of those earlier times. The "self" had no place in the dominating group orientation of normal Japanese life and thought. (Only in the more obscure aspects of Zen could it be found elsewhere.) The batsu (the group, see page 76), the kokutai (national policy, see page 94), the very belt system of judo, are all structures trying to ignore the needs of the individual and elevate the value of the group above all else. The individual is only important as a part of the group, not as a person in his own right.

By putting self-help (the two characters mean literally "self profit") before the group advantage (kyo ei means mutual benefit), Kano slapped a foreign concept on Japanese training (English utilitarianism) that still sits uncomfortably on the Japanese body politic. It is so "foreign" that even now, when some Japanese translate the maxim into English they "naturally" omit the "self-help" part and only mention the group aspect – mutual benefit, like for example the Kodokan Illustrated.[10]

I have already hinted that perhaps Kano became more or less disillusioned with what just "physical training" could do. Such a view is supported by the fact that later on in his life he talked about "judo in the narrow sense" and "judo in the wide sense". He meant by the "narrow sense" the judo of just physical performance. He was far more interested in the application of principles intrinsic to physical performance, i.e. strength of intent, dedication to achievement, sincerity in attitude, to the wider sphere of life – "judo in the wide sense". This development is indicated by his move away from the "physical dojo" where judo is actually done, to the intellectual training area, contained in the Cultural Association, also founded by Kano, in 1922, and also based in the Kodokan.

It seems to me that an essential step towards achieving this idealism of helping and developing the individual to become something more than when he started (doesn't matter at what) he must be encouraged and helped to create things for himself. In order to create, there must be thinking, there must be understanding: those ingredients must help towards the goal of self-realisation.

Kata is a prime area in which simple creation can take place. The individual, be he coach or player, can create a sequence to achieve a specific purpose of his very own – initially it is true, for only himself, but perhaps later it could help others too! By making, creating, kata for himself, it will help him to realise he can MAKE something. Once that idea has taken root, who knows where it could take him! If on the other hand, kata is seen simply as a traditional "mind-number" (do it the "right" way only) then it becomes a drill for a robot.

Some New Kata

The Go-No-Kata

I have taken myself at my own word, and devised kata – many of them. I have found the exercise very beneficial, for it did force me to really look at the principles and techniques involved. When I first realised the oppositional hypothesis of ju and go, I felt I just had to try and devise a go-no-kata. I knew that Kano had already devised one, (but that it was lost[71]), which gave me a real incentive to try for myself. As it was my first real attempt at making a new kata, I decided to stick to the general shape of the nage-no-kata; that is to have different sets to cover differing secondary principles (the primary principle, in this instance being of course "go"). However, I felt I had learnt from Kano's mistakes (at least what I considered were his mistakes) as well as his successes. Along with the illustration of the physical manifestation of "go", I also wanted to show – all in the one kata – how that same principle worked out in all aspects of competitive judo, e.g. nage and katame-waza, linked attacks – in both grappling and throwing situations. I did not want to put these aspects in different kata, as Kano had done, where the implication could be taken that somehow nage and katame-waza manifested the principles differently.

I have already tried to show what I feel "ju" to be – the utilisation of a primary force by a lesser, secondary force. In "go", the initial conditions are the same; that is the primary force is launched, in a pre-determined direction. The opposition then contains that force (momentarily), assesses it in terms of magnitude and direction – and then applies a secondary force, which is greater (than the primary) and is applied in the opposite direction (in practice that may not always be precise). Why I call "go" the domination (of force) by force.

As Shao said, each one, each principle, has a legitimate part to play in every aspect of life. There is a time to use "go" as there is a time to use "ju". The movement by President Kennedy against the Cuban missile bases in 1962 was an example of international political "go", just as the Chamberlain appeasement policy towards Hitler in 1939 was an example of "ju". The use of either principle in the wrong situation can be disastrous, just as the ability to use the appropriate one in the right situation can be successful. So in judo. The competitor must be able to decide when one, or when the other is to be used. If he judges wrongly he loses – but then that's what competition is all about!

Of course good fighters have recognised these two principles from the very beginning. It is nothing new to them. Their acquired instinct in training has "told" them when they must give way to a "bigger-than-both-of-us" situation and when they must fight back against a set of circumstances that they know if only they can accumulate enough energy, power, effort – call it what you will – they will win. The restriction is that because he has (probably)

had it dinned into his head that judo is "giving way", he feels vaguely "guilty" when he starts crashing in with power and strength. The "guilt" feeling can limit his commitment, so that he does not use everything he has (sei ryoku zen yo), and therefore it hinders his efficiency. What I want to show by this kata, is that such "guilt feelings" are not necessary. If fighters want to use power to beat the opponent that is fine – as long as they know when and how to use it!

FIRST SET
SIMPLE INITIATION
LOCALISED FORCE
As in the nage-no-kata, it is the task of uke to establish the general conditions. He starts the movement, initiating the primary force; he sets pace and direction of force (e.g. the force is not always parallel with the ground).

WHAT IS TO BE ILLUSTRATED
How a localised (limb) force, can be overcome by a total (body weight) force.
Abstract, shown in physical terms.
Uke and tori face each other, about 6 feet apart. They raise their arms shoulder height, with the palms facing forward. They come together, so that the palms are touching and the elbows bent. Uke pauses, then begins to push tori back by EXTENDING THE ARMS ONLY. Tori contains the push, then drops one of his legs back, and by leaning forward, using his body-weight to overcome the push of just the arms.

Uke will of course be tempted to drop one of his feet back to get the push, but this he must

Fig. 30

resist. The idea is to show just the arm/limb push. Similarly tori must not jump and drive, only use the leaning body weight, figure 30.

FIRST ILLUSTRATION
OUCHI-GARI

Static situation. Uke and tori hold in standard (right) manner. Uke pushes forward with both hands. Tori drops his left foot back and thrusts forward, along the left arm of uke, finishing with ouchi-gari – directly backwards (see figure 31).

Movement situation. They move around freely at a fast pace. Uke can crouch a little if he wants, and pushes forward with both arms. Tori drops the left foot back in the same way, and thrusts through the push and throws with ouchi-gari.

Practical Comments

Sometimes tori will pull hard on uke's collar, ensuring – as much as possible – that uke's pushing left arm is really jammed into the chest. The moving of tori's left foot, to a position where it can "absorb" the push of uke's left arm is very important.

Fig. 31

Fig. 32a. Uke is on left; notice Tori's left-hand hold

Fig. 32b. Notice how the hips are right across

SECOND ILLUSTRATION. SODE-TSURIKOMI-GOSHI

Static situation. Uke and tori hold in the standard (right) manner. Uke pulls in slowly but strongly with both hands. Tori pulls back, but more with his left hand — he tries to straighten uke's right arm (but not necessarily with any success). By using the tension created by the opposing forces, tori moves his left foot across for a pivot, swings the right foot back and throws uke FORWARD with LEFT SIDED tsurikomi-goshi. (See figures 32a and b.)
Movement situation. Much as above, only now uke is moving backward when he pulls, in order to reinforce the pulling action of the hands. The pace will be a little slower than the first, but will still be comparatively fast.

Practical Comment
For the illustration, uke's right hand should hold high on tori's collar at the beginning, and of course the bending of that arm should not be allowed to go beyond a right angle. The throwing attack by tori should be when the arm is around 120°. The containment and tension between the arms/bodies is of course critical.

THIRD ILLUSTRATION
UDE-GARAMI (NE-WAZA)

Static situation. Uke is on his back. Tori begins
to pin with kuzure-yoko-shiho-gatame. Uke
gets both hands under tori's chest and begins
to push up (so making space for himself to
turn in and escape). Tori, by adjusting his feet,
drives down into uke's left hand, forces it
down onto the ground. The arm lock is applied
see figure 33.

Movement situation. Uke and tori should start
in a half-kneeling position (see figure 21). Tori
turns uke onto his back and goes for a pin. The
pace is fast. From then on the procedure is as
for the static situation.

NOTE: This example should be the same as
that in the "trad" katame-no-kata, but is not;
because "trad" kata generally chooses "ju" as
the applied principle, which if followed
produces the WRONG situation, i.e. if uke
pushes (as he does) and tori avoids that push,
uke's (left) arm STRAIGHTENS, so making a
BENT arm-lock very difficult.

Practical Comments

This is of course a very elementary example.
Very few experienced players would push in
this way, although as always sometimes they
can be tricked into making such an elementary
mistake.

I included it, because it was an application of
the arm lock, shown over the past many years,
even by the people who were great ad-
vocators of "ju" only — they never seem to
realise that it was a good example of force
overcoming force.

Fig. 33

Fig. 34a　　　　　　　　　　　　　　　　　　　　　Fig. 34b

THE FOURTH ILLUSTRATION. O-GOSHI

The static situation. Uke and tori hold in the standard (right) manner. Then uke changes the position of his left hand (on the sleeve) and moves it to the collar – now he is holding both hands on both collars. Uke then pushes obliquely (forward) and downwards. Tori bends his knees, lets go with his right hand, moves forward under the arms of uke, getting his right arm round uke's waist, and lifts straight up. (See figure 34a and b.)

The movement situation. Essentially, this is a static throwing action; that is o-goshi is normally only done when the opponent is stationary (if he was not, he could easily move away from the lifting hips). However, for a general effect, uke and tori can move around, again, quite fast, then in a way they can sort out for themselves, they can come to a sudden stop and repeat the static situation throw. Such a "stop" moment can be created by a feint attack (by tori); by a quick change in direction (by both); or by a quick – unsuccessful – attack (by uke). Let the participants use their own imagination!

Practical Comments

O-goshi (or something very much like it!) if it is used in good class competition is used frequently as a counter. The attacking action of the opponent often has the effect of fixing the man's position (because it failed) and usually the forces exerted are downwards – either the man tries to drop his weight down (minimising the lifting possibility) or does actually push down trying to keep HIS opponent down. The counterer then has got to be able to rally enough power to lift this down-pushing weight/force.

Fig. 35

THE FIFTH ILLUSTRATION
YOKO-GAKE

Yoko-gake as a counter-attack.

Static situation. Both face each other in standard (right) hold. Uke attempts tai-otoshi, but only manages to make tori step over blocking (right) leg. Realising it has failed, mainly because the arms have been extended (so creating too much space between the bodies), uke attempts to retrieve the situation by pulling the arms back towards his body. Tori steps to uke's left with his driving (right) foot, (see figure 35), and throws uke – to his right – in spite of the arm pull which is towards uke's left.

The moving situation. Uke attempts the tai-The moving situation. Uke attempts the tai-otoshi as tori is moving forward. The pace is fast. A quick "stabbing" tai-otoshi attack by uke, tori easily steps over it. So on, as with the static situation.

Practical Comments

Tai-otoshi, as a type of throw, can be done at any pace (one of the reasons why it's so popular). When it is done at a fast pace, a common mistake is to push the arms out trying to "lever" the opponent over the blocking leg. The throwing spaces are opened (not closed as they should be) and avoidance or escape is the usual result. The hands must be kept close to the body to be successful (figure 36).

Tori must not try to jump straight into the yoko-gake throwing position. Jump over the leg first, assess the withdrawing force of uke, THEN go into the throwing position.

Comments on the Set

Unlike the standard nage-no-kata, specific opportunity for uke to offer is not mentioned or insisted upon. This I would generally want to leave to the participants to work out.

However, if a general guide is needed, I would suggest the following as something to start with (later perhaps different opportunities could be tried).

1. Ouchi-gari, uke to have his right foot back.
2. Sode-tsurikomi-goshi, uke to have his right foot forward.
3. O-goshi, uke to have both feet level.

4. Yoko-gake, uke to have the right foot forward of the left foot.

Because the primary force is produced only by the arms (bending or straightening) the initiating movement is quite small; this indicates generally that pace is fast. Certainly it can be appreciated that in this, the first set, the pace is fast for all.

Of course, there is a variation within the set, the last one is slower than the first, the fourth is usually – but not always! – faster than the second. But again relative pace can be worked up and discovered by the participants.

Fig. 36. Tori, on right, starting the left foot (the driving leg) back for power

SECOND SET
DYNAMIC BODY FORCE
COMPLEX INITIATION

The object of this set is to try and show how a body weight force can be overcome by a dynamic body movement: abstract, shown in physical terms.

Uke and tori stand as before, about 6 feet apart. As before they raise their arms, palms facing. They come together till the palms are touching and the elbows are bent. Uke steps back with one of his feet (so he is in a lunging position), and pushes forward, using the falling body weight. Tori contains the force, assesses it, JUMPS one of his feet back and drives right through uke with his thrusting body weight, figure 36.

Uke's force is the result of a gravity reinforcing weight push; tori's is the result of dynamic thrust from the back foot.

SIXTH ILLUSTRATION.
ASHI-GURUMA

Static situation. Uke and tori hold in the standard (right) manner. Uke pulls his whole right side back — hand and foot — into a half crouch, trying to pull tori's left side forward. Tori pulls back hard with left hand. The pulling back is the containment and the assessment. Having done that, tori crosses his left foot, spins, and throws uke with (right) ashi-guruma.

The moving situation. Uke is moving backwards at about a medium pace, using the direction of movement to reinforce the body turn that is making the pull back. Tori starts to pull back against the pull of uke; assesses, then spins in for ashi-guruma.

Practical Comments

In competition, this type of attack is sometimes used on a change of direction. Uke pushes forward, tori gives way, uke cautiously over-reacting pulls the side back and goes back. Tori uses the direction of movement he has already started and pulls forward. The situation is now as above.

Fig. 37. Tori-otoshi

SEVENTH ILLUSTRATION.
TAI-OTOSHI

Static situation. With tori holding in standard (right) manner, but uke is holding with both hands on tori's collars. Uke, by moving his left foot forwards thrusts hard at tori's right side. Tori "stamps" in hard for tai-otoshi, throwing uke almost backwards.

The movement situation. Uke moves around, upright, but defensively, keeping his right foot back. Both arms, although bent, are trying to keep tori's weight onto his right foot, by pushing on to it. Tori will contain that defensive force, and when he has assessed it, stamp in and drive right through it. The pace will be slow to middle.

Practical Comments

This illustration is trying to show several things at the same time. For example, what are normally considered forward throws can be — in the right circumstances — backward throws (in relation to the opponent). How an opponent can be defensive when standing up straight; how he can make a mistake by trying to pin his opponent onto the wrong foot.

EIGHTH ILLUSTRATION.
HON-KAMI-SHIHO-GATAME

Static situation. Uke is on the ground, tori attacks with hon-kami-shiho-gatame. Uke gets hands underneath tori's chest and pushes upwards (again trying to make space, so that an escape is possible). Tori plants his feet wide, raises his body and then drives down hard, alternatively on each pushing arm. The push

from uke is not just from the arms of course, the whole body is rocked into each push that uke gives. It is for this reason that tori stamps and drives his body weight down on each of uke's hands/arms in turn. Gradually the "space-making" push of uke is destroyed and the pin is achieved.

Movement situation. Again both can start in a half-kneeling position, see figure 21. Tori "throws" uke onto his back, moves into the pinning position, and the thing completes as above. Pace is middle to slow.

Practical Comments

In competition, this is a system that, small as it is, can be worked in many circumstances. Many situations in ne-waza are when one man pushes the other — with his hands, body, feet, knees, elbows, etc.; the attacker has got to be able, not only to brace against such pushes, but must be able to produce a stronger push back. Alternatively driving from the feet, is a good method.

NINTH ILLUSTRATION.
TANI-OTOSHI

Static situation. Tori holds in standard (right) manner. Uke holds both collars (or thereabouts) with both hands. Uke by having his right foot forward, thrusts forwards and downwards, keeping his body upright. Tori pushes back, evaluates, brings his right foot back and drives hard against the thrust of uke. (See figure 37.)

Movement situation. Uke is driving and moving forward, trying to maintain space between the bodies. Tori is pulling in (with the

arms only) trying to ensure that the push of uke's is strong and consistent. Those arms will still be pulling in when the total driving body weight surges up the stiff arms of uke — throwing him backwards. The pace is slow.

Practical Comment

This is a very typical example of a right-handed player trying to keep off a left-handed player. The stronger(?) left-handed player will be attacking the space on his own right side in order to get the control necessary to throw the opponent to HIS LEFT. The opponent, realising this, tries to keep the space open on his right by pushing the dominator away. By going right through that very strength (the domination of force!) tori can bring off a throw to his opponent's RIGHT!

Fig. 39. Final uchi-mata

Fig. 38. First sasai

Movement situation. The pace is slow, and the whole thing very strong and powerful. The movement of tori from the first feint to the throw must be deliberate and quite slow. Accuracy is essential! If there are faults in foot positioning, the push of uke WILL knock tori down. The feint has got to be strong enough to act as a threat to uke, who will then respond by changing his line of defence. "Go" is a very important principle to understand, when the pace is slow and strong.

Practical Comments

The idea of using a feint which pretends to utilise the "giving way" attack of one side, in order to get an even stronger "domination of force" on the other side, is a very practical one. It can be developed for many many situations, both in terms of attack (combination) and defence (kaeshi-waza).

COMMENTS ON SET

The approach as before. The details are really left to the participants. As for opportunity, well most are stipulated anyway (have to be, because of the driving body weight). The pace is again mostly by definition, slow. The thrust that can be utilised from lunging body weight is best done when moving slowly. The dynamic power to overcome that must equally come from a fast aggressive stamp and drive, done at a slow controlled overall pace.

TENTH ILLUSTRATION.
UCHI-MATA – AS A LINKED ATTACK

Static situation. Again tori holds in standard (right) manner, uke is holding both collars and is in a half-crouch defending position.

Uke thrusts forward to his own right front corner, tori feints by stepping to the left side of uke and attacking with right sasai-tsurikomi-ashi (see figure 38). To "kill" that attack, uke switches his push, and now drives hard, forward, to his left front corner. (He hopes to push tori over in that direction.) Instead tori, swings the left foot right round, takes up the pushing force of uke and throws against that force with uchi-mata. (See figure 39.)

Fig. 40a. Tori (on right) pushing uke off . . .

Fig. 40b. Uke "breaks", and tries for arm-lock, but tori spins . . .

Fig. 40c. . . . into a side pin.

Fig. 40a

THIRD SET
DYNAMIC INTERACTION
WHAT IS TO BE ILLUSTRATED?

Emerging from the last illustration is the idea of using these principles of opposites in the form of a pattern to establish particular (required) situations. Again such a mixture of uses is fairly common among very skilful players (although I don't suppose for one moment they would consciously recognise that is what they do!), but again the business is seldom taught. It is left to the individual to find out these things on his own – which of course he may do, but on the other hand, he may not! Because the principles are mixed up, it means the pace is variable throughout. Again this gives a good opportunity for the trainee to try out his own ideas of pace change to see if they work, and then – if they do – he can try to transfer that general experience to other situations.

Abstract

Uke and tori come together as before, palms to palms, with elbows bent. Uke pushes with body weight, tori responds with dynamic drive. Uke retreats, giving way to tori's superior power. Uke then avoids tori's line of force (attempting to use "ju"), but in getting out of the way of tori's force, uke loses some control. Because of that loss, tori quickly changes direction, and again hits uke with a dominating force, which drives uke completely back.

A complex pattern of course. The palms of the hands should not break contact. In other

words, the pushing and change of direction should be very smooth and continuous. If the pattern becomes jagged, the hands will separate and the continuity will be affected. The sequence is: primary force, overcome by bigger secondary force; primary avoids to utilise secondary but loses control. Secondary changes direction – into new line of primary force – and overcomes primary again. Finish. Because it is movement it cannot be shown in still photographs, but I did show it in some films I made (see end of bibliography).

ELEVENTH ILLUSTRATION.
OSOTO-GAKE

Static situation. Uke pushes forward, tori lunges back to overcome that push. Uke gives way and retracts, tori pursues due to weight commitment. Uke breaks line of retreat and tries a right tai-otoshi. However, because of "careless" avoidance, uke's weight is allowed to swing too far round and finishes on uke's LEFT foot. This allows tori to avoid the attack easily (by jumping over uke's outstretched right leg). Tori drives hard, and pushes uke over the outside edge of his left foot. Uke moves one or two steps in order to try and regain control, but before he can do so, tori steps in and throws with LEFT osoto-gake. *Movement situation.* In this, the last set, there is little difference between the static and movement situation (not as much anyway as in the first two sets). But what IS different, is the variation of pace and control of movement. For example, the first push of uke will be slow to middle, the reaction of tori will be fast

and strong. Uke will give way slowly but then more quickly as he retreats, hoping that tori will also speed up (uke will probably pull too, to encourage a loss of control). Tori will speed up, so allowing him to jump over the tai-otoshi when it is tried. Tori will now slow the pace right down, so that he can get the power to overcome uke's positional strength, and bring off the throw. Perhaps too, as experience is accumulated, uke instead of just swinging out of the line of tori's response drive (and then trying a throw) actually changes direction first, getting tori to change direction too – by using his grips extensively. Then when tori has changed direction, uke can try the tai-otoshi attack. Again tori can jump over, but now how does the change in pattern affect the final throw – if at all?

Practical Comment

There are many variations possible on this simple change of principle pattern.

TWELFTH ILLUSTRATION.
UCHI-MATA

Static situation. Both uke and tori hold in the standard (right) manner. Uke crouches and begins to pull downwards. Tori moves, gets underneath the arms of uke and starts to push up (against the downward pull of uke). Uke allows himself to be pushed up and then suddenly begins to pull up and goes for kosoto-gari on tori's right leg. Tori moves, swings his left foot (his driver) well back, pushes down, now with both hands (against uke's upward lift) and throws with right uchi-mata.

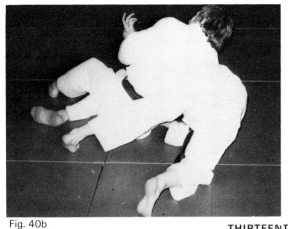

Fig. 40b

Fig. 40c

Moving situation. Again it is a matter of extending the movement pattern of the sequence, in order to see the ebb and flow of power. Uke could illustrate the downward pull as he moves backwards in a wave-like action, pull release, pull, release. Tori picks up the rhythm, as uke pulls down he suddenly moves in and drives up. Uke changes direction, from going backwards he now swings to the side of tori (and goes slightly out of control as he does so). In order to try the kosoto, uke makes tori move a couple of steps to his (tori's) right before the actual kosoto is tried. Tori moves outside the upward lift of uke and throws downwards with uchi-mata.

Practical Comments

Again a complicated, but fairly common type of sequence among skilled players. The great "secret" is not to be afraid of moving through the pattern. The novice (even of a year or so) may tend to try and keep the movement sequence tight and compact. For this kind of series it's the wrong sort of attitude. The whole thing has got to be allowed to "flow". There must be a rhythm from one action to the other. A slow, strong pace to start with, tori tries to quicken it up when he drives up, uke quickens it up again to get in the kosoto attack. Tori slows it right down again at the end, for his uchi-mata.

THIRTEENTH ILLUSTRATION. KUZURE-YOKO-SHIHO-GATAME

Static situation. Tori lies on his back. Uke attacks with a right side pin (i.e. on tori's right), tori turns towards him and pushes uke off with his arms (trying to create space), uke tries to hold tori's push, and then suddenly releases and tries for waki-gatame. Tori pulls his (left) arm back, turns onto his front, pushes uke onto his back and pins him with kuzure-yoko, (figures 40a, b and c).

Movement situation. As always with the newaza sequences, let the two – uke and tori – start in the half-kneeling position. Now it is uke's turn to "throw" tori down. He drives in fairly slowly for the side pin, tori pushes back much at the same pace. But when uke "breaks" to try for the arm lock he takes the pace up fast. Tori responds even quicker, by pulling his arm back and taking advantage of the slight loss of control suffered by uke when he took the pace up too fast. Tori quickly turns uke onto his back and pins him at a slow pace.

Practical Comments

The loss of control I try to illustrate in the sequence, is typical if too much of a pace change is tried. Sometimes of course the sheer surprise of an extreme pace-change pays dividends, and works like a charm (so I am not saying don't EVER try it), but it can easily lead to a momentary loss of stability and is therefore hazardous. Like so many other things, if the hazard is known to exist it is comparatively easy to avoid it. If it is not known, then the hazard can cause disaster!

FOURTEENTH ILLUSTRATION. UTSURI-GOSHI

Static situation. Uke and tori hold in the standard (right) manner. Uke pulls back with body weight. Tori suddenly drives hard backwards trying to pull uke unexpectedly forward. Uke resists the pull, then again suddenly breaks and pushes tori backwards, and tries osoto-gari. Tori holds the attack, tori then counters with utsuri-goshi.

Movement situation. Uke starts the pull back at a medium pace. Tori counters with a slower paced dragging of uke forward. Uke quickly ups the pace, pushes forward and tries for the osoto-gari. Tori changes direction, swings his driving left foot back, drops the pace right down to slow and completes the utsuri-goshi.

Practical Comments

A good example of a contestant who, in the excitement of what he thinks is a fortuitous set of conditions – takes advantage of (what he thinks) is a spontaneous situation, and in so doing forgets the basic fighting factor, and attacks the opponent's "pivot" leg, without due care and attention given to throwing direction. For, whereas, he should be throwing tori to his (right) side, in the excitement of the moment, he tries to throw straight back – disaster! It is in such exciting moments at this, when caution and preparation can be swept aside in the sudden heightened moment of drama – that basic factors are forgotten and mistakes made.

FIFTEENTH ILLUSTRATION.
IPPON-SEOI-NAGE

Static situation. Uke and tori hold in standard (right) manner. Uke begins to push tori in a curved shape (towards uke's left). Tori suddenly pushes back along the same curved path, but in the opposite direction. Uke breaks away from that curved direction and goes directly backwards. Tori quickly follows, causing uke to lose a slight amount of control. Nevertheless, most other things are O.K. so uke tries ouchi-gari. Tori lifts his left leg well over the sweeping right leg of uke; then as uke is trying to regain his stability tori nips in quickly and throws with ippon-seoi to uke's right rear side.

Movement situation. Uke starts fairly slowly. Tori's response is slower but stronger. Uke "breaks" from the curve fast – as is the ouchi-gari attempt. Again tori slows it all down to ensure the ippon-seoi to the rear scores.

Practical Comment

Circular sideways movement is fairly common in competition, because it helps to close up the side spaces and make throws like uchi-mata somewhat easier. So it is useful to have this basic kind of movement pattern in a kata layout. Again without doubt perspicacious fighters will be able to devise their own answers to this "basic" situation. Note also that if the situation is "right", the direction of the throw does not have to be orthodox!

CONCLUSION ON THE KATA

As can be appreciated this kata has a much "looser" shape than the traditional ones. That's how I like it, for I would want the participants to supply their own particular – and peculiar! – parts to the performance. I have not said anything about doing the whole series the opposite way round. But that goes without saying, all the moves should be repeated the other way, left and right. If however, anyone feels too lazy to bother, well they can blame that on the fact that I left the "opposite performance" out of my description! Also I have not spoken about how to get from one set to another. As I do not feel this is very important, I leave that to the performers. The kata is a training scheme for the participants – to improve their competitive skills – it is not for the benefit of spectators. Therefore as far as I am concerned, how the sets or illustrations are joined up is immaterial. I am sure he "drillers" will find a "nice" way of doing it! I do hope the reader will agree it is a worthwhile kata to try and learn. I have tried to make it as comprehensive as possible. I hope I have not tried to get too much in, and hence confuse rather than clarify. But by including direct attacks, combinations and counters all in the one short sequence, with the forces going horizontal, vertical, and in circles, instances of most competitive situations are illustrated. And then what is most important of all, is the attempt to show it is the interplay of basic principles – not just one principle – that can make a skilled performance exciting.

Being used as a training aid I would not expect the total sequence to be rigidly adhered to at every performance. There may be times, when only parts are used: for example, if beginners are being trained, then perhaps only the static movement would be taught; if the trainees were more advanced then perhaps only the movement situations need to be used. It has already been said how the individual can experiment with pace and direction of attacks in the various sets and illustrations, and that could just as easily apply to the kata as a whole. Kata, to do its real job, must be virile and alive. The objectives of it must be clearly understood. If these qualities are fulfilled little can go wrong!

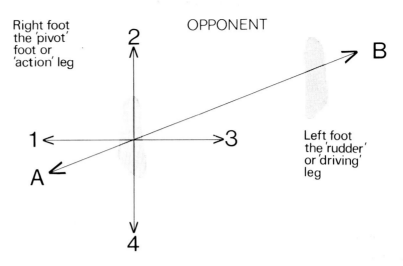

Right foot the 'pivot' foot or 'action' leg

Left foot the 'rudder' or 'driving' leg

Fig. 41

Senjitsu-No-Kata

This is another kata I devised; the purpose of which is to illustrate the various tactical factors contained in competition. As has already been seen the go-no-kata is a very much "loosened off" shape from traditional kata, loosened because I want the needs of the individual incorporated into the performance. The kata of tactics is "loosened" off even more, indeed it is really only a sequence of factors, the actual illustrations are left almost completely to the performer. There is something of an analogy with art here; in the classic school pattern and style was very much dictated – close foreground, going into populated middle distance, disappearing into far misty distance. Subjects and story were also specified quite clearly by the "establishment". The Impressionists broke the classic tradition and painted as they thought they saw and felt. That went in its turn, and along came "pop art", when representation of the "outside" (of them) became so real, so practical that real objects were included in their painting. In this kata of tactics, the performer can incorporate his own "real parts": he does not have to perform movements which may not be, probably are not, his own; having once got the idea of what is needed, he produces his own "thing"!

Senjitsu is Japanese for tactics. Whether the kata needs such a "traditional" title is itself open to question. I have done so mainly for old times' sake, but I doubt very much if it is really

necessary. The title, a tactical kata, would do just as well. Its uses could be various, ranging from a basis for a lengthy training plan, where every illustration is considered in depth, with lots of self-devised examples included in each part, through to a "shopping list" use, where a fighter quickly goes through the list in his head just before he starts an actual contest, just to remind him of the things he has to look for and do.

FIRST SET
BASIC TACTICAL FACTORS

FIRST ILLUSTRATION
THE RUDDER LEG

The need to know the opponent's driving leg. One leg, usually (but not always) the nearest one, is the pivot or action leg. The other, usually the furthest, is the driver or rudder leg. When attacking the man will pivot on the forward foot, swing the other leg into position where it will drive the attacker's weight into the direction of the throw. The pivot foot, then becomes the action leg, for it can go on to sweep the other man's legs from under him or to act as some kind of block over which he is rolled.

If the forward foot (the pivot) is attacked, then the back leg is "ruddered", first to maintain stability and then to become the driving leg, if a counter-technique is actually used. See figure 41 for how to attack the pivot foot.

If an attempt is made to sweep or move the (opponent's) right foot in any of the four directions—very hazardous—the opponent will "plant" the foot, swing or rudder the driving leg into throwing position, and counter. By throwing towards A or B, this "ruddering" ability will be minimised.

SECOND ILLUSTRATION
HEAD CONTROL

Controlling the head, in terms of being able to restrict its movement of turning and nodding, is important in both nage and katame-waza. In throwing actions it is usually done by the collar hand, holding high round or nearly round the opponent's neck. If the collar-hand is high, care must be taken to ensure that the elbow is kept low, to protect the space on that side. If the elbow is allowed to "float" high, space develops between the bodies, and the opponent can turn into that unprotected space (if he does so – a throw is usually the result).

Controlling the head, raises the subject of which side to throw on – the collar or sleeve side? Orthodoxy maintains that sleeve-side throwing is the only really viable side, for it exercises maximum control over the opponent on the throwing side (i.e. it fixes the arm, so that the opponent cannot pull it free and make space in which to escape). Perfectly true of course, by and large throwing on the sleeve side (the side on which the sleeve is being held) is the best, because of the control already mentioned. But nevertheless, many skilled players do throw on the collar side in spite of its apparent weaknesses. Why? Head control seems the answer. True, the control over the arm – and hence the side – is not very good (possibly allowing the opponent to pull the arm away, create space, and so avoid the fall), but head control is good. By holding deep round the back of the (opponent's) neck, the head can be pulled in very tight when the throw is attempted. Knowing the weakness of the throwing direction, related to lack of side control, all that is needed is to ensure that the turn to throw is very tight. If space is allowed to appear between the bodies on the throwing side, the falling man will – at best – be able to put the hand down onto the floor and avoid any high score. With the head pulled in tight, the hand should not be able to reach the ground.

In ne-waza too, fixing the head is important, not only in actual technique (i.e. in most of the pins, fixing the head is critical), but in general space control too. For example, for movement to be really effective in ne-waza, the head must be able to guide the direction (of movement) and emphasise force. If there is no freedom of movement, then effectiveness of total body movement decreases considerably. However, it should be realised that on some occasions restricting the opponent's head can restrict the attacker's head movement also. In which case training will have to be put in on that part of skill where the opponent's head movement is limited, but maximum freedom is retained by the attacker.

THIRD ILLUSTRATION
SPACE AND THE USE OF IT

What sort of space does the man need? Side spaces, top, bottom, variable, constant; all these would be good to know. A very general guide could be as follows. It indicates the sort of thing to check on.

SIDE SPACES:

(a) closed side spaces (sleeve pulled in) could mean osoto or kouchi attacks, ogurumas, certain types of uchi-mata. If very tight, sutemi-waza or a tai-otoshi type could be the threat.

(b) open side spaces: (sleeve pushed back) could mean ouchis, tai-otoshis and kosotos.

Top spaces: closed (crouching): dropping onto knees, shoulder throw, up-the-middle-uchi-mata, ouchi and kouchi-gakes, sutemi of the rolling type, i.e. sumi-gaeshi, tomoe-nage, etc.

Top spaces: open (straight): harai-goshi, most types of koshi-waza (i.e. tsurikomi-goshi, ogoshi, etc.). If pace is fast enough any sweeping attack could be tried, i.e. ankle sweeps of all kinds, osoto-gari, etc.

It must be stressed the above is only a guide, each player will need to complete his own list. For his own shape, pace and movement quality will decide what he is to do and what he can expect the other man to do.

Inexperienced players will find that the "old hands" will "punch" their way into creating space. It must be expected! There should be no surprise when such an approach is met (certainly they must not "choke" when it happens). Such rough (unfair if you like) methods should not be allowed to cloud the view of the weakness and strength that lies beyond the roughness. The inexperienced must be able to go right through the curtain of "hardness" and attack what is behind it.

FOURTH ILLUSTRATION.
TURN AND TWIST OUT

This refers mainly to avoiding scores, or the cutting down of a fall by at least one stage. This means, if a man is thrown for ten, by twisting in the air, he can reduce that initially hoped for score to a real seven or even five. Twist outs are usually for forward throws/falls, and means the man can either twist out by going with the throw or against it (see figure 9). If the throw/falls are backwards, then the man can usually turn out (see figure 10 and 11). Whether twists or turns are used, the object — and this is all important — is to keep off the back! The concept of "keeping off the back" is a good one to stress in both nage and katame waza. It is true of course that some men in ne-waza do fight well from a position of being on their backs — but they are very few! By and large it is a "rule", always to stay off the back, whatever the circumstances! If by any unfortunate chance, the man does find himself on his back, he should make it a habit to get off it as quickly as possible — quicker in fact! When twist outs and avoidances of all kinds have become second-nature, the next stage is to transform the movements into counters. That is comparatively easy to do, so I will not elaborate upon it here.

FIFTH ILLUSTRATION.
THE MULTI-BITE

This refers to the ability (of a fighter) to repeat the throwing action WITHOUT repeating the attacking action. This means the individual's best direct throwing skills must be practised in such a way that they can be repeated until a high score is achieved. The points to be considered are:

(a) The first and only attacking action must be done with maximum stability; that is the driving leg does not have to go directly to the correct, first position; it can be kept back out of harm's way (minimising counters). The hands need not be pulling in tight, or the weight fully committed.

(b) The (attacker's) hands/grip relax, allowing the driving leg to hop to a position closer to the final, required one; as the foot lands in the new position, the hands pull in tight.

(c) Again the hands relax, the driving foot moves into its final, correct position. As it does so, the hands pull in tight again, and the throw is completed.

NOTE: There is no fixed number of hops — from one to six, or as many as needed! The attacker must keep pressurising the opponent throughout the whole hopping series. The hands relax and tighten in co-ordination with the hopping foot — relax, hop, tighten, relax, hop, tighten. The opponent must not be given a moment of peace in which he can rally his defence and start countering. Used with discretion, accuracy and courage, it is a very useful throwing skill.

THE SECOND PART
MATCH CONTROL

SIXTH ILLUSTRATION
DOMINATION

Precise ways to achieve domination will of course depend upon each individual – and his personality! However, here are a few tips.

Be positive, get the grip first, then hustle! Push him, drive him, in jerky spasms onto his rudder leg. Try and keep the opponent's shoulders moving (by pushing and pulling on them), don't let him settle. Try not to back off (psychologically poor); go AT the man all the time. Changing the grip, hard and often, can be very disconcerting.

The inexperienced player must be prepared for the "madman", the fellow who rushes out from the starting bow, flailing arms and legs like a pepped up windmill. It may be real, it may be false; inadvertently(?) the inexperienced man may get a blow in the face, a finger in the eye, a kick in the groin – all of course an accident! He must not let this put him off his job. The referee may stop the "madman" – he may not – if it is after the blow (or whatever) it doesn't really matter for the injury has been done anyway! Be prepared to tuck the head down and weather the storm. Some "madmen" keep the rush up for the whole of the match (although very few are that fit); most will use it in fits and starts. As soon as there is a lull in the storm, the other man should start fighting back hard. Don't let the "madman" start again!

Do, and expect, the unexpected. Many judo players are very conservative; they only do those things that ought to be done (whatever that is!). If their expectancy is smashed, and something quite different is used, their opposition frequently crumbles, simply because things are different – not necessarily because things are better!

Having said that, do not let the gimmick be the only score-earning trick. A good, steady, sound scorer – whether the opposition knows it or not – is always the prerequisite of the champion!

SEVENTH ILLUSTRATION
ATTACKING FIRST OR SECOND

Every man should KNOW which he is: both ways have advantages and disadvantages. If the "attack-first" man makes a good attack, and it MUST be good – that is it must get the opponent's feet off the ground – then the psychological advantage can last out the match. On the other hand, if the "attack-second" kills the other man's first attack, not only does he get a psychological advantages, but he also acquires a lot of tactical information (i.e. type of throw, opportunity, pace necessary, etc., etc.). Armed with that, it can make his first attack – when it comes – that much stronger. The "attack-first" must put in a lot of training on "snap" attacks. A fast judgement of the situation, and then into a 100% effort. It must be right! The "attack-second" must start with maximum caution in case the first attack he had to weather is the last!

EIGHTH ILLUSTRATION
PACE CONTROL

Does the opponent move at a faster, slower or the same pace? How is the differing pace to be controlled? By grips and body drag? By "hanging" on the opponent the pace can be slowed, by "lightening" the load (i.e. stand up straight, pull in instead of downwards), pace can be encouraged to go faster. Change of pace is critical; the player should develop a large degree of sensitivity towards this factor. Sometimes it is assumed, wrongly, that fast pace change is the province of the smaller man. No, no. Some of the best pace-changers I have seen have been big men: Glahn of West Germany, Ruska of Holland jump to mind. A point to remember, if a man wants to use a lot of pace change he will need to be fit!

NINTH ILLUSTRATION
BACK AND FRONT FIGHTING

This aspect of tactics has been discussed at some length already in previous parts of the book, so I will not go over it again here. Again remember a style that requires a lot of hustling, particularly "back fighting", will also need a lot of fitness to make it really effective.

TENTH ILLUSTRATION
SET PIECES

Again the idea of set-pieces has already been discussed at length, so here in the kata, the performer will put his own favourite pieces in. Having several of them, say one for each general situation (i.e. start of the match, on the

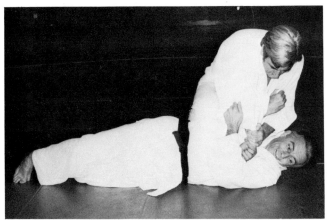

edge, after a score has been lost, etc.). He can practise each of them to get them "smooth". Similarly in ne-waza set-pieces should be organised (much easier here, for the ground itself limits the action to "horizontality"!). Let me give two general ne-waza examples, but before doing so, I would like to make a small deviation regarding some learning theory; it is called Hicks Law. Hicks Law says, "the greater range of alternatives, the longer the response time". This in judo terms means that if an attacker makes an attacking movement, which has several possibilities intrinsic to it (i.e. in relation to, for example, direction of throw), the opponent will take longer to respond to that attack because he has to first decide which direction is the true one. It is a "trick" well known of course; in tennis, a man like Rosewall will make a forehand stroke, but disguise right up to the moment of impact which way he is going to hit it. His opponent, instead of anticipating the direction (which of course he may do anyway — and guess wrong) has to wait until after the ball has been hit before he can move to intercept — which may be now far too late. So in judo, a skilful fighter will launch an attacking move and disguise its ultimate destination till the very last split-second, hoping that by doing so, the opponent will have to wait too long before deciding what to do.

This has a very common application in ne-waza, a typical "set piece" where the attacker will move in such a way that it is difficult to tell if he is going for a pin or a lock, by the time the

By controlling the opponent's right arm, the attacker can go after . . .

. . . a pin, or . . .

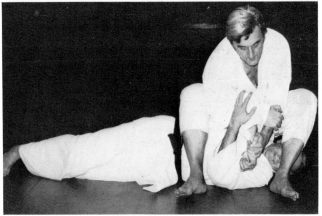

. . . on to a straight arm-lock (ju-ji-gutame), by dropping back.

opponent has decided what he THINKS it is going to be, the attacker has finished. A slightly different application of the same principle is also much used in ground play. Here the attacker forces his opponent into a situation that has two alternatives. The attacker has a sequence based upon each alternative. Whichever choice the opponent takes, the attacker will simply take the opposite one. For example in figure 42a, b and c the attacker has got himself into a position where he can either arm-lock or pin. If the opponent decides

to defend against what he thinks is an arm-lock attack, he gives a bigger opportunity for the pin. If he defends against the pin-attack he gives away the arm-lock.

A corollory of this multi-choice approach to attacking tactics is that relating to the recipient in terms of defence. The more that is known by him (the opponent), the more likely he is to be able to make the correct choice (of what the attack is) and so give the correct response quicker than if knowledge and experience is limited.

Fig. 43a. The man between the legs has
started making space

Another useful set-piece to have well covered in ne-waza is the "between-the-legs" position (see figure 43a). There are many ways for the man between the legs to get out, but fundamentally it is a matter of space. The man on his back will be trying to keep the space between the two bodies small (so the other man cannot get the room to move away), whereas the man between the legs will be trying to make space between the bodies. A common fault emerging from this situation is when the man eventually does break out from between the legs, he is so keen to get up towards the other man's head (for control), that he allows the space between the bodies to get smaller again, and suddenly he is back where he was before! (see figure 43b). Once space has been made in order to escape, it must be maintained — and even enlarged.

Fig. 43b. The top man's right hand is
checking the other man's hip movement

THE THIRD PART

Location within the fighting area. The whereabouts in the area will affect the type of skill used.

ELEVENTH ILLUSTRATION.
EDGE OF THE MAT

(a) Arriving at the edge unknowingly.
This should never happen to a good competitor. After all he can lose the match (and the championship!) by simply putting a foot outside the area, so he should never be in a position to do it. He must "learn", by body sensation, how far the edge is away from the middle of the mat. One way is to step the distance out with a blind-fold on. Keep doing that until the distance is "felt". Then move around freely, but still keep going through the same distance. Eventually the man should have a built in alarm bell that (when he gets near the edge) rings in his head!

(b) Arriving at the edge knowingly.
There are three general reasons for this happening, the good competitor should recognise them all.
1. Aggressive purposes.
One man will manoeuvre the other man up against the edge so that he can control his direction of movement. Because the (other) man will not be able to go over the edge, he will have to move away from the edge in a limited number of directions, which will favour the attacking action of the aggressor.
2. The losing man will himself move to the edge of the mat — and stay there. By being able to cover very defensively any other direction not covered by the edge of the mat, he can block any remaining attacking directions.
3. Time-wasting.
By manoeuvring to the edge, try an attack, break to the middle, repeat. Ways will have to be found to beat this negative tactic.

TWELFTH ILLUSTRATION

Fighting in the centre of the contest area. This is a much more straight forward affair. Here is the place for the big direct attack — where it doesn't matter if a part of the high-speed revolving body shape goes spinning off taking up a lot of space! Here is where the long string of continuous attacks are started — trying to achieve fatigue or victory! The middle of the mat is the place for imagination and flair, the edge of the mat for caution and organisation!

THE FOURTH PART
Refereeing

Because the referee and the (two) judges do control the match, they must be considered as a part of the training scheme.
Points to consider:

13. Do not try and do the referee's job for him! In other words, he will decide what score the attack deserves. The fighter should keep going, should keep trying to win until the referee tells him he has won! — or lost! Don't stop after a throw because YOU think it has scored 10; keep going!

14. The referee's decision is final. The easiest way of acquiring the referee's favour is to plant the opponent on his back! As quickly as possible!

15. Watch the score board carefully and KNOW what the position is. Does a particular referee tend to score high or low? Does he only give five, when others give seven, or does he give five when others give nothing? (I can hear the referees protesting. They will say, "But what scores five is clearly defined. How can it score anything else?!" But let's be honest fellows, even referees, are fallible!) The competitor should know the kind of referee he's up against and attack accordingly.

16. Keep a "who's who" of referees; know what their idiosyncrasies are — use them! Is that one hard on stepping off the mat? Does that one have his "blue-eyed boy"; if so who is he? Is he so fair, that he is actually harder on the people he knows than those he doesn't know? Any and all such information about contest officials could be critical in certain matches. It is foolish to train hard, to develop a high class skill, and then throw it all away, because it wasn't known before the match that that referee penalises a man who holds in such and such a way.

FINAL COMMENTS

No doubt the traditional kata man will read the above and say how can I take such a conglomeration of ideas, performances and tricks and call it kata? There's very little pattern to it, there certainly is no ritual, there's no precision, in fact everyone does it how they want, putting in mostly their own material. It just is not kata! Of course I would differ. (It does remember, conform to old man Shao's definition!) Of course it is a lot different from nage-no-kata, but then it has a much different subject to cover – tactics and not just throwing. One of its main purposes is to show the diversity of kata that is possible. When I studied nage-no-kata I used an inductive approach: that is I looked at the many details in that kata and drew a lot of very useful general conclusions from them (see my book, "Anatomy of Judo") when (and if!) people study the senjitsu-no-kata, I hope they will apply a deductive approach and draw specific conclusions from the very general statements made, and conclusions which are of benefit to each individual.

CONCLUSION

Buried in the whole concept of kata and its functions as a skill training programme, are the two long-standing arguments found in learning-theory in general. One is the distribution of practice and the other is accuracy v. speed. Is it better to practise a skill (whatever it is) for three hours at a time, twice a week, or every day for one hour? Is it best (especially in the early days of learning) to start practice with the emphasis on speed and let accuracy develop in its own time, or is it best to start being accurate and let speed catch up as best it can?

Much time can be wasted discussing the pro's and cons of the two arguments, in practice it would appear to be a "non-problem". In the "distribution" argument much depends on what is meant by practising period related to time-off periods in between. (Doing something once a month would be a very slow way of improving an ability). Factors like boredom, arousal, interest (motivation) would play a critical part in deciding what is a "practising period" and what is a "rest period"! Similarly with accuracy v. speed, if the indifference to one, in order to get high absorbtion-rate (of learning) for the other, is disproportional then the neglected one will eventually sabotage the other. The two must develop hand in hand, especially if they play an equally important role in the final skill (as they do in judo) so therefore the trainer, coach, player, must give each an equal time allotment in the training programme.

Arguments of this type, where defintions of terms are not clearly stated at the outset can easily get built up into something which they are not and hence waste time and effort. General statements can only too often, with the passing of time, get transformed into a specific comment of fact, without there being a realisation that a change has happened. Certainly as far as human performance is concerned the only general statement that can be made with any longstanding conviction, is that there is no general statement which can cover all individuals' performance! But what is accepted by all is that practice is necessary to improve skill. But yet again it is not just a question of "practice makes perfect"; it's the quality of practice which is critical. Is the rationalisation of the practice sound? Are the individual's needs considered adequately? Only when these considerations are taken into account can the practice of the skill, by and for the individual be devised effectively. That is the job of kata! There is very little benefit in using kata as a Cyclops' bed – do you remember how he made everyone fit his bed. If they were too short he would stretch them on the rack; if they were too long he would chop off anything that stuck out ! – it is no good dogmatising about every tiny detail and making all conform; that only produces robots or morons (or worse still moronic robots!) Kata must be flexible, just as Shao said 900 years ago; the form is finite, the content infinite. It must be able to cater for any developing pattern of "new" skill; it must be

able to help each individual to improve his
own skill in his own way. It will offer guide-
lines, it will offer templates of performance
standards, it can even offer a ritual that by its
very nature will help towards the achievement
of a high standard of performance. In many
places it will overlap into randori – and indeed
shiai too – just as the other two areas of skill
improvement will overlap into kata; often it
will be difficult to distinguish where one sort
of training starts and another stops. (When is
the first day of spring?) Only man tries to draw
stiff lines of demarcation between two types
of information; the result is invariably frustration, deception, injustice and intolerance.

It's try and keep ''pigeon-hole'' thinking out
judo!

A Conclusion

So to conclude, I hope I have done what I said I would do in the introduction. But what about purpose? That I did not mention; can I bring it into this conclusion?

The purpose for doing judo is to experience enjoyment and satisfaction through the sense of achievement of having created something. It seems as if one of man's basic drives is to create; it also appears that value, utility, intent of that creativity is immaterial. If it works out giving a little more benefit to the greater number, so well and good; but if it does more harm for the greater number, so be it! Creation itself is what is important; "progress" is the excuse for building, whether it is physical architecture, or abstract political structures. The H-bomb and the poison gas is created with just as much gusto and conscientiousness (and acclamation) as the symphony and the hospital – Bernard Shaw would say more! But like all talents, all the people are not given the same ration of potentiality to satisfy that ubiquitous urge to create. Indeed many may not realise they have it at all. While others, because life nudges their proclivity in a slightly different way have their urge to create diverted into an urge to destroy. For love is to hate as creation is to destruction.

The word "creation" has overtones of making or building massive designs and projects; what Mumford calls the megamachine.[28] Creation is not normally applied to such mundane activities as gardening or knitting, but on the continuum scale of creativity all such activities have a place and all comply with the definition of creation. A definition which says that something exists now that did not before the activity took place, and has the hallmark of the individual's personality stamped on it. Sport is, or can be, a medium for creativity, perhaps not of the higher orders, but it can provide a certain type of person with the opportunity to express himself (another way of saying creativity). By developing a skill, a physical skill of their very own, the basic need to create something from and for themselves can be satisfied. It could be said that physical skills are a very ephemeral creation, of less value than the longer-lasting works of say music and painting, ephemeral because the art (if there is any) in the skill dies as it is being created. But for the individual that is not important. However brief, however tenuous, is his act of creation, in that moment when he produces something that has never been done before and will never be done again, he touched the stars! Fragile as it is, it is his contribution to the totality of man's creativity and achievement. Something that he can be proud of, something which would not have been possible without sport. For whereas one man's talent is for manoeuvring numbers, another for juggling with bits of noise, another for juxtaposing colours, so another can use his body – as an implement – better than many others.

"The creative act is not an act of creation in the sense of the Old Testament. It does not create something out of nothing; it uncovers, selects, reshuffles, combines, synthesises already existing facts, ideas, faculties, skills. The more familiar the parts, the more striking the new whole."[72]

The task of the educator – call him teacher, coach, what you will – is to lay bare as many of these ideas, skills and stimulants as possible, so that the potential creator can use or find something from among them, to "trigger", to fire off, his own act of creation. If the educator buries or hides such sources of stimulation, either accidentally or intentionally (and the latter is criminal) then he is not doing his job. If the educator tries to cover up his own indolence, his own indifference to the needs of others, by replying to all queries "because that's how it has always been done" – or something similar – then he is a traitor to cause he pretends to have allegiance to – cause of helping others to find themselves. One of the difficulties of creating a stimulating environment for the development of a creative ability, is the unintentional discouraging effect of the established creator. The syndrome roughly as follows. An individual (usually with a high level of creative ability) is faced with a problem, a problem produced by a class of factors in a moment of time. The person all his scattered pieces of experience and knowledge, tosses all into the "synthesising machine" in his head, and in time and with "luck" a solution pops up. The quality of the "synthesising machine" is of course critical, is what the mystics have been dealing with for centuries, and what they have been trying to explain for the same period of time. It is the satori of Zen, the ghost in the machine of Koestler, the dedifferentiation of Ehrenzweig, the lateral thinking of de Bono.[75] It is what makes the act of creation look like magic, and can deceive the ignorant by its very apparent simplicity.

It is this aura of magic that is the bane of the educator's task. So often the followers of any one creator (and I only mean followers in time, not as disciples) are lazy or timid or both and therefore use the "magic" as an excuse not to do the work necessary to build a "synthesising machine" of their own. Instead they seize upon the discovered solution, as THE solution. They see it as final, as absolute! No need to work out solutions for themselves, for their own problems for their own times; it has all been done for them. But to make the excuse appear honourable, the solution (which after all was only a transcient solution) has got to be given the permanency of "official" recognition. It is therefore frozen into an ice-cube of false tradition, for all to see and imitate – if they are that dull! No attempt is made to realise that time has not been frozen; time with its constituents of multi-variables is still producing problems, but different problems. Problems that will need different solutions from those frozen in the ice-cube.

The leaders, the educators, to deserve their name of leader and educator must retain their ambition to create their own "synthesising machine". They must be very aware of the dangers of wearing blinkers and blindfolds. They must try and develop the ability to an-

ticipate problems, and not wait till they trip over them. They must not fall back on robot-kata as a reason for doing nothing themselves and thereby stifling creativity.

What I have tried to show in this book, is the scope and range of judo knowledge. To do that I have spent more time on some aspects than others. Sometimes the scrimping has been due to lack of space, sometimes for the lack of knowledge, but I hope the faults are excused if the purpose has been even partly achieved. Already there are a few judo writers who are producing some original thought, who are expanding the limits of judo knowledge, which I find very gratifying, for it may be the start of a new wave of development. Judo is a very fragile plant, it has had something of a hypochondriachal existence. (It nearly died in the 1930's and after World War II.) It could still die unnoticed and unsung. (Whatever happened to 10 pin bowling?) And die it will if the leaders of the sport do not encourage new acts of creation. Creation, ostensibly for the sport itself – in terms of new ways of presenting competition, new training methods, new ways of producing skills – but really for the benefit of the individual participant. If he is not given the opportunity to create in proportion to his capability and ambition he will go on his way. He will look for other challenges, other problems that he can solve by his own creative genius, but which he considers are not to be found in judo.

An Appendix

Although I have tried to cover many of the aspects of judo in the body of the book, there are still a few which I have not touched upon, and which I feel would be remiss of me, if I ignored. For example, I am often asked if the "old" training of judo differed in any great way from that of the present training. An intriguing question, and one difficult to answer, because of the paucity of information. But again let me make some points, based upon my discussions with middle-aged judo teachers in Japan in the 1950's. But in brief, the answer would appear to be "little change over the years".

Before the last war the feudal approach to physical training was very much in evidence in Japan. After all, officially it was only 50 years back (some of my friends' fathers carried swords – for real!). Such training was based mainly on a master/pupil relationship. The ambitious student would live with the master, become his servant and his payment was the secrets of the trade. A feudal apprenticeship. I met several judo teachers who had been trained this way.

The benefits of such a method are obvious; learning takes place when both are ready: it can take place over breakfast, or even in the street. There is no need for motivation; the life style is that. Disadvantages are just as numerous. It is very expensive on time; no-one is in a hurry; the master teaches as and when he feels like it; it is expensive on numbers, only one or two at a time can take advantage of the teacher. It develops discipline, but encourages sloppy methodology.

Fig. 44. The Kenshusei, research students

At first sight it may appear as if such a system was contrary to what I talked of earlier, the group-orientation of Japanese society. But in fact no, for the master is a part of the group, and so too, by affiliation, is the pupil. The master's status is largely judged by the pupil he produces. This in judo meant that when the young fellow practised his skills in "competitions" he was not really showing his own ability off, but that of his master. The teachers would look on benignly, perhaps one of them would even condescend to "teach" something to another master's pupil, also in "free competition", but the young man would never dream of beating the master (even though he could probably have done so with "one hand tied behind his back"). It was not done; it was against the group's norms.

Kata would no doubt be done by the older men/teachers, whilst the younger ones tried out their "open skills" in open competition, for kata appeared to be the "physical notebooks" of the teachers. It was here that they "jotted down" their ideas on technique and skills, showing each other what they had thought of recently, and exchanging ideas on that performance. As a research student of the Kodokan (see figure 44), I was taught kata by various masters, and even when it was just the nage-no-kata, each was different from every other. That to me is how it should be, and the move by the Kodokan in 1962 to standardise (fix) this kata, was, in my opinion, ill-advised and against the whole spirit of developing skills.

The Belt or Kyu/Dan System

There are still some people who think this is a judo monopoly. Quite wrong of course. It exists in all Japanese indigenous arts and crafts, ranging from chess and flower-arrangement to judo and fencing. It is sometimes quoted, in the West, as an excellent example of motivation for skill improvement. Certainly in Japan that is not its purpose. There it is mainly an indication of the individual's status within the particular structure. Of course skill plays a part in the qualification, but only a part. In Britain it is used mainly as a stimulant for improvement and as a "money-spinner" for the organisers. The only catch with the stimulous approach is, if the next higher grade is not won. The backlash is formidable indeed! So much so, that much of the dissidence among national judo organisations in Britain, is the result of squabbles over grade awardings.

The kyu grade, usually referred to as the "pupil" class, varies in number and colour throughout the world. In Japan usually there are only three coloured belts before "black", whereas in Britain there can be six colours, or even more. The black-belt is called "dan", and although there used to be – "on paper" – 12 of them, now, for all practical purposes there are only 9, (about 3 or 4 Japanese have this high ranking). Up to 4th or 5th Dan (black belt) competitive ability is usually the main qualification, after that, contributions to the sport – in terms of knowledge and service – becomes the major factor.

6th–8th Dan, in fact officially wear a red and white "black" belt, whilst 9th Dans wear an all red one.

Competition

I have already spoken how the concept of "competition" can vary between cultures, i.e. Japan and Britain. Perhaps the "sudden death" idea contained in judo came from the fact that the pupils were not really fighting for themselves (as they are in the West), but for their teachers. Therefore "winning" becomes almost symbolic, something that simply indicates a GENERALITY – at this moment in time, this man is better than that man.

There have been periods in Japan when the best of three points was the way of deciding (this method was also used in Britain after the war). I even heard that at one time it was the best of three points, with no time limit! This meant that a match could, and occasionally did, go on for over an hour!

However, now the Japanese favour one major point only. As the (major) point is won, so the match ends.

The Influence of the Past on the Present

The feudal attitude towards training still hangs on in Japan. Worse still, it has even been brought over to Britain and Europe. It is bad enough in Japan, where even there the social conditions have changed almost out of recognition over the last hundred years, but in Britain, we have had nothing like it for eight hundred years!

This feudal approach has come to mean the "traditional" way of teaching judo (in spite of all Kano's efforts to inject "modern" ideas into the sport). Because it is both anachronistic and foreign, its effect upon judo growth in the West has been extremely debilitating. It would appear to go without saying that a teaching method should be structured to accommodate the general characteristics of the people for whom it is intended. Why Britain, and indeed Europe, have to inherit such an antiquated system; one so out of touch with the needs of the present (i.e. indicated by such things as sports halls, comprehensive schools), that I am left bewildered by the apathy of it all.

A Teaching System

Having said that a "new" teaching system is wanted, what should it do? It seems to me that the two aspects of skill development need to be catered for – the organised and the spontaneous.

In the good old days, no doubt the masters felt they had to produce pupils with "flair" (both in terms of physical skills and personality prowess). To get that, he felt the training would need to be strict and disciplined. In order to achieve that, because of the many feudal restraints, he felt the best way was to stress the accuracy of isolated movement, and ignore the need for realisation of the whole skill. The result was the opposite to that intended! The "flair" was drilled out of the individual, and in addition he had no awareness of totality, i.e. tactics.

I have gone after the stressing of organising a broad skill range – quite opposite to that contained in "traditional" skill training. In doing that I realise fully that I too may be running the risk of losing "flair", somewhere along the production line. How to get it in the system, and keep it there?

Somehow there has to be a physical equivalent of de Bono's mental "lateral thinking".[73] The fighters have got to be trained how to play "lateral fighting"! Not only has he got to be able to organise a whole sequence of fighting schemes, based upon observation (of the opposition) and experience (in both training and competition), but also he must be able to produce the unexpected, unknown, spontaneous, skill, for the right moment at the right time.

The coach has got to produce schemes and methods that will force the player to move and act unconventionally. How can he throw without holding the jacket? Can he get BEHIND his opponent (as in Koshiki-no-kata) and throw him from there? Can he do a fast tempo throw at a slow tempo? That should put the other fellow off!

Judo in Britain

After all judo has been in Britain now for over fifty years; there should be some originality available by now! After the last war, in 1948 the British Judo Association was founded, subsequent to that other national bodies were established. Each in their own way was trying to promulgate "traditional" judo. In 1951 the European Judo Union was formed, and soon after that the International Judo Federation. These organisations all arranged their own level of competition, which did much for the growth of the sport of judo.

The expansion in Europe was slow. France, Britain, Holland were the countries which lead the way in the early 1950's, but by the 1960's the Germans and the Russians were all in on the act. At the present most of the European countries are a part of the European judo competitive scene. But the Japanese feudal training system still hangs on most of them like a blight. Still the countries are struggling to produce sophisticated skills with the tools of a medieval craftsman. Sure, some individuals have broken through this "bamboo curtain" of obfuscation, but by and large improvement is tortuously slow. In the World Championships of 1971, I thought Europe had grown-up when it managed to beat some of the Japanese (not all of them) but by the Olympics of 1972, the Japanese had restablished their superiority, and Europe had dropped back to "second best". Why is this? Europe has the sporting experience, it has the ambition, it has the money; why can't it improve faster than it is?

As important as this question is, and I think it is extremely important, very few people in the high places of judo seem to bother to even ask the question, let alone find an answer for it. The establishment in Britain still does not appear to be interested in developing improved teaching and coaching methods. It appears to be quite satisfied with the success it has had in the past, and therefore sees no reason for change. The methods I advocated during my time as national coach, have had a major influence upon the growth of judo in Britain, but will the spirit that this influence has engendered be strong enough to offset the moribund existing structure? I do hope so. Otherwise judo will go the way of collar and sleeve wrestling!

Bibliography

1. A. Solzhenitsyn. *One Word of Truth*. The Nobel Speech. The Bodley Head Press.
2. J. Kano. *The Contribution of Judo to Education*. A lecture given to the University of S. California, 1932.
3. *Readings in Physical Education*. Published by the Physical Education Association.
4. H. H. Clarke. *Application of Measurement to Health and Physical Education*. Prentice Hall.
5. A. Ehrenzweig. *The Hidden Order of Art*. Paladin.
6. E. H. Gombrich. *Art and Illusion*. Phaidon Press.
7. G. R. Gleeson. *Better Judo*. Kaye & Ward Ltd.
8. G. R. Gleeson. *Anatomy of Judo*. Kaye & Ward Ltd.
9. Messrs. Mifune, Kudo, Matsumoto. *Judo Koza*. Vol. II. Hakusui Sha.
10. *Illustrated Kodokan Judo*. Kodokan, Japan.
11. S. Muruyama. *Dai Nippon Judo Shi*. Kodokan, Japan.
12. *Judo Koza*. 5 volumes. All Japan Judo Association.
13. K. Mifune. *Do to Jitsu*. Shibun Doshin Gensha.
14. A. Geesink. *The Gokyo*. W. Foulsham & Co. Ltd.
15. G. R. Gleeson. *Judo for the West*. Kaye & Ward. Ltd.
16. B. Knapp. *Skill in Sport*. Routledge, Kegan & Paul.
17. M. D. Vernon. *The Psychology of Perception*. Pelican.
18. E. L. Schurr. *Movement Experiences for Children*. Appleton-Century-Crafts.
19. P. Barnett. *Judo to Win*. United States Judo Association.
20. T. Kawamura. *Judo Combination Techniques*. W. Foulsham & Co. Ltd.
21. H. T. A. Whiting. *Ball Skill*. G. Bell & Sons Ltd.
22. K. Kingsbury. *Notes on Physical Training*. British Judo Association.
23. P. V. Karpovich. *Physiology of Muscular Activity*. W. B. Saunders Co.
24. Davidson & Passmore. *Human Nutrition & Dietetics*. E. S. Livingstone Ltd.
25. C. G. Jung. *Man & His Symbols*. Dill Publishing Co. Inc.
26. S. H. Hook (Ed.) *The Labyrinth*. Society for Promoting Christian Knowledge.
27. J. Huizinga. *Homo Ludens*. Routledge, Kegan & Paul.
28. L. Mumford. *Myth of the Machine*. Secker & Warburg.
29. J. L. Henderson. *Ancient Myths & Modern Man*. Dill Publishing Co. Inc.
30. Lord Raglan. *The Hero*. Thinkers Library.
31. G. R. Taylor. *Rethink*. Secker & Warburg.
32. K. Clark. *Civilisation*. B.B.C./Murray.
33. M. Eliade. *Myths, Dreams & Mysteries*. Fontana Library.
34. C. Wilson. *Occult*. Mayflower.
35. E. Cassirer. *Language & Myth*. Dover Publications.
36. C. C. Chang. *The Practice of Zen*. Reden & Co.
37. T. S. Eliot. *Selected Essays*. Faber.
38. Cozens & Stompf. *Sports in American Life*.
39. J. Kano. *Judo Kyohon*. Kodokan. Japan.
40. I. Yamashita. *Kogakko Judo Kyosai no Jissai*. Kodokan, Japan.
41. G. Koizumi. *My Study of Judo*. W. Foulsham & Co. Ltd.
42. J. Oda. *Judo Taikan*. Vols. I & II. Tokyo Kokubun Sha.
43. *Judo Koza*. Vol. I.
44. Ogilvie & Tutko. *Problem Athletes & How to Handle Them*. Pelham.
45. Lord Moran. *The Anatomy of Courage*. Constable.
46. J. C. Maloney. *Understanding the Japanese Mind*. C. E. Tuttle Co.
47. E. Berne. *The Games People Play*. Penguin.
48. A. Graham. *Zen Catholicism*. Collins.
49. Hu Shih. *Chan (Zen) Buddhism in China; its History & Method*. Philosophy East & West. Vol. III No. 1. University of Hawaii Press.
50. J. Needham. *Science & Civilisation in China*. Vol. II. Cambridge University Press.
51. Fung Yu-Lan. *A Short History of Chinese Philosophy*. McMillan & Co.

52. Dumoulin & Sasaki. *The Development of Chinese Zen.* The First Zen Institute, New York.
53. A. Flew. *An Introduction to Western Philosophy.* Thames & Hudson.
54. J. Needham. *Science & Civilisation in China.* Vol. I. Cambridge University Press.
55. Plato. *Phaedo.* Penguin Classics.
56. H. P. Bowie. *On the Laws of Japanese Painting.* Dover Publications Inc.
57. D. T. Suzuki. *Zen & Japanese Culture.* Routledge, Kegan & Paul.
58. C. Stanislavsky. *An Actor Prepares.* Geoffrey Bles.
59. Newton & Handley. *A Guide to Teaching Poetry.* Unibooks.
60. G. K. Piovesana. *Recent Japanese Philosophic Thought 1862–1962.* Enderle Books, Japan.
61. D. Bergamini. *Japan's Imperial Conspiracy.* Panther.
62. G. B. Sanson. *The Western World & Japan.* Cresset Press.
63. E. H. Norman. *Japan's Emergence as a Modern State.* University of British Columbia, Canada.
64. B. H. Chamberlain. *Things Japanese.* John Murray.
65. N. Ike. *The Beginning of Political Democracy in Japan.* J. Hopkins Press.
66. R. Storry. *The Double Patriots.* Chatto & Windus.
67. B. J. Cratty. *Movement & Behaviour & Motor Learning.* Lea & Febiger.
68. B. W. Robinson. *Arms & Armour of Old Japan.* V. & A. Museum.
69. P. McIntosh. *Physical Education in England since 1880.* Bell.
70. Maekawa & Hasegawa. *Studies on Jigoro Kano.* Bulletin of the Association for the Scientific Studies of Judo, Vol. II. Kodokan, Japan.
71. C. Otaki. *Judo.* Saishin Sports, Tokyo.
72. A. Koestler. *The Act of Creation.* Pan.
73. E. de Bono. *The Use of Lateral Thinking.* Jonothan Cape.

FILMS

Written and directed by G. R. Gleeson.
Teaching Judo I and II. Sports Films, Eskdale, Totteridge Lane, London, N.20.
Judo in six parts, produced by Gerard Holdsworth Productions Ltd., 31 Palace Street, London, S.W.1.
(The first of the set won an International Sports Film Festival Prize in Germany in 1973.)

Appendix

The following records have been compiled as fully and accurately as possible. However, official records are difficult to find and the publishers would be pleased to hear from anyone who can supply missing information.

EUROPEAN CHAMPIONSHIPS The first event took place in Paris in 1951

Key   A = Austria   B = Belgium   C = Czechoslovakia   EG = East Germany   F = France   H = Holland   I = Italy   P = Poland   GB = Great Britain   WG = West Germany

L = Lightweight   M = Middleweight   H = Heavyweight   LM = Light Middle   LH = Light Heavy

	1st Dan	2nd Dan	3rd Dan	4th Dan	Open	Team
1957 Rotterdam	Newman GB	Sinek WG	Dan	Dan	Geesink H 7	GB
1958	Bourgain F	Newman GB	Dazzi F	Geesink H	Geesink H	GB
1959 Vienna	Rossain F	Nottolat F	Rabut/Legay F	Courtine	Open	GB
1960 Amsterdam	Franceschi F	Desailly F	Guldemond B	Outelet B	Geesink H	H
1961 Milan	Niemann EG	Ierland H	Desailly F	Tempesta I	Geesink H	H
1962 Essen	Etienne B	Kibrozaschvilli USSR	Petherbridge GB	Desailly F	Geesink H	F

	L	M	H	Amateur Open
Olympic Weight Categories	Bourreau F	Grossain F	Niemann WG	
European Weight Categories	L	Courtine F	Geesink H	Kiknadze USSR

1963 Geneva	L	M	H	Open
Amateur	Bogolyubov USSR	Norris F	Geesink H	Geesink H
Olympic	Bourreau F	Leberre F	Glahn WG	Nitz EG Team USSR
1964 Berlin				
Amateur	Bourreau F	Bondavenko USSR	Niemann EG	Kiknadze USSR
Open	Bogolyubov USSR	Grossain F	Geesink H	Geesink H Team USSR

	L	LM	M	LH	H
1965 Madrid					
Amateur	Stepanov USSR Open Kiknadze USSR	Bourreau F	Hofman WG	Kibrotsachvilli USSR	Niemann EG
Professional	Iljouchin USSR Open Meier WG	Kouspiche USSR Team USSR	Poglajen H	Youdine USSR	Chikwiladze USSR
1966 Luxembourg	Suslin USSR Open Kiknadze USSR	Stepanov USSR Team USSR	Snijders H	Gouweleeuw H	Ruska H
1967 Rome	Suslin USSR Open Geesink H	Desme F Team WG	Pokatajen USSR	Herman WG	Ruska H
1968 Lausanne	Marktkoplischvilli USSR Open Saunin USSR	Magaltadze USSR Team F	Hofmann WG	Hermann WG	Glahn WG
1969 Ostend	Feist F Open Ruska H	Rudman USSR Team WG	Bondarenko USSR	Snijders H	Ruska H
1970 Berlin	Mounier F Open Hennig EG	Hendel EG Team USSR	Jacks GB	Pokatajew USSR	Glahn WG
1971 Gotenburg	Mounier F Open Kusnetsov USSR	Hendel EG Team GB	Auffray F	Howiller EG	Ruska H
1972 The Hague	Mounier F Open Ruska H	Hotger EG Team USSR	Goche F	Parisi GB	Ruska H
1973 Madrid	Melnichenko USSR Open Novikov USSR	Hotger EG Team USSR	Jacks GB	Rouge F	Ojeda Spain
1974 London	Melnichenko USSR Open Novikov USSR	Kruger EG Team USSR	Coche F	Zuvela Yugoslavia (LM)	Onashvilli USSR

WORLD CHAMPIONSHIPS

	L	LM	M	LH	H
1958 Tokyo (The first event)	Sone J				
1961 Paris	Winner Geesink H				
1963					
1965 Rio de Janeiro	Matsuda J	Okano J	Okano J (M)	Inokuma J (Open)	
1967 Salt Lake City	Shigeoka J Open Matsunaga J	Mintoya J	Maruki J	Sato J	Ruska H
1969 Mexico City	Sonoda J Open Shinomake J	Minatoya J	Sonoda J	Sasahara J	Suma J
1971 Ludwigshaven	Minomi J Open Minomiya J	Nomura J	Jujii J	Soto J	Tagaki J

OLYMPICS

J = Japan   K = Korea

	L	LM	M	LH	H	Open
1964 Tokyo	Nakatani J		Okano J		Inokuma J	Geesink H
First official full participation of judo						
1972 Munich	Kawaguchi J	Nomura J	Sekine J	Chochoshvilli USSR	Ruska H	Ruska H